Founding the Criminal Law

Founding the Criminal Law

Punishment and Political Thought

in the Origins of America

Ronald J. Pestritto

Northern Illinois University Press

DeKalb 2000

© 2000 by Northern Illinois University Press
Published by the Northern Illinois University Press,
DeKalb, Illinois 60115
Manufactured in the United States using acid-free paper
All Rights Reserved
Design by Julia Fauci

Library of Congress Cataloging-in-Publication Data
Pestritto, Ronald J.
Founding the criminal law : punishment and political thought in the origins of
America / Ronald J. Pestritto.
        p.   cm.
Includes bibliographical references and index.
ISBN 0-87580-260-5 (alk. Paper)
1. Punishment—United States—History. 2. Criminal law—United States—
History. I. Title.
KF9225.P47   2000
364.6'0973—dc21   99-32841
CIP

To Barbara

CONTENTS

ACKNOWLEDGMENTS

A SINCERE DEBT OF GRATITUDE is owed to many who have helped to make this book possible. While I acknowledge them here, I must emphasize that any deficiencies in this work are entirely my own responsibility.

The book was written during my tenure at two institutions, the University of Dallas and Saint Vincent College, and I wish to thank both for their support. In particular, I am grateful to my colleagues in the Politics Department at the University of Dallas for the rich intellectual environment they provided. Jack Paynter and Tom West read portions of the manuscript and made much appreciated suggestions. I also thank the Center for Economic and Policy Education at Saint Vincent College for its numerous forms of support, financial and otherwise. Gary Quinlivan, the center's executive director, and Bill Boxx, the center's Fellow in Culture and Policy and chairman of the Philip M. McKenna Foundation, were a tremendous source of encouragement and help. Andrew Herr, the center's Fellow in Economics and Policy, took the time to read the manuscript and to offer advice at a critical stage.

My friends at the Claremont Institute for the Study of Statesmanship and Political Philosophy, where I serve as an Adjunct Fellow, have taught me much about the American founding and have helped to make possible this and many other of my endeavors. I thank especially the Institute's director of research, Glenn Ellmers, for the time he put into reading portions of this manuscript, offering important suggestions, and encouraging the project from the very beginning.

I also owe a debt of gratitude to the Earhart Foundation for a fellowship research grant that supported a critical summer of research. The John M. Ashbrook Center for Public Affairs and its director, Peter Schramm, have graciously supported several pieces of my writing over the last two years. Joseph Bessette and Christopher Manfredi read this entire manuscript, more than once, and made helpful suggestions too numerous to count. Their time and energy is deeply appreciated. Thanks also go to Stanley Brubaker, whose comments on the manuscript were very helpful.

Many have helped to produce the book. I thank the staff at Northern Illinois University Press, especially Martin Johnson for his constant encouragement, as well as Susan Bean and Pippa Letsky. I also thank my student research assistants for their contributions, particularly John Grant, Ann Marie Lund, Liz Kaczmarski, and Gary Stofko. Margaret Friloux, a librarian at Saint Vincent College, was a great help in facilitating so much of the research for the book.

In general, little of what I have done in this project or in other academic endeavors would have been possible without the advice and friendship of Charles Kesler, my teacher and mentor. Along with Joe Bessette, Jim Ceaser, Harry Jaffa, Jim Nichols, and Jack Pitney, he has provided an education for which I am very grateful. Finally, I thank my wife, Barbara, to whom the book is dedicated, for her reviews of the manuscript and especially for her devotion and patience from the very start of the project.

Founding the Criminal Law

Introduction

THE DEBATE ABOUT CRIMINAL PUNISHMENT was one of the liveliest political debates of the American founding era, and in many ways it is a guide to the political principles that were most influential during the founding. This book seeks to illuminate the political thought during the American founding by analyzing the significant changes that took place in the criminal laws and punishments of the time. The manner in which the founding generation approached criminal punishment provides lessons about the broader questions involved in interpreting the political thought of the new republic.

Although scholarly works on the founding-era punishment debate have not been numerous, there have been several important contributions in recent decades. Most of these works, however, have been written by historians and have naturally addressed the questions relevant primarily to the discipline of history. This book is primarily a work of political science, and especially political theory. As such, it makes use of historical research into the founding-era punishment debate in order to answer questions that are fundamentally political. The book seeks to fill a gap in the scholarly literature by providing an analysis of the key events of the founding-era punishment debate from the perspective of political theory. Such an analysis is inextricably linked to key historical questions, yet the issues it addresses are, in many respects, different.

These issues are not only of relevance to the past but are also a contentious element of our contemporary politics. Crime and criminal punishment are among today's most important public policy questions. The current significance of the issue is most evident at the state level, where new criminal laws have been moving through state legislatures at a rapid pace in the last few years. "Three-strikes" laws have been most prominent, and the debate over them proves instructive in studying the contemporary politics of punishment. Given the national attention it received, the debate that took place over three-strikes in California is of particular interest; California's law is also one of the most far-reaching in the nation.[1]

It is clear that, during California's three-strikes debate, the public was intent on increasing criminal punishment for a wide variety of crimes, but there was no clear agreement on *why* punishments should be made more severe. In California, there were several widely publicized cases that drew attention to the rising problem of violent crime. Both the Kimber Reynolds case in 1992 and the Polly Klaas case in 1993 presented the public with brutal killings of young girls carried out by parolees each with a long list of prior convictions for serious offenses. As a consequence of these and other cases, a successful campaign was initiated to adopt a three-strikes law in California.

There were two distinct arguments in favor of implementing the three-strikes law. Some argued from the perspective of public safety. Governor Pete Wilson, supported by a large segment of the public, contended that increased punishments were necessary in order to keep dangerous offenders off the streets. Many noted the obvious point that, if the killers of Reynolds and Klaas had been incarcerated for lengthy periods for any of their past convictions, neither would have been free to commit these most recent murders. Some also argued from the perspective of just deserts. Many wondered why men who had committed so many serious crimes did not deserve to be in prison for the rest of their lives. Not only was public safety an issue, but it was also thought that the criminal law was no longer "doing justice."

After the passage and implementation of three-strikes in California, those who opposed the law approached the debate from different perspectives. Some contended that the punishments were simply too severe for the crimes. They noted that even a minor felony could count as a third strike and could send someone to prison for a minimum of twenty-five years (where twenty years must actually be served). The law provided for penalties that were beyond what offenders actually deserved. Others argued against the law from a more utilitarian cost-benefit perspective. The most well known of these arguments was made by the Rand Corporation. It reasoned that the object of the criminal law should be to protect the public at a reasonable cost. Rand believed that the cost of increased incarceration under three-strikes would far exceed any benefit that might be derived in terms of crime reduction.[2]

The California case is merely an example of the larger competition of ideas about criminal punishment in contemporary American politics. Although great public attention has been focused on the issue of punishment, there is still much confusion and debate about why, exactly, society punishes criminals. What are the principles that underlie criminal punishment? What is its aim? Although it is quite clear that the trend has favored longer sentences for a wide variety of crimes, the intended purpose of such sentences is less clear.

The four justifications for criminal punishment that are most commonly mentioned in the contemporary debate are just deserts, deterrence, incapacitation, and rehabilitation. To the extent that one can generalize, the rehabilitation view argues that society itself is the "root cause" of much of today's criminal behavior and that criminals, therefore, do not necessarily deserve punishment. Instead, society has an obligation to rehabilitate the criminal. Such a view, dominant in the 1960s and 1970s, has essentially been abandoned in political circles. Rehabilitation is, however, undergoing a revival of sorts in the academic arena.

Most common in the contemporary politics of punishment are the utilitarian approaches of deterrence and incapacitation. The deterrence approach seeks to identify the sorts of punishments that will make potential criminals think twice about committing future crimes, appealing to the criminal's self-interest in avoiding punishment. The assumption of the deterrence approach is that potential criminals rationally consider the costs and benefits of their behavior. The assumption that criminals act on the basis of such a rational, cost-benefit calculation is tenuous, however. A lack of confidence in this fundamental principle of deterrence has led many to retreat from it and to turn instead to incapacitation, which does not require any assumption about the motivations of criminals but merely asserts that, if a criminal is behind bars, he is unable to commit additional crimes against the public. This view, for example, drove much of the three-strikes movement. Both deterrence and incapacitation are fundamentally utilitarian because the most important question in formulating punishment policy is how effective such a policy will be at reducing future crime.

The focus on utilitarian concerns is what distinguishes deterrence and incapacitation from the just deserts approach. As often as one hears that punishment must protect society from future crimes, it is also common in the contemporary politics of punishment to hear that our policy must be to "do justice" to the criminal. In other words, punishments must be formulated so that the criminal receives the punishment he *deserves*. Such a view has grown out of recent revelations about how little time many violent criminals actually spend behind bars. The argument behind the just deserts approach is that punishment should not only be directed at protecting society but, even more important, should be designed to give the criminal a punishment commensurate with the moral gravity of his offense.

There is, of course, no reason that punishment policy cannot seek both to prevent crime and to give criminals their just deserts, but these two views have deep roots in the Western political tradition, and the tradition is polarized in its approach to punishment. In the modern era, both the just deserts approach and the utilitarian approach are pushed to their respective extremes. The modern roots of the just deserts approach lie in the moral idealism of Kant and Hegel. In an argument that is more accurately defined as mere retribution, Kant in particular rejects all utilitarian considerations. Instead, he believes that punishment policy must be crafted upon the principle that punishing criminals is inherently good, regardless of any benefit it might bring to society in terms of crime reduction.

The other extreme—embraced by Hobbes, Bentham, and especially Cesare Beccaria—asserts that the politics of punishment must be based only upon societal self-interest, narrowly understood. These "reform" theorists reject any notion of a moral foundation for the criminal law, arguing that only those punishments necessary to protect society from future crime are justified. In addition to these extremes, the contemporary rehabilitation approach also has its roots in the modern era, in the political thought of Rousseau and the British political writer William Godwin.

To find a more comprehensive approach—an approach, I argue, that is at least partly reflected in the formation of America's political principles—one must look to an earlier period in the Western political tradition. In ancient and medieval political thought one finds a coherent mixture of just deserts, utility, and even rehabilitation. In the writings of Plato and St. Thomas Aquinas, as well as of others from the classical and medieval periods, there is an understanding that the criminal law relies upon a higher moral law and, consequently, that justice requires the punishment of criminals. Accordingly, criminal punishments must reflect the moral transgressions inherent in crimes, and public policy must attempt to punish in a way that considers what the criminal deserves. Both Plato and Aquinas rely heavily upon utilitarian considerations, arguing that the protection and preservation of civil society are vital elements in the understanding of justice. Finally, justice must also take into consideration the good of the offender. Although it does not focus on the "root social causes" of crime in the way that the contemporary rehabilitation school does, ancient and medieval political thought does consider it the responsibility of society to reform the souls of its wayward citizens. In general, the more comprehensive approach of these traditions reflects a broader notion of political justice, in which society punishes those who deserve it, protects its citizens, and concerns itself with their souls.

This coherent mixture of the more extreme approaches to the criminal law helps to shed light on the fundamental principles of the American political order. The politics of punishment was an important part of the larger political debate that took place during the American founding. The politicians and political thinkers of that time found themselves in the midst of a battle of ideas, and the debate about criminal punishment was one such battle.

In the political science literature, sharp differences have arisen over the fundamental influence on the political theory of the founding. Much of the debate has centered on the extent to which Enlightenment rationalism defined founding-era political thought. One school of thought in political science argues that the founding rests almost entirely upon enlightened self-interest. Focusing particularly on *The Federalist*, the argument is that the founders realized they could not rely upon the virtue or civic spiritedness of either the citizens or their rulers; the political system had to rely instead upon each individual's pursuing his own self-interest. Such a pursuit of self-interest, as explained most explicitly in *Federalist* numbers 10 and 51, would allow for ambitious interest groups and public officials to counteract each other and to reduce the risk of majority faction while the government kept to the limited but fundamental task of protecting life and property. Thus the founding, according to Martin Diamond, was "low but solid"; the founders' understanding of the challenge of government was not terribly different from that of Thomas Hobbes, even if their solution to that challenge took a different form. For government to achieve its primary aim of self-preservation, it would abandon the task of ennobling its citizens and would concentrate instead on protecting them by appealing to their enlightened self-interest.[3]

A second school of thought on the founding, while admitting the obvious influence of enlightened self-interest in the founders' political thinking, contends that arguments such as Diamond's focus too narrowly on modern thought. The founders, according to this second view, considered virtue, civic education, character formation, and statesmanship to be essential elements of our political order. Classical political philosophy thus combined with the "improved science of politics" of the Enlightenment to make the founding a nobler enterprise than Diamond suggests.[4]

Finally, there are many political scientists (as well as historians) who have read the Enlightenment out of the founding almost entirely. Rejecting the influence of Hobbes, John Locke, and the centrality of individual natural rights, this group of scholars argues that traditions such as classical republicanism and religion formed the primary basis of the founding. While some would extend that argument only to the Revolution of 1776 and not to the subsequent constitutionalism of 1787, the rejection of Enlightenment rationalism as an important influence on the founding is a dominant theme of this school.[5]

Among historians, who primarily have been responsible for the literature that exists on the founding-era punishment debate, the role of Enlightenment penal reform philosophy is also a central question. Several historical works place the Enlightenment at the heart of what takes place in criminal punishment during the founding.[6] Many of these works have noted the proximity of the American Revolution to the rise of Beccaria's utilitarian penal reform philosophy and have asserted a close connection between the two. Beccaria's *On Crimes and Punishments* was, after all, published in 1764 and was first translated into English in 1767. Just as American political principles derive largely from Enlightenment political thought, some scholars argue, so too do early American approaches to punishment get their guidance from Beccaria's Enlightenment penal reform philosophy. Recently, a few historical works have been published that question the extent of Enlightenment influence on the reform of criminal punishments in the early republic,[7] although several of these tend to emphasize the penal reform that took place after the founding in the Jacksonian era. So the question of the Enlightenment's influence during the founding remains a central issue in both the historical and the political understanding of the early republic.

With respect to the political thought of the founding and the early American punishment debate, I argue that there is, in general, too much emphasis on the exclusive role of Beccaria and the Enlightenment. Although it is certainly the case that the politics of punishment during the American founding was influenced by Beccaria, many have overlooked the importance of other approaches—just deserts, in particular. An analysis that looks at both the penal reform movement during the founding era and the writings of the relevant statesmen reveals that a complex synthesis was at work. Contrary to the almost exclusively utilitarian principles espoused by Beccaria and other early modern theorists, the politics of punishment during the American founding bears a degree of resemblance to the synthesis of approaches in the ancient and medieval traditions.

An examination of the politics of punishment in founding-era Pennsylvania—where the prominence of Benjamin Rush and William Bradford made that state a center of penal reform—indicates that there were many competing ideas. Although Beccaria certainly had his admirers among Pennsylvania's reformers, much of the change in criminal punishment there can also be attributed to religious beliefs, which Beccaria strongly believed should play no role at all in formulating punishments.

Many scholars also point to Virginia as an example of the Enlightenment's influence, particularly because of the sweeping changes that Thomas Jefferson proposed to the state's criminal code. An examination of Jefferson's writings on the subject suggests, however, that he was at least as much concerned with just deserts as he was with questions of utility. Consider that Virginia's colonial punishments—in line with those of most other colonies—were amazingly harsh; for some time, the criminal law in the Virginia colony stipulated the punishment of death for stealing fruits or vegetables. Jefferson's writings on the criminal law indicate that his aim was to restore a proportional relationship between crimes and punishments, that is, to give criminals the punishments they *deserve,* no more and no less.

A study of the official documents, including state constitutions, as well as of other important writings during the founding era reveals an understanding of the criminal law much broader than Beccaria's narrow utilitarianism. The founders were indeed concerned with issues of deterrence and incapacitation and learned much from Beccaria and others along these lines, but they did not confine themselves to this approach. They also believed that the criminal law is founded upon a higher moral law, and, consequently, criminal *desert* was a critical element in the early American politics of punishment. This synthesis of principles, along with elements of the rehabilitation approach that became more pronounced with the rise of the penitentiary movement, indicates that the competition of ideas in the American punishment debate was more complex and thoughtful than many acknowledge.

STRUCTURE OF THE BOOK

This book is divided into parts. Part I addresses the case for penal reform, including, in particular, the changes in the founding-era criminal codes of Pennsylvania, Virginia, and New York, and the writings of some of the most prominent reformers. Part II traces the roots of the penal reform debate in the Western political tradition. It begins by considering the Enlightenment political thought that is said to be at the heart of the American penal reform movement and moves on to address the alternative philosophic approaches to punishment. Part III reexamines the founding-era debate and argues that there was a much broader understanding of criminal justice at work than is suggested by the narrow penal reform approach of the Enlightenment. The conclusion addresses the contemporary punishment debate and suggests that the comprehensive founding-era approach has much to teach us about our current situation.

In asserting that the political thought during the founding holds important applications today, I contend that ideas transcend historical circumstances. A study of the important historical events constituting the founding-era punishment debate is a central tool for this book's analysis of founding-era political thought. Yet the political principles at work in the punishment debate are not the property of a single historical age; otherwise, studying the ideas of the past becomes little more than an exercise in antiquarianism. The premise of this book is that the principles of the founding era reflect many important themes in the principles of past historical epochs, in addition to putting forth their own unique teaching. In articulating the defining principles of our country, the founders did not aspire to speak of standards for their age only but rather to discover those principles that define just government for all ages.

Part One

Reform in Early America

CHAPTER ONE

The Pennsylvania Experience

IN A COLLECTION OF LETTERS by one of the signers of the Declaration of Independence, there is an entry from 1787 describing an encounter on the streets of Philadelphia. This statesman recounts coming upon a group of prisoners from the city jail who are chained together and performing hard labor. Struck with sympathy, the statesman shares a beer with the prisoners and remarks in his letter that one of them showed great affection for a stray dog that happened by. The statesman concludes that this affection was evidence of the prisoner's capacity for reforming himself, reasoning that "a heart is not wholly corrupted and offers at least one string by which it might be led back to virtue that is capable of so much steady affection even for a dog."[1]

That statesman was Benjamin Rush, who, in addition to signing the Declaration of Independence, was a member of the Continental Congress from Pennsylvania, founded an antislavery society with James Pemberton in 1774, and was responsible for bringing Thomas Paine's *Common Sense* into print. He was perhaps most well known, however, for his involvement in Philadelphia's penal reform movement. In addition to interacting with chain-gang prisoners and working to undo the law that required such public labor, Rush frequently expressed his belief in penal reform by sending watermelons to Philadelphia's prisoners. A 1797 entry from his autobiography reads:

> This day gave two dollars to the keeper of the new Jail to buy water melons for the prisoners, and accompanied it with the following note: "A citizen of Philadelphia requests to the prisoners in the new Jail to accept of some water melons. He requests no other return for this small present than that they should consider that God, by disposing the heart of one of his creatures to shew them an act of kindness, is still their Father and their Friend."[2]

He repeated this donation in 1800, writing to the prisoners that God is "ready to receive them into his favor upon repentance and amendment of their lives." In 1801, and again in 1802, he gave the jail money to purchase corn for the prisoners.[3]

Rush's concern for penal reform, and in particular his objections to the 1786 Pennsylvania law that required prisoners to perform public hard labor, led him to join a reform group that had organized in 1787 calling itself the Philadelphia Society for Alleviating the Miseries of Public Prisons.[4] The prison society came together in 1787 for the express purpose of pursuing a change in Pennsylvania's penal statutes and of effecting improvements in Philadelphia's jail. The subsequent changes in Pennsylvania criminal law were largely the result of the prison society's lobbying of the state legislature.

It is significant that both Rush's encounter with the prisoner chain gang and the organization of the prison society took place in Philadelphia during the year 1787. Not far away, in the very same city, fifty-five political leaders were gathered to fashion a new government for the United States. Two great reform movements were coming to fruition at approximately the same time and place: first, a political and institutional reform on the basis of natural rights and popular consent, and second, the amelioration of the criminal law to provide for the more just and humane treatment of criminal offenders. In this book our interests lie in the joining of these two reform efforts in the constitutions, laws, and political writings of the new nation and its states; in whether the two movements are related in principle; and if so, what that relatedness might teach us about the philosophical influences on early American political thought.

The Philadelphia penal reform movement in which Rush and the prison society were important players has a long and instructive history. Pennsylvania was, without a doubt, home to the most prominent penal reformers in America, and the history of its criminal law is one of remarkable change. For those other states that reduced the severity of their criminal laws during the founding era, Pennsylvania was often the model. Harry Elmer Barnes, a historian of penology, goes so far as to say that "no community has been more significant in the history of penology than this commonwealth."[5] The journal of the most important and influential prison society during the founding era contends that "few of the United States can boast of an earlier, or more rapid amelioration of the severe criminal code of Colonial times than Pennsylvania."[6] Long before other colonies or states even considered moderate reductions in their criminal penalties, Pennsylvania was making drastic reductions. At the colony's inception in the late seventeenth century, its penal code was probably the mildest in the civilized world.

Not only did Pennsylvania have the mildest of penal codes, it also led the way for the reduction of criminal penalties during the founding period. Pressures from the British crown meant that Pennsylvania adopted a severe penal code throughout most of the eighteenth century, but it returned to reform shortly after independence. Of all the changes that took place in criminal codes in the origins of America, the Pennsylvania changes were probably the most consistent with the Enlightenment ideals of Cesare Beccaria and others.

Michael Meranze has recently published a thorough history of the penal reform movement in Philadelphia, focusing on the development of the penitentiary. Meranze acknowledges the influence of the Enlightenment in Philadelphia's reform movement, but he also has a sound appreciation for the complexities of the competing theories of punishment at work in early America. He remarks that "Philadelphia was a crucial site for the elaboration of Enlightenment ideas in America" but also understands that "all the world is not Philadelphia."[7]

Our interest here is to get to the root of the competing influences on punishment in the origins of America. The first task is to examine reform ideas in Pennsylvania. This requires an understanding of the influences on the development of Pennsylvania's criminal code, beginning in the colonial period.

THE DEVELOPMENT OF PENNSYLVANIA'S COLONIAL CODE

There are three basic stages in the development of Pennsylvania's penal code prior to the Revolution. The first set of laws was actually promulgated before William Penn left England. The so-called Hempstead or Duke of York laws took effect in Pennsylvania in 1676. These were the first formal statutes in the colony, and they reflected the harshness of the English common law. The Hempstead laws were replaced by the early Quaker laws, once Charles II granted a charter to Penn. Most of these famous mild statutes were enacted by the Chester Assembly of Quakers in 1682 before they set sail for the New World. In 1718 the mild laws were thrown out, however, and Pennsylvania enacted a set of harsh penal statutes closely resembling English common law. The harsh laws remained in effect until the state began its penal reform in 1786. Roberts Vaux, a founding-era penal reformer, wrote regretfully that Penn's mild laws were "ahead of his age."[8]

The Hempstead laws were passed under the direct authority of the British crown. The Duke of York acted on behalf of Charles II when he initially promulgated the code in New York on March 1, 1664. He exercised the lawmaking authority for all of the territory that he had conquered for the British by defeating the Dutch. The Hempstead code was predominantly an imitation of the laws of the New Haven colony, whose statutes of 1642 and 1650 largely imitated English common law. The Hempstead code was applied to Pennsylvania in 1676, during the governorship of Edmund Andros.[9] Under the Hempstead laws, the following were capital crimes: "to deny the true God and his attributes," murder, using a sword to kill a defenseless person, killing by lying in wait, buggery, sodomy, kidnapping, bearing false witness in a capital case, treason, invasion of towns and forts, and smiting one's father or mother. To be convicted of smiting one's father or mother, it was only necessary for one's parents to file a complaint, which would serve as sufficient evidence to warrant the death penalty: "At the complaint of the said Father and Mother, and not otherwise, they being sufficient witness thereof, that Child or those Children so offending shall be put to death."[10] In cases of arson, the court was allowed either to enforce the death penalty or to force the offender to pay full damages to the injured party. The Hempstead laws directed that there be at least a four-day period between sentencing and execution and that the body of the offender be buried near the place of execution.[11]

The Hempstead laws also addressed noncapital crimes. For assaults, the court was allowed to choose any corporal punishment it deemed appropriate, except for death or dismemberment. The punishment for fornication was "Marriage, fine or Corporal punishment, or any of those According to the discretion of the Court." Those convicted of forgery were to suffer the pillory for three days and to pay double damages to the injured party. They were also disqualified from being a future witness in court. There was a three-tier set of punishments for burglary and robbery. On the first offense, the law required branding on the forehead; the second offense merited branding and a "severe" whipping. On the third offense, the criminal would finally be put to death. For larceny, which the code defined as the theft of minor items such as fruits and vegetables, offenders were to pay triple damages to the injured party and to be whipped.[12] Fines, imprisonment, and the stocks were reserved for such crimes as excessive drinking.

The Hempstead code was replaced by the laws of William Penn, once Charles II granted him a charter for a Quaker colony. The charter required that the laws of the Pennsylvania colony be "as neare as conveniently may bee agreeable to the Lawes, Statutes and rights of this our Kingdome of England."[13] To ensure that the colony's laws were indeed made consistent with those of England, the charter required that all colonial laws be subject to review by the crown.

A transcript or Duplicate of all lawes which shall be so as aforesaid, made and published within the said province, shall within five yeares after the makeing thereof, be transmitted and delivered to the privy Councell. . . . And if any of the said Lawes within the space of six months . . . be declared by us, or heires or successors, in our or their privy Councell, inconsistent with the sovereignety or lawful prerogative of us, . . . the said Lawes shall be adjudged and declared to bee void by us.[14]

Penn promulgated a constitution for the colony once the king granted the charter. The constitution—written in England—included a criminal code. Vaux comments that the criminal code was, contrary to the dictates of the charter, quite unlike the British criminal code.[15]

Pennsylvania was indeed the exception among the British colonies, most of which closely imitated the harsh criminal code of England. Whereas Connecticut's infamous Blue Laws listed fourteen capital crimes, in Pennsylvania under Penn's new code only murder was punishable by death. The two unique aspects of the Pennsylvania code were the reduction in the number of capital crimes and the use of imprisonment and hard labor instead of corporal punishments. Although the code was certainly mild, it did regulate many petty types of behavior that were offensive to the Quaker religion. Minor punishments were enacted to deal with sexual misconduct, profanity, gambling, smoking, drinking, and dueling. Penn himself drafted the criminal code of the Quaker colony and officially submitted it to the Assembly of Quakers in Chester for approval; it was approved without alteration.

When Penn promulgated the "Laws Agreed Upon in England," he also had to establish some sort of prison, since punishment by imprisonment was a rather new idea. The code directed that "all prisons shall be workhouses for felons, vagrants, and loose and idle persons; whereof one shall be in every county. . . . All prisons shall be free, as to fees, food, and lodging."[16] Murder remained a capital crime, and Penn had to establish penalties for other felonies, which were ordinarily capital under the English common law. The Pennsylvania code dictated that felons were to pay double damages and that all of their property was subject to forfeiture in order to pay the damages. Those offenders who were not able to pay were to be imprisoned in a workhouse "till the injured party be satisfied." For those convicted and put to death for murder, their property was to be divided between the injured party and their own next of kin, one-third to the former and two-thirds to the latter. Penn ordered the publication of the criminal laws in the courthouse and a reading of them once a year in public. He also stipulated that two witnesses were required for any conviction.[17]

Various other crimes were addressed by the "Body of Laws" approved by the Chester Assembly in 1682. The punishment for taking the name of the Lord in vain was five shillings or five days in prison with only bread and water. Cursing was punishable by half a crown or three days in prison. For "defiling the marriage bed," one was punished by a public whipping and one year in prison at hard labor; the second offense merited life in prison. The spouse of the offender was allowed a divorce. The punishment for incest was forfeiture of one-half of one's estate; the second offense was punishable by life in prison. The first offense of sodomy or bestiality merited a forfeiture of one-third of one's estate, six months in prison, and a whipping; the second offense required life in prison. Bigamy was punished by life in prison. Drunkenness was fined five shillings on the first offense and ten shillings on the second offense. Arson required payment of double damages, one year in prison, and whatever corporal punishment the court deemed appropriate. For burglary, the offender was required to pay quadruple damages and to serve three months in prison. If the offender was unable to pay the damages, he was subject to seven years in prison. Children convicted of assaulting a parent were to be put in prison at hard labor for as long as the parent desired.[18]

When the colonial assembly convened in Pennsylvania in March 1683, it added the punishment for manslaughter to the criminal code. Offenders convicted of manslaughter were to be punished at the discretion of the court, excluding death and forfeiture of more than one-half of the offender's estate. Penn also changed the traditional definition of murder in the 1682 code. Under the common law, murder was defined as acting with "malice aforethought." This legal term included not only clear planning and intent to kill but also any killing that occurred in the commission of another felony, even if there was no premeditation. Penn changed the words of this definition when he drafted the 1682 code, requiring that all those convicted of murder must have acted "willfully or premeditately."[19]

Vaux praised Penn's mild criminal code. He contended that there was no increase in crime during years when Penn's code was in effect (1682–1718). "No evidence exists, that offences were of a more flagitious nature, or of more frequent occurrence, than in the neighbouring Colonies, where rigorous penalties were inflicted."[20] The British crown was not as pleased with Penn. He was relieved of his proprietorship from 1692 to 1694, after King William and Queen Mary ascended to the throne. The crown placed Benjamin Fletcher in control of the colony in Penn's absence. The colonial assembly was ordered to enact new penal laws, but Governor Fletcher allowed the enactment of a criminal code almost identical to Penn's.[21]

When Penn was restored to power, he undertook another revision of the criminal laws. Although slightly more severe, the code was still decidedly milder than English common law and the laws of the other colonies. Herbert William Keith Fitzroy claims there was "an overzealousness on Penn's part to adopt a code acceptable in England."[22] He refers to the increase in corporal punishments in Penn's revised code, but he fails to acknowledge that the punishment was not much more severe than the 1682 laws and that in every other British colony most of the crimes in question were punishable by death. Indeed, even though Penn was restored as the colony's proprietor, the crown began to invoke its privilege to review colonial laws. In response to the mildness of Penn's laws, the British Privy Council nullified much of the colonial criminal code during the last decade of the seventeenth century and the first decade of the eighteenth century.[23] Some of the negative British reaction to Penn's measures even seems to have been fueled by complaints from non-Quakers in Pennsylvania.[24]

Events of 1709 and 1714 led to a radical change in Pennsylvania criminal statutes in 1718. Quakers were essentially pushed out of public office in Pennsylvania because Queen Anne closed a loophole in the law that had previously allowed Quakers to serve without swearing oaths. For religious reasons, Quakers were in the practice of taking affirmation, which the crown had found acceptable until 1709. In that year, and again in 1714, the queen nullified this exception in Pennsylvania law.[25] The Quakers were advised by the governor that the best way to return to the good graces of the crown was to enact penal laws similar to those of England. William Bradford wrote later that the assembly was "assured by the Governor that the best way to secure the favor of their Sovereign was to copy the laws of the Mother Country." This they did in 1718 and, as Bradford remarks in reference to Penn's death, "thus ended this humane experiment in legislation, and the same year, which saw it expire, put a period to the life of its benevolent Author."[26]

When the crown suspended the privilege of affirmation, the government of Pennsylvania was thrown into turmoil, primarily because most of its officials were Quaker. Governor Gookin attempted to enforce the new law vigorously. He was replaced by Governor Keith, who tried to settle the crisis by advising the assembly to adopt English-style criminal statutes. The bill that accordingly altered the Pennsylvania criminal code was enacted on May 31, 1718.[27] The new code was a radical change. Barnes comments that the 1718 code was even more severe than the Hempstead laws of 1676. "Though the right of affirmation was guaranteed, this concession was much more than offset by thorough acquiescence in the barbarous severity of the criminal code of England and of the Puritans in other American colonies."[28] The act defined twelve crimes as capital, which was still somewhat milder than the British law because larceny (a capital crime in Britain) was made punishable by flogging, imprisonment, or branding. The Pennsylvania law also allowed for the benefit of clergy in a number of capital crimes.[29] Fitzroy believes that the increased harshness of the 1718 criminal code was due not only to the suspension of affirmation privileges but also to the increased violence of the time period. He notes that many of the recent immigrants to the colony were poor or were social misfits.[30]

The preamble to the 1718 criminal code, entitled "An Act for the Advancement of Justice and the Administration thereof," noted that under the charter to Penn, the laws of the colony were to reflect those of England. The preamble emphasized the failure of the colony to adhere to the British code for capital crimes. According to the preamble, "some persons have been encouraged to transgress certain statutes against capital crimes [as defined in the British code], and other enormities, because those statutes have not been hitherto fully extended to this province." The new law established the death penalty for the following felonies: arson, concealing the death of a bastard child, burglary, murder, premeditated mayhem, petty treason, bestiality, rape, manslaughter, robbery, sodomy, and witchcraft. The first six were specifically named in the 1718 statute, while the last six were automatically made capital because the new statute adopted the punishments from the British common law. All death sentences were to be carried out by hanging, except for the crime of petty treason. This crime—traditionally defined as the murder of a master by his servant or the murder of a husband by his wife—required death by drawing and burning. One of the most criticized elements of the new code was the provision dealing with the death of a bastard child. If a bastard child was found dead, the statute stipulated that the mother had the burden of proving that she had not intentionally killed the child. If she could not prove that the child was stillborn, she was presumed guilty of petty treason.[31]

Four years after the 1718 revisions, the colonial assembly addressed the crime of counterfeiting. Offenders were to be put on the pillory, to have both ears cut off, to be whipped publicly thirty-one times, and to pay all damages plus £100. If offenders could not pay the damages, they were to be sold into service for up to seven years.[32] Lawrence Gipson summarizes the state of the Pennsylvania penal code after the acts of 1718 and 1722: twelve crimes punishable by death, five by branding, one by the loss of ears, eight by whipping, two by servitude, thirteen by forfeiture, twelve by imprisonment, and five by fines.[33] These penalties remained essentially the same throughout the remainder of the colonial period. The American Revolution and the subsequent freedom of the new states to craft their own laws opened the door for reformers such as Benjamin Rush to press their agenda.

BENJAMIN RUSH

Many believed that the Revolution and Pennsylvania's new independence from the crown presented the perfect opportunity to revise the severe colonial criminal code. Among those advocating reform was Benjamin Rush. Rush studied medicine at Edinburgh and was one of the first American physicians to earn an international reputation. Michael Meranze, the editor of a collection of Rush's essays, argues that Rush's time in Scotland turned him into a product of the Scottish Enlightenment. Meranze also contends that Rush was not as radically democratic as many in Pennsylvania, despite his fierce support of independence.[34] In the 1780s and 1790s, Rush turned his attention to Pennsylvania's criminal code.

Although Rush was certainly a penal reformer, his campaign on behalf of reform in Pennsylvania was not simply an extension of the European penal reform movement led by Beccaria and other Enlightenment writers. In his biography of Rush, Donald J. D'Elia emphasizes the influence of Christianity in his thinking. For D'Elia, Rush combined revolutionary Enlightenment ideals with the precepts of Christianity. D'Elia explains that Rush was on a "Christian revolutionary mission . . . in an era when revolution and Christianity were hardly thought compatible. Revolution and Christianity were compatible in Rush's thinking."[35] Rush's Christianity, of course, differed significantly from the Puritan version, which served as the foundation for much of the severe punishment against which he argued. Rush advocated a system of criminal law that would seek both to deter future crime and to reform criminals. There was in his system, in other words, an element of Enlightenment utilitarianism, along with what Meranze rightly describes as a belief "that social problems could best be contained through the transformation of individual character."[36] This latter belief turned Rush into a proponent of the penitentiary, which placed an emphasis upon the inner conversion of criminals. Rush's own approach to punishment brought utilitarianism together with reformation and forgiveness and made them all part of the larger mix of reform views in Philadelphia.

Rush rejected the extreme just deserts approach to punishment, calling it "revenge." He did not believe that vengeance can be an element of justice. There is no way, Rush argued, that punishment—particularly capital punishment—can provide justice for victims. Writing to Thomas Eddy, a

New York penal reformer, Rush said, "it is in my opinion murder to punish murder by death. It is an act of legal revenge, for it does justice to neither the injured friends of the deceased nor to the state."[37] Taking issue with the Thomistic view, Rush contended that God does not require vengeance as a condition of salvation; God does not require that the stain of sin be removed by human punishment. "It is impossible to advance human happiness," he said, "while we believe the Supreme Being to possess the passions of the weak or wicked men and govern our conduct by such opinions." In a letter to Jeremy Belknap, he cited St. Luke's Gospel (9:56): "'The Son of Man came not to destroy men's lives, but to save them,' is a passage that at once refutes all the arguments that ever were offered in favor of slavery, war, and capital punishments."[38]

Taking issue with the philosophy that underlies retribution, Rush asserted that humans cannot have any a priori knowledge of the just punishment for a particular crime. Since the two most important purposes of punishment are the reformation of the criminal and the prevention of future crime, society must try new ways of punishing criminals and judge the propriety of such punishments by their consequences.[39] In addition to accepting this utilitarian formulation, Rush also gave a Beccarian argument against punishment based upon the moral law. Like Beccaria, he implied that such an approach to punishment led to intolerable excesses: "The same false religion and philosophy, which once kindled the fire on the altar of persecution, now doom the criminal to public ignominy and death." He believed that the old forms of punishment were "melancholy proofs of the feeble operation of reason and religion upon the human mind."[40] Consequently, Rush did not accept the Platonic or Thomistic contention that bodily suffering leads to reform of the soul. Instead, solitude and prayer are the means of reform. Whereas the old school saw punishment as a means for preparing the soul for salvation, Rush viewed punishment as a means to prepare the individual for a return to society.[41]

Rush was one of the few penal reformers who, like Beccaria, advocated the complete abolition of capital punishment. Rush, citing Beccaria as support for his argument, contended that abolishing the death penalty for all crimes would not lead to a reduction in deterrence or lead to a higher crime rate. Rush also cited an associate—Dr. Moore—who had recently traveled to both Rome and Tuscany. Moore reported that in Tuscany, where capital punishment had been abolished, the murder rate was negligible. In Rome, where public executions were the norm, the murder rate was very high. Rush claimed that all other factors were essentially the same in Rome and Tuscany, and therefore "the abolition of death alone, as a punishment for murder, produced this difference in the moral character of the two nations."[42] Public executions harden the citizens, exposing them to murder and leading them to murder, which accounts for the higher crime rate in Rome. Quoting Euclid, Rush said that "murder is propagated by hanging for murder." In a letter to Jeremy Belknap, Rush expressed outrage that America was behind Europe in the progress of enlightened penal reforms: "How disgraceful to our republics that the monarchs of Europe should take the lead of us in extending the empire of reason and humanity in this interesting part of government."[43]

Like Beccaria, Rush believed that the proper aim of punishment could be attained without the death penalty. Since the proper measure of punishment is not based upon proportionality to the crime itself but upon the punishment's utility, abolition of the death penalty does not detract from the purpose of the laws. "If society can be secured from violence, by confining the murderer so as to prevent a repetition of his crime, the end of extirpation shall be answered."[44]

Rush wrote in his essay "An Enquiry into the consistency of the punishment of Murder by Death, with Reason and Revelation" that the death penalty is contrary to reason and to social utility. It lessens the horror that should be associated with the taking of human life and thereby leads to additional murders. Rush claimed that capital punishment might lead those who are "tired of life" to murder someone so that they can deliver themselves to the authorities for execution, in order to avoid committing suicide. Capital punishment makes convicting murderers more difficult, because juries are less willing to send someone to their death. In general, Rush's argument in this part of the essay is utilitarian; he did not believe the death penalty serves society's aggregate self-interest.[45]

In addition to narrow utilitarian arguments, there are other principles of punishment at work in Rush's writings. In particular, he often implied that offenders might not be entirely responsible for their criminal behavior. He argued that there is a direct connection between physical disease and crime. Physical ailments lead to moral ailments, which is why reformation must be an important goal of the criminal justice system. The criminal is not necessarily to blame for his behavior, and modern science may possess the means to cure him. Just as it is possible to cure physical ailments, it is also possible to cure moral ailments that are probably caused by physical ailments in the first place. In "The Influence of Physical Causes Upon the Moral Faculty," Rush cited many physical conditions that he believed led to differences in the moral faculty. He listed climate, diet, drinks, hunger, disease, idleness, and solitude.[46] With regard to climate, he contended that "not only individuals, but nations, derive a considerable part of their moral as well as intellectual character, from the different portions they enjoy of the rays of the sun."[47] Diseases in general "dispose to vice." The correction of vice cannot, therefore, come from punishment in the traditional sense. "It is vain to attack these vices with lectures upon morality. They are only to be cured by medicine."[48] Rush's view on the physical causes of human behavior serves to demonstrate the variety of principles contained in his thought, many seeming incompatible. If he followed Beccaria and the utilitarians, then he must have believed that humans possess the requisite freedom to make rational decisions; but if their behavior is caused by physiological elements beyond their control, they can possess no such freedom.

In turning away from the utilitarian perspective, Rush also raised some moral and religious questions surrounding capital punishment. He took up the contention that societies, as a whole, favor the death penalty. Social approval does not make an institution moral, he countered. Societies also trade slaves, but this does not mean that the slave trade is moral.[49] This view led Rush into an analysis of the oft-cited biblical authority for the death penalty: "He that sheds the blood of man, by man shall his blood be shed."[50] Rush argued that this was only a "prediction," not a "law." He believed that this was a biblical warning that murder will only beget murder.[51] Referring to the law of Moses,[52] Rush contended that Moses had to use many ill-conceived laws because the Jews at the time were prone to sinful behavior. Rush pointed to many elements of the Mosaic law that were not followed by modern Christians—and properly so, in his view. Adultery was no longer punished by death, as commanded by Moses, and neither was blasphemy.[53]

Rush based his call for abolition upon the New Testament. He suggested that the imperfection and the severity of Old Testament laws were intended as a contrast to the New Testament—to the beneficent nature of the salvation brought by Christ. The intention of the Old Testament laws was "to illustrate the perfection and mildness of the gospel dispensation."[54] Capital punishment is contrary to divine revelation because individuals are commanded to forgive. "A religion which commands us to forgive, and even to do good to, our enemies, can never authorise the punishment of murder by death. . . . It is equally an usurpation of the prerogative of heaven."[55]

Perhaps the most interesting of Rush's arguments against capital punishment is the one that combines Christianity with Enlightenment ideals. Rush believed that the triumph of Christian principles would represent society's progress and acceptance of reason. "This triumph of truth and Christianity over ignorance and Judaism will mark an era in the history of mankind."[56] For Beccaria, human progress makes us increasingly aware that murder is not in our interest. For Rush, the progress of Christianity will mirror the progress of reason. Both Christianity and reason will make it clear that the death penalty is immoral and irrational. When society executes someone for murder, Rush believed, it relieves him from the guilty conscience that God wants him to have. Society relieves the murderer of all of his duties, such as his duty to support the victim's family.[57] One wonders why it is appropriate for an offender to have a guilty conscience, or to be obligated to support the victim's family, if (as described above) Rush questions whether offenders are ever to blame for their crimes. Yet while a guilty conscience is God's just punishment, Rush said, society can pay no attention to an offender whose guilty conscience drives him to request his own execution. Such offenders are not truly driven by conscience but suffer from the "effect[s] of prejudice and education. . . . The acquiescence of murderers in the justice of their execution," he said, "cannot flow from a conscience acting in concert with reason or religion—for they both speak a very different language."[58] Murder does not permanently alter the character of one who commits it. Ultimately, it is possible for the offender to come into compliance with reason and revelation.

Rush rejected capital punishment partly because it precludes the possibility of reforming the offender, and he saw a direct relationship between physical disease and immoral behavior. While he strongly believed in reformation—saying that "the great art of surgery has been said to consist in saving, not in destroying, or amputating the diseased parts of the human body"[59]—Rush admitted that he was not so sure which cures would prove effective on particular criminals. This is why he urged an experimentation with different punishments, in order to judge them by their effectiveness.

Faith in human reformation was a central tenet of Rush's thought throughout his life. In his autobiography, he reflected upon his days as a schoolchild. He admired in particular the Reverend Dr. Samuel Finley, who lectured misbehaving schoolchildren on the wrongness of their actions:

> In the infliction of punishments in his School, he always premised them by a discourse upon the nature, harmoniousness, or tendency of the offence. Sometimes he made all the Scholars in the School give their opinions upon the nature of an offense, before he gave his own, and now and then he obliged them to pronounce sentence of punishment, before he inflicted it.[60]

This corresponds to Rush's contention that reasoning with offenders—persuading them that they have acted wrongly—is the best punishment. The manner in which Rush raised his own children also illustrates his belief that corporal punishment does not work on humans beyond their first two or three years of life. Solitude—making them reflect on their wrong—is a more effective punishment. He believed that this applies to all humans, children and adults. He wrote to Enos Hitchcock that he had used solitude as a punishment in his family "with the greatest success. My eldest son . . . has more than once begged me to flog him in preference to confining him."[61]

Rush believed that criminal punishment should proceed much the same way, which is why he joined the Philadelphia Society for Alleviating the Miseries of Public Prisons. He believed that prisons could be designed to achieve the maximum reformative effect. Prisoners could be reformed if they would turn to God and take up the Christian work ethic. While older approaches to punishment (St. Thomas Aquinas's, in particular) often took the view that the most effectual way to reform an offender's soul was to have him pay for the crime, Rush's approach aimed to change the offender so that he could be productive. Both methods are, in different ways, concerned with offenders' improvement. Rush's encounters with and donations to Philadelphia's prisoners demonstrate his approach to reform.

With his emphasis on reformation, Rush argued that the length of criminal sentences should be discretionary. The board or court responsible for determining sentences should visit the penitentiary once or twice each year to observe the reformative progress of the offenders, and the length of time served should be based upon this observation.[62] Rush was not concerned about the costs of building and running the type of penitentiary system he envisioned because he was confident the focus on reformation would significantly reduce crime.

In correspondence to Thomas Eddy, Rush laid out his plans for a penitentiary. He explained the importance of solitude, which is intended to "awaken delicacy," as opposed to public punishment, which only hardens the offenders. He wrote that a proper diet is crucial because a healthy body is critical to the reform of one's mind. In preparation for returning to society as productive citizens, the prisoners should occasionally be allowed to eat fine foods funded by private donations. This will demonstrate to them that their social bonds will not be entirely absent when they leave prison. Providing them with such meals will lead prisoners to concentrate on the good in society, not on their anger toward society for having convicted and punished them.[63]

According to Rush's plan the penitentiary should be a large building divided into apartments. It should provide the opportunity for work and exercise. In a 1794 entry in his autobiography, Rush wrote approvingly of the "new jails," designed after protests over the so-called wheelbarrow laws, which ordered public labor for prisoners. He noted that the prisoners were hard at constructive work; there was also "care of morals: preaching, reading good books, [and] cleanliness in dress."[64] The prisoners received some small amount of compensation for their work, so they could see how honest work actually pays. All of this was an improvement in Rush's view over the laws that had required public labor by prisoners; he did not believe such punishments to be reformative. "This I hope will pave the way for the adoption of solitude and labor as the means of not only punishing but of reforming criminals."[65]

Rush was adamant that punishments not be carried out in the public view. Beccaria and other Europeans argue against torture, but many of them see value in milder forms of public punishments because they would serve the utilitarian end of demonstrating to others that crime was not in their interest. Rush went beyond Beccaria's utilitarian argument by rejecting all forms of public punishments. Even hard labor, he reasoned, should not be performed on the public streets but rather behind the walls of a penitentiary. Public punishments do not, in Rush's view, satisfy the goals of reformation and deterrence. "All public punishments," he said, "tend to make bad men worse, and to increase crimes, by their influence upon society."[66]

Rush gave several reasons as to why he believed that public punishments make bad men worse. Such punishments destroy an offender's sense of shame, because they make him infamous. Public punishments are too short in duration to produce any of the necessary changes in habit. They also increase the offender's propensity to recidivate; the offender "has nothing valuable left to lose in society." Indeed, on top of his old vices, society adds by public punishment the desire for revenge against the community. Rush also discussed why public punishment does not deter others from criminal behavior. Fortitude is a virtue. When we see an offender endure punishment with fortitude, it weakens our hatred of crime. It also desensitizes the public. The level of fear decreases because punishment is not a mystery. Furthermore, when the public sees the suffering of the criminal, it naturally develops a sympathy for him. When this ceases to be the case (that is, when the criminal is so contemptible that we do not pity him), it is an indication of unhealthy passions among the citizenry. Rush argued that "we must love the whole human race, however diversified they may be by weakness or crimes. The indignation or contempt which is felt for this unhappy part of the great family of mankind, must necessarily extinguish a large portion of this universal love." Rush argued that employing prisoners in public labor would give labor a bad name; it would "render labour of every kind disreputable."[67]

In general, Rush put faith in the progress of enlightenment, assuming that it would move society beyond the "present tide in favor of errors." In a letter to John Adams, he cited the example of William Bradford, a prominent Pennsylvania statesman. Bradford had initially ridiculed Rush's proposed reforms, particularly those concerning the use of the penitentiary instead of corporal punishment. Rush boasted that Bradford had since come around to agree with the recommendations;

Bradford even wrote a pamphlet in favor of reform.[68]

Reflecting upon his life in another letter to Adams, Rush painted himself as the enlightened progressive fighting the prejudices of the day. He was willing to stand up to the old order—to the traditional view of punishment. Rush gave several reasons as to why others had hated him, noting his friendship with Adams and John Hancock and his signing of the Declaration of Independence. There was also his opposition to Pennsylvania's public punishments and his attack on the blood punishment of the old tradition, which drew the wrath of "Old Testament divines and saints." Rush was proud of his "writing against monkish learning, commonly called the Latin and Greek languages."[69] He rejected the past and put his faith in the future. Consequently, both religion and enlightenment contributed to Rush's confidence in the effectiveness of deterrence under mild punishments and in society's ability to reform offenders through penitentiaries.

CHAPTER TWO

The Success of
Pennsylvania's Reformers

WILLIAM BRADFORD

WHILE BENJAMIN RUSH was a prominent and forceful advocate of penal reform in Pennsylvania, the movement itself really gained momentum when more mainstream politicians joined the effort. William Bradford, in particular, was instrumental in legitimizing penal reform. In fact, many point to Bradford's 1793 pamphlet, *An Enquiry how far the Punishment of Death is Necessary in Pennsylvania,* as the primary example of reform philosophy during the founding period, even though Bradford took his cue from Rush and others. Indeed, Rush boasted of *An Enquiry* as proof that Bradford had finally come around to Rush's point of view, even though Bradford's approach seems more strictly utilitarian than Rush's. As attorney general of Pennsylvania, Bradford drafted the state's first penal reform statute in 1786. Once Bradford became chief justice of Pennsylvania, the governor requested that he write a report on the effectiveness of the 1786 law. This report, and its recommendations for changes in the code, formed the basis of Bradford's published pamphlet. Vaux believed that the pamphlet had a strong influence on the state assembly and that it was a primary factor in moving the assembly toward further revisions of the penal code. Vaux attributed Bradford's writings to the influence of Philadelphia's prison society.[1]

Bradford pointed to Beccaria and Montesquieu as the important influences on the modern view of punishment. He believed that the general principles upon which penal laws must be founded had been "fully settled." He took care to say that these principles had not been settled by the ancient theorists of justice but by Beccaria and Montesquieu. Their modern view of penology had become accepted by "the enlightened writers on this subject."[2] Referring favorably to the French Revolution, Bradford wrote that the "enlightened patriots" in France's first National Assembly implemented Beccarian penal reforms in their fundamental law. The French had long witnessed the severity of the criminal law and were anxious to guard against such severity in the new republic. Borrowing a passage from the French first National Assembly, Bradford wrote that "the law ought to establish such punishments *only* as are *strictly* and evidently *necessary*."[3]

Like Beccaria, Bradford explicitly rejected the strict just deserts approach to punishment:

> It being established, that the only object of human punishments is the prevention of crimes, it necessarily follows, that when a criminal is put to death, it is not to revenge the wrongs of society, or of any individual—it is not to recall past time and to undo what is already done: but merely to prevent the offender from repeating the crime, and to deter others from its commission, by the terror of the punishment.[4]

This reasoning is the basis for his argument against the death penalty for most crimes; if the penalty does not correspond to the principles of deterrence, there is no justification for it. Bradford also attacked what he saw as the vengeance-driven punishment for rape. Since the crime is so repulsive and involves the theft of female innocence, Bradford commented, this leads to a strong desire for revenge. He urged society to use reason instead, which should show that rape is more likely a crime of passion and does not indicate some permanent defect of character. "This offense, arising from the sudden abuse of a natural passion, and perpetrated in the phrenzy of desire, does not announce any irreclaimable corruption." Bradford referred to William Penn, who believed that imprisonment and hard labor were sufficient punishment for the crime of rape. Bradford remarked that the state of Vermont no longer counted rape as a capital crime. Ultimately, his position comes back to a rejection of the strict just deserts approach. "If any one, mistaking the end of punishment, and more intent on vengeance than the prevention of crime, deems this chastisement too light, a visit to the penitentiary house lately erected as part of the [jail] of Philadelphia, will correct the opinion."[5]

Rejecting the strict just deserts approach, Bradford embraced the utilitarian standards of Beccaria, that "the preventing of crimes is the sole end of punishment." He asserted that "every punishment which is not absolutely necessary for that purpose is a cruel and tyrannical act," but he also admitted that there is an appropriate role for the just deserts approach, as a limitation to the severity of utilitarian punishments. First, a punishment must be determined by its utility as a deterrent; second, the principles of just deserts—or proportionality—must ensure that the punishment is not too severe. Like Beccaria, Bradford argued that moderate punishment makes the most effective deterrent. Strict and consistent enforcement of moderate punishments provides a greater deterrent than severe punishments, which are by nature subject to arbitrary enforcement. Also like Beccaria, who contends that individuals fully aware of the consequences of criminal behavior will rationally choose obedience, Bradford urged that citizens be better educated about criminal penalties. A sound crime-control strategy should include "a *diffusion of knowledge* and a *strict execution of the laws.*" Bradford pointed to Penn's original penal code as an example of how to make the consequences of criminal behavior well known to the citizens. Bradford described Penn's laws as requiring parents to instruct their children in reading the Scriptures by age twelve. The laws also required that a copy of the criminal code, "simple and concise," be used as a schoolbook. Bradford noted similar laws in Connecticut, where children were "taught the laws against capital offenses."[6]

For purposes of deterrence, pardons concerned Bradford; he argued they "should be rarely, *very rarely*, granted."[7] When criminals are sent to prison, the punishment should be sufficiently severe to instill in them a desire never to return. "Their treatment ought to be such as to make their confinement an *actual* punishment, and the remembrance of it a terror in the future." Prisoners should not be allowed to sit idly behind bars at taxpayers' expense. "The labor, in most cases, should be real *hard* labor—the food, though wholesome, should be *coarse*—the confinement sufficiently long to break down a disposition to vice—and the salutary rigor of *perfect solitude, invariably* inflicted on the greater offenders."[8] If punishment of this sort is consistently enforced, there will be no need for more severe, corporal penalties. Bradford noted that, in 1752, the British wanted to increase the terror associated with their punishment for murder—for purposes of deterrence. Accordingly, they ordered that the bodies of those executed for murder be "delivered at Surgeons Hall, to be dissected and anatomized." Bradford conceded that there was some shock for a short time because of the punishment's novelty; but once the novelty wore off the murder rate did not change. Bradford expressed regret that the U.S. Congress chose to use this punishment in its Crimes Act of 1790.[9]

In general, Bradford argued that terribly severe punishments had not been effective as deterrents. He took up the punishment for the "crime against nature" (sodomy). This crime is so rare, he contended, because there is so little natural temptation to commit it. Accordingly, there is no need for severe penalties to deter the behavior. His argument fits nicely with Bentham's formulation that the penalty for the crime must rise in accordance with the temptation to commit it. The enlightened legislator realizes that severe penalties are not consistent with the proper goals of punishment. Such "laws might have been proper for a tribe of ardent barbarians . . . which are wholly unfit for an enlightened people of civilized and gentle manners."[10]

Bradford also made utilitarian arguments with regard to the effectiveness of punishments for burglary, robbery, and counterfeiting. He found himself responding to the charge that the state legislature's reducing the punishment for burglary and robbery had actually led to an increase in the incidence of these crimes. He attributed the apparent increase to two causes, both of which explained the concentration of these crimes in the city of Philadelphia. First, he noted that many had been pardoned of these crimes under the old laws. The pardons led to a lack of certainty and a weakening of the punishment's effectiveness. Second, many burglars and robbers had previously been punished on the pillory or whipping post. These punishments of the old law actually hardened and embittered the offenders, leading them to commit additional crimes. Had milder laws been enforced more consistently, the incidence of robbery and burglary would not have increased. Bradford used statistics from the city of Philadelphia to prove his point. He noted that of sixty-eight people convicted of burglary and robbery prior to 1790, twenty-nine had escaped, thirty had been pardoned, and five had been executed for other capital offenses. Bradford argued that almost no offender had been consistently punished in accordance with the law. When the defects of the system were corrected in 1790, the deterrent effect of the law was much improved. Bradford made special mention of the reform of the pardon power, which was confined to the hands of a single magistrate. He also pointed to the two-year periods both before and after 1790, showing that there was a considerable decrease in crime during the latter period. Also applying a utilitarian calculus to the crime of counterfeiting, Bradford argued that the temptation to commit the crime had reduced as the sophistication in the art of minting had grown. Capital punishment for counterfeiting therefore went well beyond the bounds of necessity.[11]

In addition to Bradford's utilitarian arguments, his faith in enlightenment contributed to his case for reform. He wrote approvingly of those in Europe who had listened to the voice of "reason and humanity" by undertaking a "progressive amelioration of their criminal codes." Like Beccaria, he wrote of the increasing rationality of the human mind. "A spirit of reform has gone forth . . . and the progress of liberty, by unfettering the human mind, will hasten" penal reform. He contended that sanguinary punishments were products of a "barbarous age"; because of the enlightened progress of reason, he contended, society must recognize that many punishments are not useful. "The progress of freedom, science, and morals renders them unnecessary."[12] Beccaria claims that history brings the human mind to higher stages of rationality, whereby milder punishments will achieve a strong level of deterrence.

Bradford, because of his faith in enlightenment, emphasized knowledge and education as the best means of preventing crimes. He praised the policy of other states that required education. This policy "deserves attention and imitation." The more individuals understand that criminal behavior will result in consequences contrary to their own interest, the more likely they are to rationally avoid committing crimes. In both New England and Scotland, he contended, executions were rare. This is "owing to the diffusion of knowledge. . . . Early education prevents more crimes than the severity of the criminal code."[13]

There appears to be no clear moral distinction between criminal and noncriminal for Bradford. Instead, it seems, he believed that those who behave criminally have not been sufficiently shown that crime is not in their interest. In a way, society is culpable for crime, because it has not provided education sufficient to deter it. Praising education as enlightenment, Bradford urged Pennsylvania to follow the dictates of its constitution, which called for the establishment of a public education system. The "enlightened legislator" would be able to overcome whatever obstacles existed to implement this constitutional provision.[14]

Bradford's faith in the progress of enlightenment translates into an argument against the death penalty for most crimes. The increasing rationality of individuals "may hasten the period, when, in the progress of civilization, the punishment of death shall cease to be necessary."[15] Bradford's argument against the death penalty is the same as Beccaria's—not that the penalty is unjust but that it is not necessary in order to deter. Bradford did not go quite as far as Beccaria because he did not believe that the complete abolition of capital punishment was yet possible. He did say that it is *almost* always unnecessary. "One would think," he argues, "that, in a nation jealous of its liberty, . . . the infliction of death, the highest power that a man exercises over man, would seldom be prescribed where its necessity was doubtful." He contended that there are other punishments that would have the same utility, such as "perpetual imprisonment." With life in prison, there can be the possible payment of reparation to the victim; there can also be swift punishment, which (for reasons he left unexplained) is not otherwise possible. Finally, imprisonment allows for the potential reform of the offender. If "the offender becomes humbled and reformed, society, instead of losing, gains a citizen."[16]

Bradford analyzed capital punishment by the standard of utility. He believed the death penalty was not generally the most effective punishment. When juries know that the punishment for a crime is death, they are much less likely to convict. This creates an uncertainty in the punishment; like Beccaria, Bradford argued that certainty is more important than severity in producing deterrence. "The prospect of escaping detection and the hopes of an acquittal or pardon, blunt [the death penalty's] operation and defeat the expectations of the Legislature." In contending that certainty is more important than severity, Bradford referred to the works of the "most enlightened men of Europe." These men argue that "the imagination is soon accustomed to over-look or despise the *degree* of the penalty, and . . . the *certainty* of it is the only effectual restraint."[17]

Bradford referred to experience with the death penalty in order to demonstrate its ineffectiveness. In the most successful stage of the Roman republic, no one was punished with death other than the slaves. He referred also to East India, "where the gentlest of punishments are said to be a curb as effectual as the most bloody code in other countries." England, by contrast, had a number of very severe and bloody punishments, yet had a greater crime rate than anywhere else in Europe. Bradford also looked at the different experiences of the American states. He remarked that some states implemented the death penalty for horse stealing, forgery, robbery, burglary, and other such crimes. He argued that there was no evidence that such crimes had been prevented more effectively in those states that used the death penalty than in those that did not. He looked at horse stealing in particular. Generally speaking, the states north of Pennsylvania treated horse stealing like other kinds of simple larceny, whereas states south of Pennsylvania treated it as a capital crime; yet the rates of horse stealing showed little difference. In Virginia, Bradford said, horse stealing was the most frequently committed crime, even though it was punishable by death. The same analysis applied to the case of forgery, which in New York was considered a capital crime but in Pennsylvania was not, with a similar outcome.[18]

Bradford advocated the abolition of the death penalty, because of its ineffectiveness, except "in the higher cases of treason and murder." He noted that many Europeans had argued for the total abolition of capital punishments. He also said that some Americans had argued similarly, and he named Rush in particular. Bradford's standard was "whether it is *necessary* for the peace, order, and happiness of society."[19] He believed that where there is no hope of pardon, execution for murder will be rare, but the penalty should be maintained for murder because Bradford could not yet be confident that other punishments would prove as effective:

> I do not affirm that it is *absolutely* necessary, or that a milder one will be insufficient. It is possible that the further diffusion of knowledge and meliora-

tion of manners, may render capital punishment unnecessary in all cases: but, until we have more experience, it is safest to tread with caution on such delicate ground.[20]

Bradford considered the argument that a long life of imprisonment might seem a more terrible alternative than a quick death, and hence prove a more effective deterrent, and he ultimately rejected this contention as untenable. He reasoned that this argument might have some merit in those countries with sharp class distinctions, where a man's life in a less-favored class might be so wretched he would easily risk death to improve it. In America, Bradford believed, death was still the most feared penalty. Death is easy to imagine, creating a terror in one's mind. Life in prison is more vague—it is hard to conjure up a great fear of it because it is unknown and imprecise.[21]

Bradford wrote favorably of Pennsylvania for making penal reform one of its priorities. He specifically mentioned the abolition of the death penalty for many crimes.[22] He believed the lower crime rates proved the effectiveness of reform. It is in America, of all places, that penal reform should enjoy the most success, he argued. It is a new country, with morals and institutions that have not been corrupted like those of Europe. Why is it, he asked, that most criminal codes in America continued to adhere to the old laws, copied from the British?[23] He praised Virginia, as well, where the Committee of Revisors had recommended the abolition of capital punishment in all cases other than treason and murder.

Referring to the historical development of Pennsylvania's laws, Bradford noted that William Penn had no choice but to imitate the laws of England. He cited the charter, which directed that the laws of the Pennsylvania colony be made consistent with those of England. Bradford praised Penn for resisting this directive as much as possible. Penn was "a philosopher whose elevated mind rose above the errors and prejudices of his age, like a mountain, whose summit is enlightened by the first beams of the sun, while the plains are still covered with mists and darkness." Penn was a reformer because he was more enlightened than his time. Of Penn's great and enlightened acts, Bradford mentioned his prohibition of religious intolerance and his prohibition of forfeiture in cases of suicide. Penn's first penal code was enlightened because it prescribed punishments "calculated to tie up the hands of the criminal—to reform—and to hold up an object of terror sufficient to check a people whose manners he endeavored to fashion."[24] Bradford argued that, during the thirty-five years that Penn's mild penal code was in place, the penalties were not any less effective. Since these laws were often before the legislature, he reasoned, there would have been ample opportunity to amend them had they been ineffective.[25] Bradford attacked the colonial legislature, implying that it was cowardly for eventually caving in to British pressure. Reflecting one of the primary motives for American penal reform, he wrote that "the severity of our criminal law is an exotic plant and not the native growth of Pennsylvania. . . . The religious opinions of many of our citizens were in opposition to it: and, as soon as the principles of Beccaria were disseminated, they found a soil that was prepared to receive them."[26] The irony is that Beccaria was vigorously opposed to the influence of religious principles in lawmaking.

Bradford made some criticisms of specific sections of the state penal code. He wished that distinctions had been made for different degrees of robbery and burglary, particularly with regard to the use of a deadly weapon. He wrote favorably of Milan, where such distinctions were on the books. Bradford argued that Milan was enjoying great success under these statutes, according to an account given to him by a nephew of Beccaria who had been visiting the United States. Bradford also attacked the laws against petty treason in Pennsylvania. The effect of the law was to implement different punishments for men and women; men were to be hanged, whereas women were to be drawn and burned. "Is not this distinction unjust?" he asked. He attacked the barbarity of execution by burning. He suggested that Pennsylvania might adopt a statute like that of the federal government, stipulating that all executions were to be carried out by hanging.[27] Bradford called for a statute differentiating degrees of murder. For the purpose of creating a more terrible impression upon the imagination, the punishment for the highest degree of murder "ought to be *widely* different from that of every other crime."[28] Such a statute would deter criminals from murdering in an effort to eliminate witnesses to a lesser crime. (This should be compared with Beccaria's argument for punishing attempted crime less severely than crime actually committed.)

Bradford's writing was influential on other reformers of the day,[29] including Roberts Vaux, who became prominent for his work in prisons. For Vaux and others who were part of the reform movement, prevention and reform became the most important goals of the criminal justice system. Vaux wrote: "It will not, at this enlightened period, be denied, that one of the first duties, as well as the true policy, of every government, is to adopt measures *for the prevention of crime;* not that the most powerful instrument for effecting this important object is *universal education.*"[30] Vaux referred to the "rude age" when offenses "were avenged at the will and by the power of the injured party." He praised Penn for his help in bringing about the enlightened age of penal reform. Vaux noted that Penn's code focused on deterrence, not on vengeance, and was consistent with the views of the most "enlightened" men and thinkers in America and Europe.[31]

POST-REVOLUTIONARY REFORM IN PENNSYLVANIA

The first post-Revolutionary reform of Pennsylvania's criminal code came in 1786, pursuant to the state constitution of 1776. When independence was declared, the Continental Congress recommended to the states that each establish a form of government. Edwin R. Keedy comments on the influence of the Whig Society, which he describes as "patriotic and liberal," in drafting the Pennsylvania constitution. This society was influenced by French philosophers, particularly Montesquieu and Voltaire. Keedy identifies Thomas Paine, Charles Willson Peale, David Rittenhouse, Timothy Matlack, Dr. Thomas Young, and James Cannon as members of the Whig Society; of these, Cannon, Rittenhouse, and Matlack were appointed to the committee responsible for drafting the new frame of government.[32] The constitution called for the future reform of the state's penal laws: "The penal laws as heretofore used shall be reformed by the legislature of this state, as soon as may be, and punishments made in some cases less sanguinary, and in general more proportionate to the crimes." To accommodate the anticipated reform, the constitution also stated that "houses ought to be provided for punishing by hard labour, those who shall be convicted of crimes not capital." The purpose of such "houses," according to the constitution, was "to deter more effectually from the commission of crimes, by continued visible punishments of long duration, and to make sanguinary punishments less necessary."[33]

The preamble to the 1786 law entitled "An Act Amending the Penal Laws of This State" made it clear that the revisions were founded upon a fulfillment of the 1776 constitution:

> Whereas by . . . the constitution of this commonwealth it is declared, "That the penal laws as heretofore used should be reformed by the legislature of this state as soon as may be and punishments made in some cases less sanguinary and in general more proportionate to the crimes." And . . . that, "To deter more effectually from the commissions of crimes by continued visible punishment of long duration, and to make sanguinary punishment less necessary, houses ought to be provided for punishing by hard labor those who shall be convicted of crimes not capital, wherein the criminal shall be employed for the benefit of the public or for reparation of injuries done to private persons."[34]

The preamble stated that the goals of the criminal code were "to correct and reform the offenders, and to produce such strong impression upon the minds of others as to deter them from committing the like offenses."[35]

The main focus of the 1786 reform was to abolish the death penalty for many crimes and to implement instead "continued hard labor, publicly and disgracefully imposed on persons convicted of [crimes], not only in the manner pointed out by the convention, but in streets of cities and towns, and upon the highways of the open country and other public works." These were the famous wheelbarrow laws, which required chain gangs of prisoners to perform labor on the streets of Philadelphia during the late 1780s and early 1790s. The new law moderated the penalties for robbery, burglary, sodomy, and buggery. The penalty for each became forfeiture of property in order to pay damages, plus a term not to exceed ten years in prison. For horse stealing, offenders were required to return the horse, to pay the value of the horse to the victim, to pay the same amount to the commonwealth, and to serve a prison term of no more than seven years. The statute also created the category of simple larceny, defined as a theft not to exceed twenty shillings in value. Punishment for this crime was restoration of the goods, payment of double damages (half to the victim, half to the commonwealth), and a prison term of up to three years. The statute shifted the burden of proof for infanticide to the prosecution, meaning that a woman who had concealed the death of a bastard child did not have to prove it was stillborn in order to avoid a murder conviction.[36]

The 1786 statute laid down the rules for those who were to be punished with imprisonment. They were to be put to hard labor, preferably in the public view, on the various public works projects in the respective county. The statute directed that prisoners should be adequately fed and clothed. When the prisoners were working in public, they were required to have some indication on their garment of the crime they committed so that the public could see for itself the consequences of criminal behavior.[37] Although the requirement for public labor was urged by many reformers, they eventually became convinced that such labor was counterproductive. Caleb Lownes, one of the original members of the prison society who later wrote a firsthand account of the new penitentiary, complained that the law, "however well meant, was soon found to be productive of the *greatest evils:* and had a very opposite effect from what was contemplated by the framers of the law." Lownes contended that because the public was exposed to the prisoners' "drunkenness, profanity and indecency," the level of public disorder actually increased.[38] The perceived problems with the 1786 law actually led to the formation of Philadelphia's prison society in 1787.

Moderate revisions of the 1786 code were undertaken in 1789 and the early 1790s. In 1790 the legislature enacted a code that essentially reiterated the penalties of the 1786 law but also effected a prison system that concentrated more heavily on solitary confinement. The law directed that prisons should be divided into cells or apartments. The law also provided for the sanitary condition of prisons, stipulating that "the walls of the cells and apartments shall be whitewashed with lime and water at least twice in every year and the floors of the said cells and apartments shall be washed once every week or oftener." The law prohibited jailers from keeping together those awaiting trial and those already convicted of felonies.[39]

In 1791 the legislature passed a revision that mainly addressed criminal procedure, but the new act did effect the moderation of some punishments. It repealed the extension of the British punishment for the crime of witchcraft, taking it off the books entirely. The law also repealed the old punishment for adultery and fornication, which had consisted of "whipping, imprisonment at hard labor, or branding." It set limits for any new punishment that might be imposed for these crimes at a fine not to exceed £50 and a prison term of between three and twelve months.[40]

In 1794 Pennsylvania enacted laws that Vaux characterized as the most progressive reforms ever made.[41] During 1793 and 1794 the Pennsylvania Assembly debated a proposed overhaul of the penal code. William Bradford's pamphlet served as a commentary on the 1786 code and suggested potential corrections and improvements. Much of the debate focused on the writings of Bradford, who was then chief justice of the Pennsylvania Supreme Court. Governor Mifflin recommended Bradford's pamphlet to the legislature as a guide for crafting new statutes.[42]

The revision was enacted on April 5, 1794, and was entitled "An Act for the Better Preventing of Crimes, and for Abolishing the Punishment of Death in Certain Cases." The preamble of the act restated the goal of the criminal justice system: "to prevent the commission of crimes, and to repair the injury that hath been done thereby to society or the individual." The statute is most well known for reducing the use of the death penalty, stating that "the punishment of death ought never to be inflicted where it is not absolutely necessary to the public safety."[43]

The 1794 act directed that "no crime whatsoever, hereafter committed (except murder in the first degree) shall be punished with death in the state of Pennsylvania." The statute also eliminated the classification of some murders as petty treason; all first-degree murders were to be punished similarly. For those crimes that were to be punished by means other than death, the statute laid out sentences: from six to twelve years in prison for high treason; from five to twelve years for arson; from ten to twenty-one years for rape; from five to eighteen years for second-degree murder; from four to fifteen years for counterfeiting; from two to ten years for intentional maiming and also for voluntary manslaughter. For the crimes of counterfeiting and intentional maiming, fines of up to $1,000 were also made part of the punishment. The code gave prosecutors the discretion to prosecute involuntary manslaughter as a misdemeanor. As

Bradford had urged, the statute directed that anyone put to death for first-degree murder should be executed by hanging.[44]

The 1794 statute was the first criminal statute in the new American states to create degrees of murder. It established both first-degree and second-degree murder, defining the former as "perpetrated by means of poison, or by lying in wait, or by any other kind of willful, deliberate or premeditated killing, or which shall be committed in the perpetration, or attempt to perpetrate, any arson, rape, robbery or burglary."[45] Juries finding offenders guilty of murder were also to decide upon the degree of murder involved. For offenders pleading guilty, the law directed the court to determine the degree of murder.[46]

DEVELOPMENT OF THE PENITENTIARY

The reform of the penal law in Pennsylvania coincided with the development of the penitentiary. As Rush had urged, Pennsylvania prisons became focused on rehabilitation by hard labor, solitude, and prayer. There were three main stages in the development of Pennsylvania's detention system. The first type of jail in the Pennsylvania colony was the typical detention jail, where those who could not pay fines were kept along with those awaiting trial; this type of jail was called for by the Hempstead laws of 1676. In 1682 the provincial council ordered the first jail to be built. The council directed officials to "build a cage against the next council-day, of seven feet long by five feet broad." The responsibility for preventing prisoner escapes fell upon Patrick Robinson, clerk of the provincial council. Robinson built a set of cages on one side of his own home, while his family lived on the other side; Robinson's cages constituted the so-called hired house.

In 1695 the process of constructing High Street Prison was undertaken, after the hired house proved inadequate. The new prison was completed in 1723, but not before modifications were made to include the various implements of corporal punishment required by the more severe code of 1718. Among these were a whipping post, stocks, pillory, and ducking stool. The famous Walnut Street Jail was authorized in 1773, but its construction was postponed because of the war. The jail was finally opened in 1784.[47]

The main force behind reforming the prison system was the prison society, of which Rush and Lownes were important members. The first president of the prison society was Bishop William White of Philadelphia's Christ Church.[48] Vaux lauded the prison society for battling the prevailing public sentiment against reform.[49] The very first article published in the prison society's journal remarked that the inception of the society took place during "a period when that mighty controversy first commenced between benevolent and intelligent reformers and the supporters of an antiquated and inhuman penal code—a code as variant with sound policy as with Christianity."[50] The constitution of the society read, in part:

> The obligations of benevolence, which are founded on the precepts and examples of the Author of Christianity, are not cancelled by the follies or crimes of our fellow creatures. . . . By the aid of humanity, . . . such degrees and modes of punishment [should] be discovered and suggested, as may, instead of continuing habits of vice, become the means of restoring our fellow creatures to virtue and happiness.[51]

The society's members were great admirers of an English advocate of reform, John Howard. The society began a correspondence with Howard in 1788, sending him a copy of its constitution. Vaux quoted from one of the society's 1788 letters to Howard:

> The Society heartily concur with the friends of humanity in Europe, in expressing their obligations to you for having rendered the miserable tenants of prisons the objects of more general attention and compassion, and for having pointed out some of the means of not only alleviating their miseries, but of preventing those crimes and misfortunes which are the causes of them.[52]

Howard wrote in one of his return letters that he wished he could establish in his country some permanent charity like the prison society.[53] One of the prison society's main complaints with the penal code (in fact, it was the reason for the society's organization in the first place) was the wheelbarrow law contained in the 1786 revisions. The society circulated a petition protesting the subjection of prisoners to labor in public. The petition generally praised the direction of the 1786 reform but advocated punishment by solitary confinement and hard labor.[54]

It was largely as a result of the prison society's efforts that the Walnut Street Jail became the nation's first model of a penitentiary. Bradley Chapin gives the prison society significant credit: "It is no exaggeration to say that by making long-term incarceration possible and giving it purpose, the Society saved the experiment in felony law reform."[55] The society was also the first to introduce religious services into prisons. These were not conducted without safety precautions, however, implemented by an apparently skeptical jailer: "A cannon was placed beside the improvised pulpit and a gunner stood by with a lighted match ready to fire into the mass of convicts at any sign of a riot."[56] The society was apparently aware that it was a leader in the penal reform movement, as it wrote regularly to the governors of other states to inform them of the success of Pennsylvania's new penitentiary system.

Lownes attributed much of the success to the establishment of regular prison inspections, which had begun pursuant to legislation enacted in 1789 and 1790. The prison society had urged the legislature to "place the prison under the inspection of some of the citizens," and Lownes credited the "perseverance" of the inspectors for the improvement in the prison.[57] The prison society was involved in the appointment of the inspectors, whose purpose Lownes recounted was to "furnish bread when necessary, . . . clothe the naked, . . . accommodate differences," and "generally to mitigate the sufferings inseparable from such places of confinement."[58] The inspectors met roughly every two weeks and appointed two of their number to be responsible for visiting the prison regularly for a period of one month. In addition to these inspections, various court officers visited the prison once each quarter. Lownes contended that these quarterly visits "strengthen[ed] the hands of the officers" by serving as an incentive for the prisoners to behave properly in the hopes of impressing the visitors and securing an early release. The prison inspectors were also responsible for overseeing the separation of the debtors from other prisoners, the separation of the sexes, the suppression of liquor, and the institution of useful labor.[59]

One of the most successful aspects of the new prison regimen, according to Lownes, was the employment of the prisoners. Men were employed "according to their abilities and circumstances," and they undertook such tasks as making shoes, weaving and tailoring, chipping logwood, grinding plaster of Paris, beating hemp, and polishing marble. Women were "employed at heckling, spinning, sewing, and washing." In addition to employment and regular attendance at religious worship, Lownes stressed the importance of improved sanitary conditions. According to the new regimen, the prison was whitewashed at least three times a year; the hallways and cells were washed at least twice a week during the summer, and once a week during the winter; clean linen was provided once a week; and the prisoners were washed each morning, with the men shaving at least twice a week. The diet of the prisoners was "plain, cheap, and wholesome, but sufficient quantity." The prospect of an occasional piece of meat served as an incentive for meritorious behavior. In fact, Lownes considered it essential that a broad system of rewards and punishments was established under the new regimen, particularly the possibility of a pardon for "long habits of orderly conduct." For disorderly conduct, which had previously been dealt with by corporal punishment, the new regimen instead provided solitary confinement. Lownes claimed that the new incentive system was responsible for the sharp decline in escape attempts, remarking that the prisoners "have now other and better hopes of obtaining a restoration to liberty, arising from a propriety of conduct which they know has been a means of procuring the liberation of many, from first offences, under the new system."[60]

Lownes was a forceful and persuasive advocate of the Pennsylvania reforms and the new penitentiary system. He remarked that he had "frequently been requested by respectable characters in other states, who wished a change in their system, to furnish some account" of the Philadelphia experiment.[61] In his arguments, he employed much of the language of the Enlightenment reform movement. He consistently emphasized the mildness of the new rules, along with their strict enforcement. Education of the prisoners about the new rules—aimed at awakening an enlightened self-interest—was the central component of the new reform efforts. "Mild regulations," he argued, "strictly enjoined, will meet with little resistance."[62]

Lownes parted company with the strict utilitarian approach, however, in his preference for indeterminate sentencing. Beccaria had advocated inflexible (though mild) penalties in order to serve as a clear deterrent. Lownes argued that such sentences are, from the perspective of a prisoner, a disincentive to good behavior and genuine repentance.[63]

The new incentive-based regimen of Philadelphia's prison excited interest not only in other American states but also in Europe. The Frenchman le Duc de La Rochefoucauld-Liancourt published a description of the Walnut Street Jail, arguing that Pennsylvania's effort had proved influential on other states and enjoyed more success than similar efforts in Europe. He praised Pennsylvania for being the only state at the time to limit the death penalty to first-degree murder, and he boasted that "the attention of the legislative assemblies, and of every philanthropic individual, in every state, have been turned upon [the Pennsylvania system]. They are uniting to collect information on the details of this new system, and the best methods of putting them into practice."[64]

La Rochefoucauld-Liancourt hoped that Europe would follow the lead of Pennsylvania and that Pennsylvania would serve "as a model, to reform the criminal jurisprudence, and establish a new system of imprisonment, in the Old World. . . . To America, it must be confessed, we are indebted for the first example."[65] For La Rochefoucauld-Liancourt, Pennsylvania was proof that the theories of the British reformer John Howard could work in practice. "Howard, thanks to the wisdom of the state of Pennsylvania, will be henceforth acknowledged to be a philosopher as acute in his observations, and as enlightened in his views, as in his disposition virtuous, and friendly to the human race."[66] In particular, La Rochefoucauld-Liancourt pointed to the jailers in the Philadelphia system as a way to contrast this system with most European systems. In Philadelphia the jailer "is not . . . , as is too often the case in Europe, an extortioner." He noted that Philadelphia jailers were better paid so that they did not have a need to extort money from prisoners as in Europe. La Rochefoucauld-Liancourt had a more favorable view of Philadelphia's jailers than others who wrote about the prisons.[67] In fact, the very purpose of having prison inspectors under Pennsylvania's penitentiary law was to ensure that reluctant jailers would comply with the new prison regimen.

Proper implementation of the new prison regimen was a primary concern for Caleb Lownes. Many, including La Rochefoucauld-Liancourt, credited Lownes as the individual most responsible for the improvement in the Walnut Street Jail. According to La Rochefoucauld-Liancourt, Lownes's "indefatigable zeal" ultimately obtained the favor of the legislature for the plans of the prison society. La Rochefoucauld-Liancourt also credited Lownes for the increasing sympathy of William Bradford. He claimed that Bradford "embraced with ardor, the new system, associated himself with Caleb Lownes, assisted him with that advice which could be given only by a man well versed in the science of jurisprudence; and shared with him his hopes, his labours, and his deservings."[68]

There were several important changes in post-Revolutionary Pennsylvania law that turned the Walnut Street Jail into the first modern penitentiary. Vaux noted that the prison society convinced the legislature to address the problem of properly separating the prisoners—into groups of those awaiting trial and those already convicted. The society also convinced the legislature to order the separation of the sexes within the prison.[69] The 1786 statute called for the separation of the older convicts from the younger ones, who "from want of a pious education are drawn unwarily into the commission of crimes and are apprehended and brought to punishment before they become so hardened as to be void of shame or beyond hope of being reclaimed."[70]

A 1789 statute addressed the issue of separating convicted felons from the other inmates. It required that anyone sentenced to a year or more be removed to a specified part of the jail, which was to be considered a separate facility; this facility was to be called the "common prison of the city and county of Philadelphia."[71] The prison society often had to obtain court orders to force the jailer to comply with the law. By Vaux's account the jailer was almost as criminal as most of the inmates.[72] By addressing such problems, the 1794 law represented a long-sought victory by Philadelphia's reformers.

CHAPTER THREE

The Spread of Reform?

The Cases of Virginia and New York

PENNSYLVANIA WAS NOT THE ONLY STATE to overhaul its criminal code during the founding era, although it was probably the most important. Pennsylvania appears to have been a model for some other states. In particular, many view the post-Revolutionary changes in the criminal codes of Virginia and New York as attempts to follow Pennsylvania down the road to reform. Both Thomas Jefferson in Virginia and Thomas Eddy in New York referred frequently to the Pennsylvania experience as they undertook their own reform efforts.

JEFFERSON AND THE VIRGINIA REFORMS

Although Jefferson's reform proposals predated the important changes in Pennsylvania, the reforms ultimately enacted in Virginia two decades later were understood even by Jefferson himself as having been improved by Pennsylvania's example. Virginia is of particular interest because its statutory revisions were based on the recommendations of Jefferson and the Committee of Revisors (of which he was a member). One of the founders most sympathetic to the Enlightenment, Jefferson advocated milder penalties in the criminal code, and he was convinced that "the reformation of offenders" was "an object worthy of the attention of the laws." This belief in reformation, in part, led him to call for milder criminal penalties, especially a reduced role for capital punishment. Jefferson contended that capital punishment "weakens the state" by eliminating many who might become productive citizens. Even if they were to remain in prison, such offenders would serve as "living and long-continued spectacles to deter others from committing the like offenses."[1]

Accordingly, the most important provision of Jefferson's proposed code was the abolition of the death penalty for all crimes other than treason and murder. This and other provisions of the proposed new code represented vast reductions from previous levels of punishment in Virginia. To understand the important influences in Virginia's undertaking such revisions, it is necessary to examine their roots in the colonial era.

Virginia's Pre-Revolutionary Penal Code

The first laws of Virginia were the "first written manifestations of the common law in America."[2] The British crown granted a charter to the Virginia Company in 1606, and the first body of law was crafted between 1609 and 1612. In the second charter to the Virginia Company in 1609, the British granted the Company's officers the authority to make the necessary laws and ordinances, "so always, as the said statutes, ordinances and proceedings, as near as conveniently may be, be agreeable to the laws, statutes, government, and policy of our realm of this England."[3] From the earliest criminal law in Virginia, it is apparent that strict discipline was a top concern. David H. Flaherty, editor of a collection of Virginia's earliest colonial statutes, argues that the founders of the Virginia colony were convinced that a lack of discipline had contributed to the failure of the Roanoke expedition in the 1580s. The Virginia Company, therefore, gave the governor of the colony great power to wield martial law in order to maintain discipline.[4]

The charter gave the colony's officers the authority to punish the following crimes with the death penalty: tumult, rebellion, conspiracy, mutiny, sedition, murder, manslaughter, incest, rape, and adultery. The punishment was to be executed without benefit of clergy, with the exception of manslaughter.[5] In addition to the punishments stipulated in the charter, the colonial government enacted several ordinances for other types of crime. The colonial statutes made it a capital crime to "speake impiously or maliciously, against the holy and blessed Trinitie, or any of the three persons," to "blaspheme Gods holy name," to utter "traiterous words against his Majesties Person, or royal authority," or to "speake any word, or do any act, which may tend to the derision, or despight of Gods holy word."[6] The colonial laws also made several other crimes capital, in some cases confirming the dictates of the charter and in others going beyond it: murder, sodomy, adultery, rape, sacrilege (stealing or robbing from a church, or trespassing in a church), robbery, burglary, and bearing false witness or taking an oath untruly. There were also several capital crimes dealing with the economic well-being of the colony: stealing from a Native American coming to trade, trading with the Native Americans without authority, embezzling or defrauding the colony, embezzling or robbing a fort, selling overpriced goods, and destroying an animal without permission of the government. The colony later extended the death penalty to such crimes as taking a fruit or vegetable from a garden or vineyard. There were several capital crimes associated with exploration and shipping: deliberately failing to return from a scouting, fishing, hunting, or trading voyage; departing by ship without permission; and selling any commodity of the colony to a departing ship.[7]

Colonial law required corporal punishments for most minor infractions. To "unworthily demeane [one]self unto any Preacher, or Minister of [God's word]" merited three whippings, plus a public begging of forgiveness on three consecutive Sabbath days. To miss church on Sunday merited the loss of a day's pay on the first offense, a whipping on the second offense, and imprisonment in the galleys for six months on the third offense. Failure to keep holy the Sabbath day—by working or playing— merited the loss of a week's pay on the first offense, a whipping on the second offense, and death on the third offense. The crime of fornication was to be punished by a whipping on the first and second offenses, and a whipping three times per week for an entire month—plus a public begging of forgiveness—on the third offense.[8] Speaking out against the government was to be punished on the first offense by three whippings, and the offender was, "upon his knees, to acknowledge his offence and to aske forgivenesse upon the Saboth day in the assembly of the congregation." On the second offense of speaking against the government, the offender was to be punished by three years in the galleys, and on the third offense by death. The laws also directed that

> no man shall give any disgracefull words, or commit any act to the disgrace of any person in this Colonie, or any part thereof, upon paine of being tied head and feete together, upon the guard everie night for the space of one moneth, besides to bee publikely disgraced hemselfe, and be made uncapable ever after to possesse any place, or execute any office in the imployment.[9]

The laws prohibited the defiling of public waterways by cleaning, washing clothes, or relieving oneself near a public water supply. Nor was anyone, "within lesse then a quarter of one mile from the Pallizadoes, [to] dare to doe the necessities of nature, since by the unmanly, slothfull, and loathesome immodesties, the whole Fort may bee choaked, and poisoned with ill aires." Such crimes were to be punished with a whipping and any other punishment determined by the martial court.[10]

The laws required that one's house be kept clean, in addition to the street in front of one's house. Failure to comply would require one to answer to the martial court for any punishment it deemed appropriate. For leaving work early, one was to be punished by having one's head and heels tied together for one night on the first offense, by a whipping on the second offense, and by imprisonment in the galleys for one year on the third offense. If any "cleaning-woman" were to steal or withhold clothes, or intentionally ruin clothes, she was to be whipped and imprisoned until she could make restitution. If any baker used inferior ingredients, his ears were to be chopped off on the first offense, he was to be sent to the galleys for one year on the second offense, and for three years on the third offense.[11] Despite, and perhaps because of, the harshness of these earliest laws, it seems, magistrates and judges were often unwilling to impose the punishments required. The penalties were left to the discretion of officers or judges, giving them wide latitude in how they were to be applied.

According to Jefferson's account in the *Notes on the State of Virginia*, the first representative form of government was formally declared in 1621, although it had existed de facto since 1619. The government consisted of a council of state, whose duty was to advise and assist the governor; this council was made up of the colony's treasurer and other officials of the Virginia Company. The government also consisted of a general assembly, which contained the council of state, plus the House of Burgesses. Each town elected two representatives to the House of Burgesses. Jefferson also notes that no law passed by the assembly could take effect until it was approved by the Company in England, nor could any provision made by the Company take effect until it had been approved by the colonial assembly. Eventually, the king and the Company quarreled, and the royal government took the place of the Company.[12]

The public law of colonial Virginia was of two types: that which was merely a direct application of British law to the colony and that which was passed by the colonial assembly.[13] Jefferson also wrote of the colony's opposition to Oliver Cromwell and Parliament. He notes that the colony was forced to lay down its arms in 1651, after a written agreement had been signed between the British and the Virginia colonists. The agreement reaffirmed the authority of the colonial assembly but stated that "nothing is to be acted or done contrarie to the government of the Common wealth of England and the lawes there established."[14]

Governor George Yeardley convened the first general assembly in June 1619, and this assembly enacted a formal criminal code. It abolished some of the most disproportionate punishments but maintained most of the previous severe penal code based upon the British common law. Among the changes, the punishment for missing church was changed to a fine of one pound of tobacco. If one missed church for an entire month, the fine was increased to fifty pounds of tobacco.[15] The new laws also altered punishment for "persons of quality" (that is, the upper class). Instead of being subjected to corporal punishments, they were to be fined or imprisoned: "Such persons of quality as shall be founde delinquent in their duties being not fitt to undergoe corporal punishment may notwithstanding be ymprisoned at the discretione of the commander & for greater offences be subject to a fine inflicted by the monthlie court."[16]

In general, most minor infractions were made punishable by various forms of corporal punishment. With regard to most crimes, the new laws followed the pattern of the common law. They were divided into the categories of felony and misdemeanor, and most felonies were punishable by death. The laws further divided felonies into those that were and those that were not subject to the benefit of clergy.[17]

Modeled after the common law, the new Virginia code maintained a hefty dose of severity. It retained the death penalty for treason, tumults, rebellion, conspiracy, mutiny, sedition, murder, incest, rape, and adultery, all without benefit of clergy; manslaughter was also punishable by death but allowed the benefit of clergy. Other crimes were to be punished by imprisonment, forfeiture of property, or corporal punishments such as the whipping post or ducking stool.[18] The common law method of execution for capital crimes, which also served as the basis for colonial law, varied depending upon the particular offense. Perhaps the most infamous methods of execution were reserved for high treason and petty treason. For high treason, male offenders were to be drawn to the gallows, hanged, cut down while still alive, have their entrails removed and burned while still alive, and finally be beheaded and quartered. Female offenders were to be drawn to the gallows and burned alive.[19] For petty treason, which could consist of a servant killing his master or a wife killing her husband, male offenders were to be drawn and hanged while female offenders were to be drawn and burned.[20] Given the importance of tobacco to the economic health of Virginia, any fraud connected with tobacco was to draw severe punishment.[21] Some minor revisions to the criminal code were made after the 1619 assembly, but this was the general nature of the laws until and through the Revolutionary period. The code was changed to include the crime of counterfeiting paper currency, for which the penalty was death without benefit of clergy.

Jefferson's Proposed Revisions

Once the colonies declared their independence, Jefferson proposed legislation to form a committee to undertake a wholesale revision of Virginia's laws. He wrote, "our whole code must be reviewed, adapted to our republican form of government. . . . It should be corrected, in all its parts, with a single eye to reason, and the good of those for whose government it was framed." The legislature adopted the proposal in October 1776 and appointed Jefferson to the Committee of Revisors, along with Edmund Pendleton, George Wythe, George Mason, and Thomas L. Lee.[22] When the Virginia state legislature (which now consisted of a House of Delegates and a Senate) approved Jefferson's proposal, it did so in "An act for the revision of the Laws." There was no special mention of the criminal laws. The bill simply stated that prior law enacted under the crown might not be applicable under the new form of government:

> It is become necessary to make corresponding changes in the laws heretofore in force, many of which are inapplicable to the powers of government as now organised, others are founded on principles heterogeneous to the republican spirit, others which, long before such change, had been oppressive to the people, could yet never be repealed while the regal power continued.[23]

The law directed the Committee of Revisors to determine and propose the necessary changes.

When the original committee met in January 1777, two of its members resigned. Both Mason and Lee reasoned that they were not lawyers and were not qualified for the work. The committee divided its work among the remaining three members. Jefferson became responsible for a review of the common law and the British statutes up until James I, Wythe became responsible for the British statutes from James I forward, and Pendleton became responsible for the Virginia statutes. Of the original members of the committee, Pendleton and Lee proposed adopting an entirely new code, but Jefferson, along with Wythe and Mason, objected that a complete replacement would prove unworkable. Jefferson argued that it was impractical to take up an entirely new system of laws. With a completely new text, he reasoned, every word would be tested and subjected to repeated judicial interpretations. This would result in the code being tied up in litigation for years. Jefferson won the argument.[24]

Jefferson claimed that all of the Revisors were agreed on the abolition of the death penalty for all crimes except murder and treason. They were also agreed that criminals should be put to "hard labor in the public works." Jefferson was later to change his view on public hard labor and wrote that such punishments, he learned, had backfired in Pennsylvania.

> Exhibited as a public spectacle, with shaved heads and mean clothing, working on the high roads, produced in the criminals such a prostration of

character, such an abandonment of self-respect, as, instead of reforming, plunged them into the most desperate and hardened depravity of morals and character.[25]

Jefferson was led to advocate hard labor behind prison walls. He also said that the advisors agreed that criminals should, in some cases, be punished by the lex talionis—the law of retaliation. Reflecting on this many years later in 1821, Jefferson apparently changed his view: "How this last revolting principle came to obtain our approbation, I do not remember. . . . The modern mind had left it far in the rear of its advances."[26]

The Revisors proposed abolishing both the benefit of clergy and the pardon. Instead of the pardon, the proposal stipulated that the court may allow a new trial if it "shall doubt that [the verdict] may be untrue for defect of testimony, or other cause." The purpose of eliminating pardons was so "that none may be induced to injure through hope of impunity."[27] In addition to this Beccarian reasoning, Jefferson referred to Beccaria more explicitly in the notes he attached to the proposal in his autobiography.[28] In the portion of the bill where Jefferson argued that the families of those who commit suicide should not be punished with forfeiture, he referred to Beccaria's chapter on suicide and expatriation. Jefferson also referred to Beccaria's chapter on "crimes of difficult proof" when he noted that bestiality was not included in the code.[29]

The Committee of Revisors worked until February 1779. It met to revise its proposal and submitted this to the legislature in June. Jefferson commented that the Revisors had kept the portions of the common law, British statutes, and old Virginia statutes that were judged good and had repealed or revised the remainder. In 1779 a few of the bills within the Revisors' proposal were passed, but the legislature's preoccupation with military affairs prevented immediate consideration of much of the plan. In 1785 the legislature finally took up the plan, and most of it passed thanks to "the unwearied exertions of Mr. [James] Madison, in opposition to the endless quibbles, chicaneries, perversions, vexations and delays of lawyers and demi-lawyers."[30] Despite Madison's efforts, however, the bill to revise the criminal code failed by a single vote, which Madison attributed to the prevailing "rage against horse-thieves."[31]

In May 1778, the Virginia legislature added a capital crime to the criminal code. The legislature had established a paper currency for the state and had directed that anyone guilty of counterfeiting the currency should be punished by death without benefit of clergy. Virginia's criminal code, which the legislature failed to alter in 1785, retained most of the colonial punishments. The following crimes were still punishable by death without benefit of clergy: high treason, murder, rape (although slaves convicted of rape could be punished by castration instead of death), petty treason, manslaughter, slave stealing, horse stealing, and arson. Both burglary and robbery remained capital crimes, as did malicious maiming.[32]

Adoption of Jefferson's Criminal Code

It was not until 1796 that the Virginia legislature reconsidered Jefferson's proposed penal reforms. George Keith Taylor, a member of the House of Delegates, was designated to draft a proposal; his proposal was based upon Jefferson's. In his *Autobiography*, Jefferson commented that his plan was adopted in 1796 with just a few changes. There were, in fact, some important differences, since Jefferson's plan did not have incarceration as a central component. Taylor's bill also called for labor in solitary confinement instead of public labor. Jefferson approved of these alterations, having since changed his mind in response to Pennsylvania's experience, particularly with the wheelbarrow law. Additionally, instead of Jefferson's proposed distinction between murder and manslaughter, the 1796 law adopted degrees of distinction within murder itself.[33]

The 1796 "Act to amend the penal laws of this commonwealth" abolished the death penalty in all cases other than first-degree murder. First-degree murder was to include murders by poison, by lying in wait, by "any other kind of willful, deliberate and premeditated killing," and any murder in the commission of arson, rape, robbery, or burglary. All other types of murder were classified as murder in the second degree. Just as in the earlier Pennsylvania statute, juries were to determine the degree of murder upon issuing a guilty verdict; judges were to determine the degree in cases of confession. In another departure from Jefferson's proposal, the 1796 law removed the distinction between petty treason and murder.[34]

For other crimes, the new law normally prescribed imprisonment with hard labor and solitary confinement. The statute required from six to twelve years in prison for high treason, from five to twelve years for arson, from ten to twenty-one years for rape, from two to ten years for voluntary manslaughter, and from five to eighteen years for second-degree murder. For many crimes, the statute also required restitution. Robbery or burglary warranted restitution, plus from three to ten years in prison; horse stealing warranted restitution, plus from two to seven years; grand larceny warranted restitution, plus from one to three years; and petty larceny warranted restitution, plus from six to twelve months. Offenders convicted of forgery or counterfeiting were to be fined up to $1,000 and serve from four to fifteen years in prison; those convicted of malicious maiming were to be fined up to $1,000 (75 percent of which was to go to the victim) and serve from two to ten years in prison. Involuntary manslaughter could be tried as a misdemeanor. The 1796 law also abolished the benefit of clergy. It directed that the jury determine the length of sentence within the boundaries prescribed by the law.[35]

Since many crimes were to be punished by imprisonment instead of death, the new statute had to address the need for additional prison space. The law called for the erection of a new penitentiary, which was to have an exercise yard. The cells were to allow adequate ventilation. Male and female inmates were to be separated. The statute also directed that some cells be constructed specifically for the purpose of solitary confinement. At sentencing the court was to determine how much of the imprisonment was to be served in solitary confinement. The statute required that prison inmates be issued clean clothing and be fed wholesome, though coarse, meals. Convicts who were particularly industrious in their labor were to be rewarded. "In order to encourage industry as an evidence of reformation," industrious convicts were to be allowed to keep excess money for use upon their release. The statute also stipulated that the prisons were to be cleaned at regular intervals.[36] Adelaide Meador Hunter points out that the 1796 law could not take effect until the state constructed adequate prison space. This was "a matter of life or death for those who were found guilty of a felony."[37] The original plan for a penitentiary had been suggested by Jefferson, and the state penitentiary was finally opened in Richmond in 1800.

PENAL REFORM IN NEW YORK

The final state to significantly revise its criminal penalties during the founding period was New York. Led also by the example of Pennsylvania, New York revised its code roughly at the same time as Virginia. Prior to the founding period, there was no real systematic codification of capital crimes in New York. Instead, the New Netherlanders imported various lists of crimes and punishments from the Dutch.[38] Penal statutes were enacted in 1788. These statutes required the death penalty for murder, rape, sodomy, burglary, robbery, arson, malicious maiming, forgery, counterfeiting, and "feloniously taking goods and chattels out of any church or place of public worship." The penalty also included forfeiture of one's estate. All other felonies were to be punished by imprisonment, fines, and corporal punishment on the first offense, and death on the second offense.[39]

The reform movement in New York was led by Thomas Eddy, who eventually became an inspector of New York City's penitentiary. Eddy was a Quaker and was influenced both by John Howard and by the events in Pennsylvania. According to Michael Kraus, many referred to Eddy as the

"Howard of America."[40] Eddy often visited Philadelphia's Walnut Street penitentiary; he also was advised by Caleb Lownes, a member of Philadelphia's prison society.[41] Eddy was interested in bringing Pennsylvania-style reforms to New York. To this end, he brought along on one of his trips to Pennsylvania General Philip Schuyler, who was a member of the New York State Senate. Schuyler, under the influence of Eddy, became the primary proponent of reform in the New York legislature.

Like many reformers, Eddy rejected the role of vengeance in punishment. He addressed this point in reference to the death penalty, where "society and the injured party are indeed, in the strictest sense, avenged on the head of the guilty offender. Justice, however, not revenge, is the true foundation of the right of punishment."[42] Unlike many in the older philosophic tradition who considered vengeance to be a legitimate part of justice, Eddy found hope in the Enlightenment. He contrasted New York's severe punishments to Enlightenment ideals and regretted that New York's punishments did not reflect the spread of enlightenment. He referred to Montesquieu and especially Beccaria as leaders of the most important aspect of the Enlightenment: penal reform. "The eloquent Beccaria roused the attention of civilized Europe, and, by his unanswerable appeal to reason and humanity, produced those successive efforts to meliorate the systems of penal laws, which constitute the greatest glory of the present age."[43] Eddy also praised the contribution of John Howard, who, he explained, was especially concerned with prisons.

Eddy associated himself with the utilitarian approach to punishment at the start of his well-known pamphlet on penal reform in New York, providing a quote from Beccaria on its title page: "A punishment to be just, should have only that degree of severity which is sufficient to deter others: Perpetual labour will have this effect more than the punishment of death."[44] Eddy also cited Montesquieu to the effect that good legislators will be more concerned with preventing future crimes than with punishing past crimes.[45] Eddy believed that the purpose of punishment is utility—to protect the aggregate self-interest of society by preventing future crimes. "The peace, security, and happiness, of society depend on the wisdom and justice of the means devised for the *prevention* of crimes."[46] Eddy argued that the prevention of future crimes would best be accomplished by a Pennsylvania-style penitentiary. In this way, society would be protected from the offender, and the offender could be reformed so that he no longer posed a danger to society upon his release. The purpose of the legislator must only be to "regard the tendency of actions to injure society." It must be left to the penitentiary system to evaluate the particular circumstances of each offender and to tailor the punishment accordingly.[47]

Eddy parted company with Beccaria on the question of pardons. Beccaria opposed pardons because he believed that they undermine deterrence (see chapter 4). Eddy agreed with Beccaria's opposition to pardons, "in theory," but argued that Beccaria assumed a perfect criminal procedure that did not exist. "It is necessary that the power of pardoning should reside somewhere, to prevent that injustice in particular cases which the legislator did not foresee, or could not avoid." There was still a need for the power of pardon and clemency, and Eddy approvingly noted that the New York constitution gave this authority to the governor. He added, however, that someone who is convicted should not simply be let off without punishment. Offenders should not be pardoned unless they have served some punishment proportionate to the actual degree of their guilt, even though such punishment may be less than the actual judicial sentence. Eddy discussed three types of situations in which he believed the pardon power should be allowed. First, the pardon should be allowed where the crime is defined by a generalized legal description that may include different acts of varying degrees of severity. In such circumstances, the pardon would allow the governor to tailor the precise sentence more closely to the specific criminal act in question. Second, pardons should be permitted where the law sets only an upper limit on time served. Eddy preferred that most sentencing discretion in such cases be left with the court, but the governor's action might be required where the court failed to exercise appropriate discretion. Finally, the pardon should be allowed where there is "unequivocal evidence of reformation in a convict." The inspectors of the prison (Eddy himself was a prison inspector) should be responsible for making appropriate recommendations to the governor.[48]

In addition to Eddy's utilitarian arguments on punishment, he also expressed a good deal of faith in reformation. He believed that reformation and deterrence are closely linked—one of the best ways to prevent crime is to reform criminals:

> The end of human punishments is the prevention of crimes. In the endeavor to attain this end, three things are to be considered; the amendment of the offender, the deterring of others by his example; reparation to society and the party injured. Of these objects, the first without doubt is of the highest importance.[49]

Like Beccaria, Eddy did not believe that severe punishments serve the ends of deterrence or reformation. "The oppression of punishment as a terror to others, is generally considered as momentary and uncertain in its effects."[50] The death penalty, therefore, does not achieve the proper goals of punishment because it precludes the possibility of reformation.

Eddy also commented specifically on the role of prisons. It was his view that one of the greatest problems with prisons was the mixing of the different classes of prisoners, which prevented the reform of those who otherwise might respond well to reformative efforts. Eddy advocated separating the prisoners into three classes: hardened career criminals beyond reform, prisoners with a good moral education but who were led by passion and bad example, and first-time offenders. "In forming an opinion of the depravity of convicts, nothing can be more unjust than to confound these different classes in the same judgment."[51] He noted that Pennsylvania-style penitentiaries were designed to make these sorts of distinctions.

Eddy claimed that the best way for prisons to effect the reformation of convicts is a "system of regular labour and exact temperance by which habits of industry and sobriety are formed." Prisoners who appear "meritorious" should be taught reading, writing, and arithmetic. Eddy was careful to write that this education should not be considered an entitlement but a privilege; it should be granted only to those who demonstrate by their conduct that they may benefit from it. Eddy also discussed the importance of religious and moral instruction. He believed prisons should offer regular Sunday services and services devoted to the prisoners' reformation.[52]

Even though Eddy consistently praised Beccaria and Montesquieu, he wrote that some Americans had been equally important to the penal reform movement. He specifically mentioned Pennsylvanians, calling Pennsylvania the model and leader for penal reform in the United States. "While the names of Montesquieu, Beccaria and Howard, are repeated with gratitude and admiration, the legislators and philanthropists of our own country deserve not to be forgotten." Eddy praised the provincial government of Pennsylvania for standing up to the British crown. He wanted to make clear to readers that the only reason William Penn eventually abandoned the mild code was to win back the privilege of affirmation for Quakers. Eddy described one of his many visits to the penitentiary in Philadelphia. While in Philadelphia, he was given a number of copies of William Bradford's pamphlet and brought them back to New York to distribute. He also mentioned his gratitude to Caleb Lownes for Lownes's advice and guidance on his trips to Philadelphia.[53] In a departure from his more narrowly utilitarian commentary, Eddy mentioned that one of the features of Pennsylvania's criminal justice system that he most admired was the close proportionality between crimes and punishments: "each crime received a punishment equitably proportioned to the degree of its enormity."[54]

Eddy's pamphlet contained a denunciation of New York for its many failures to follow the lead of Pennsylvania. Even after the Revolution, Eddy said, his state still maintained the sanguinary English-style criminal code. "This favourite child of the crown reflected more strongly than any other the image of its parent." Eventually Eddy's reform efforts bore some fruit. He wrote of his communications with General Schuyler. He convinced Schuyler to visit the Philadelphia penitentiary with him. Eddy noted that Schuyler was satisfied with "the spirit of wisdom and benevolence which presided in that institution; the cleanliness, decency, order, and tranquil industry which prevailed in every part."[55]

After his visit, Schuyler drafted a bill—"For Making Alterations in the Criminal Laws of the State, and the Erecting of State-Prisons"—and New York adopted the law in 1796. The law called for the construction of two state prisons, and it abolished the death penalty for all crimes other than treason and murder. For other crimes that had previously been punished by death, the punishment became life in prison with hard labor and solitary confinement. The remaining crimes (more serious than petty larceny) were made punishable by up to fourteen years in prison on the first offense and life in prison on the second offense. The law called for the separation of felons and misdemeanants and "wholly abolished" corporal punishments. Forfeiture was called for only in cases of treason. In order to deter escape attempts, the law mandated that anyone who escaped prison and committed a felony was to be put to death.[56] The preamble to the 1796 law stated that its purpose was to proportion punishment "to the different degrees of guilt of the offenders."[57]

Eddy noted that New York reformers were quite happy with the 1796 law but believed it still imperfect. One of the main complaints was that its punishments were not sufficiently proportionate to crimes. Almost all felonies were punished similarly—with life in prison or death. Eddy argued that each crime should have its own corresponding punishment. This was not only because different crimes require different degrees of deterrence, but also because such a uniform punishment does not reflect the differing degrees of severity in the broad range of criminal behavior. Eddy therefore objected to life imprisonment for second offenses, arguing that this penalty gives no regard to the degree of the crime. He contended that the 1796 law was an improvement upon the uniform severity of earlier statutes and that it should also be judged by how effectively it deterred crime. He admitted that it might not have been terribly effective yet, but he attributed this to an increase in immigration and other factors. Eddy expressed faith that "punishments *mild* and *certain* more effectually prevent crimes than those which are sanguinary and severe."[58]

Eddy also denounced those who advocated changing the 1796 law back to the more severe criminal code: "It is to be lamented, that many good citizens, feeling a just abhorrence at crimes, consulting the suggestions of virtuous indignation, rather than the principles of justice"[59] would advocate turning back penal reform. Notice that Eddy saw a distinction between "virtuous indignation" and "justice," in contrast with Aquinas's argument (presented in chapter 6), which sees justice as the central element of virtuous indignation.

Part Two

The Roots of the Punishment Debate

CHAPTER FOUR

The Enlightenment

Utility and Amendment

THE STATE OF THE DEBATE

GIVEN THE DIVERGENT STREAMS in modern punishment philosophy that begin branching out at the very time the United States was founded as an independent nation, is it possible to assess the relative importance of different punishment philosophies for those who founded the new American nation? Did any one philosophy dominate in the formation of the early state and federal criminal codes? Or were the early American lawmakers guided by a variety of philosophical approaches and principles? What were the potential philosophic influences on the founding-era punishment debate? With respect to the nation as a whole, Lawrence Friedman proclaims in a comprehensive analysis of crime and punishment in American history that "the post-Revolutionary age was an age of reform in criminal justice."[1] His claim is beyond doubt. But what, exactly, is meant by *reform*?

Many who have written about punishment during the founding period accept the notion that a moderation in criminal penalties necessarily implies a commitment to the utilitarian reform principles of Beccaria and Bentham. Both Morton J. Horwitz and William E. Nelson believe there was a movement away from the natural law framework of criminal jurisprudence. This, they believe, came from a growing acceptance of utilitarianism.[2] Nelson in particular notes the decline in prosecutions for moral crimes.

Harry Elmer Barnes's history of penal reform in Pennsylvania suggests strongly that the increasing importance of utilitarian considerations led to the founding-era moderation in criminal penalties. He asserts that the changes in Pennsylvania's criminal law reflected a change in the attitude of American society toward crime. He points to the activities and influence of Philadelphia's prison society as an indication that statesmen were turning away from retributive ideas of punishment. He cites the philosophical reform movement among Enlightenment thinkers in Europe as a central factor in Pennsylvania's penal reform during the founding period.[3]

Barnes asserts that in Pennsylvania's early history there was a "generally theological conception" of criminal behavior. Under this old idea, society saw fit to exact revenge. Society viewed criminals as morally autonomous. The criminal justice system "was founded upon this fundamental premise of punishment as social revenge, and the penal codes were crude and unscientific attempts to assess the mode and degree of social revenge which was appropriate to any particular crime."[4] Barnes argues that this "unscientific" approach did not consider the life circumstances of offenders. He believes that Beccarian reform philosophy was at the root of Pennsylvania's revised criminal code. The antecedents of Philadelphia's prison society "go back to the ideas and practices of the founders of the province and to the reform movements of the eighteenth century."[5]

From his study of penal reform in Europe, Marcello T. Maestro understands American penal reform to be a natural consequence of Beccaria's growing influence among Enlightenment thinkers. His reforms were well received in his native Italy, as well as in Germany, Prussia, Spain, England, and particularly France.[6] In England, Beccaria was cited favorably by the prominent legal reformer William Blackstone, although Blackstone, like many who were sympathetic to Beccaria's reforms, did not believe that capital punishment should be abolished entirely.[7] Other supporters in England were Jeremy Bentham and Samuel Romilly, who advocated Beccaria's reforms more consistently and vigorously than Blackstone (Bentham frequently criticized Blackstone for his cautious approach to English legal reform).[8]

Beccaria was most influential in France, since his strongest advocates were the French philosophers, and much of his work was an application of their philosophy to the issues of crime and punishment. Even before the French Revolution, torture was abolished in France in 1780, and additional reforms followed in 1788 regarding the circumstances under which the death penalty could be applied. As a result of the Revolution, the French instituted major criminal justice reforms. The French Declaration of the Rights of Man (1789) takes many lines almost word-for-word from Beccaria: "the law has the right to forbid only such actions as are injurious to society. . . . The law ought to establish only penalties that are strictly and obviously necessary, and no one can be punished except in virtue of a law established and promulgated prior to the offence and legally applied."[9] Maestro points to examples in American states that he believes demonstrate Beccaria's substantial influence on the new republic. He claims, "it was Pennsylvania that led the way toward a more enlightened approach to the administration of justice":

> Several circumstances combined to make the proposed alteration expedient, and among others the small and valuable gift of the immortal Beccaria to the world had its due influence and weight; for on the framing of the (then) new constitution of the state, in 1776, the legislatures were directed to proceed as soon as might be to the reformation of the penal laws and to invent punishments less sanguinary and better proportioned to the various degrees of criminality.[10]

David J. Rothman also understands founding-era criminal punishment primarily as a product of Beccaria and the Enlightenment. The focus of Rothman's *The Discovery of the Asylum* is the change undertaken in punishment during the Jacksonian era. In arguing that there was a transformation in punishment under Jacksonian democracy, Rothman contends that the change was characterized by a move away from the Enlightenment-based approach of the founding era. The foundation for the first penal codes of the new nation, according to Rothman, rested squarely upon the Enlightenment and, especially, upon Beccaria. Naming William Penn in particular, Rothman writes of the early republic as coming under the influence of "a new familiarity with and faith in Enlightenment." Key reform figures such as Thomas Eddy were absorbing Beccaria's argument: "The young republic quickly took [Beccaria's] message to heart, for it fit well with its own history and revolutionary ideals."[11]

More recently, some historical works either have rejected the idea of the Enlightenment's influence on founding-era penal reform or at least have questioned its exclusive influence. Of these, the work that places the least importance on the Enlightenment is Adam J. Hirsch's *The Rise of the Penitentiary*. Hirsch focuses part of his argument against the thesis of Rothman, who he contends mistakenly placed emphasis on the role of the Italian Enlightenment. Hirsch suggests, instead, that the real roots of the founding-era penitentiary movement can be found in sixteenth-century English workhouses. Both the American penitentiaries and the English workhouses sought to "control crime by uplifting criminals."[12] Hirsch's book, like Rothman's, is concerned primarily with the Jacksonian period.

Several other scholars in recent works on punishment in the early republic do not attribute founding-era penal reform entirely to the Enlightenment's influence, although they do acknowledge its importance in some respects. Louis P. Masur admits that the Enlightenment played a key role in the reaction against harsh punishments (particularly capital punishment) but contends that "the Enlightenment spirit alone, however, is too broad a concept to account for the opposition to capital punishment in America." In general, Masur sees American penal reform as an attempt to come to terms with the republicanism that was the dominant theme of the Revolution.[13]

Thomas L. Dumm applies Michel Foucault's framework to early America. He concedes that the founding generation understood punishment in Enlightenment terms, in that they sought to "ensure the safety of the subjects of the liberal democratic state," but argues that founding-era punishment was not true to these principles, having established instead "a complete transformation in the use of repressive power."[14] For Michael Meranze, who focuses on penal reform in Philadelphia, Beccaria and Enlightenment thought are very influential, but reform in Philadelphia was not necessarily representative of reform elsewhere in the United States. Meranze sees Beccaria as the primary factor, in Philadelphia at least, behind the push for punishment by public hard labor and for certainty in punishment as a decisive means to establish deterrence. "Pennsylvanians followed the arguments of European philosophers and argued that terror could be achieved only if punishments were certain."[15]

The political philosophy of the Enlightenment is thus central to examining the influences on the early American approach to punishment. Accordingly, this part of the book, which examines the philosophical roots of the different approaches to punishment, begins with a look at the key teachings of the Enlightenment penal reform movement. Subsequently, part two addresses the other extremes in modern political thought (most notably German moral idealism) and returns to the more comprehensive approach of the ancient and medieval traditions.

THE UTILITARIAN POSITION ON PUNISHMENT

The ancient and medieval approach to punishment was generally based on a belief that the criminal law reflects a moral law that is more fundamental than conventional. The modern utilitarian position rooted in the Enlightenment denies this connection and focuses almost exclusively on public safety: the aim of society is not to achieve "the good," insofar as such an aim would be informed by something outside of conventional politics, but rather to secure the aggregate self-interest of society's members. One does not punish to "do justice" but to protect the members of society. The strongest principle of self-interest is self-preservation. The aggregate self-interest of society dictates that threats to safety and preservation be eliminated, or at least controlled. The retributivist punishes because the offender has committed a crime; the punishment is justified by—and based on—that specific criminal act. The utilitarian punishes because he believes this will effect an increase in societal utility; the belief is normally that future crimes will decrease by way of deterrence or incapacitation. The following discussion of the utilitarianism of the early modern tradition will address six characteristics of the argument: (1) the rejection of the idea that criminal law is grounded in moral law; (2) the operation of criminal law on the basis of fear; (3) the deterrent effect of punishment, expressed in terms of precise formulas; (4) the need for swift and certain punishment, so that a tight connection between crime and punishment is created in the minds of potential criminals; (5) faith in enlightenment, which leads to an argument for milder criminal penalties; and (6) Locke's and Montesquieu's contributions to the foundation of the utilitarian argument.

Criminal Law Not Grounded in Moral Law

Beccaria's *On Crimes and Punishments*, originally published in 1764 in Tuscany and translated into English in 1767, was the first work to connect the Enlightenment's rejection of natural justice to a doctrine on punishment. Beccaria attempts to dispel the notion that punishment, or criminal law in general, can in any way be based on something other than manmade law. There is no way, he contends, to connect the law or punishments to principles of natural justice. Older theories of punishment had, in part, argued that the criminal law must be directed toward effecting an idea of justice derived from either natural or divine law. Referring specifically to the teaching of the Church, Beccaria argues that ordinary men cannot possibly understand the natural law or natural justice and that they have no business justifying their punishments by reference to it.[16] Society is based on a social contract, and one cannot consider man's "natural" duties and obligations a part of such a conventional agreement. Although Beccaria claims not to deny the existence of natural duties, he denies their applicability to political society.

Divorcing human law from a foundation in higher law leads to Beccaria's argument that punishment is justified only if it attains the conventional goals of society (security), as opposed to fulfilling the obligations of natural justice. Punishment may differ, consequently, depending on the extent to which it will affect societal utility under a given set of circumstances. Whereas retributivist punishment does not change—that is (as Kant will suggest), justice always requires that certain crimes be punished in certain ways—Beccarian punishment may change along with the aggregate interest of society. Punishment must fit the changing circumstances of conventional society, not the unchanging dictates of natural or divine law.[17]

In his argument against torture, Beccaria reveals his distrust of justice theories. One of his primary arguments is against torture that seeks "to carry out some mysterious and incomprehensible metaphysical purging of [the offender's] infamy." Beccaria is expressing a typical Enlightenment response to what were perceived as the excesses of regimes claiming to be founded on natural principles. He wants to remove the eternal or moral reasons for punishment, believing such things must be completely separated from the public affairs of men. He faults religious motives for the belief that torture might lead to the offender's expiation.[18]

Beccaria's primary disciple was Jeremy Bentham, who turns Beccaria's utilitarian approach into formulaic suggestions for legislation. Bentham too is careful to separate the objects of morality and the objects of legislation. There are certain things, he argues, that belong to the realm of morality but are inappropriate matters for legislation:

> All actions, whether public or private, fall under the jurisdiction of morals. It is a guide which leads the individual, as it were, by the hand through all the details of his life, all his relations with his fellows. Legislation cannot do this; and, if it could, it ought not to exercise a continual interference and dictation over the conduct of men.[19]

In *An Introduction to the Principles of Morals and Legislation*, Bentham does not deny the existence of punishments based on moral principles; the legislator, however, cannot impose such punishments. Bentham cites religious prohibitions against evil, where God is the one who justly punishes such crimes. The legislator cannot take the place of God.[20] Natural justice theories are accordingly little more than inventions: "A great multitude of people are continually talking about the Law of Nature; and then they go on giving you their sentiments about what is right and what is wrong."[21] To base legislation on something other than conventional utility leads to despotism. Like Beccaria, Bentham refers to what he considers the excesses and injustices committed in the name of natural and divine justice.

Although Beccaria and Bentham are the figures of modernity who write most specifically of criminal punishments, their overall approach is based largely on the teaching of Thomas Hobbes.[22] In the *Leviathan*, Hobbes contends that divine and human punishments are entirely separate. Punishment, like civil society itself, is divorced from any notion of natural justice. Instead, the conventional laws of civil society are the only things that represent "justice." Punishments are to be based entirely on these conventions. Hobbes believes it is not right to punish an act that was committed before the conventional law actually prohibited it. If conventional law did not prohibit it, then it was not a crime and does not deserve punishment.[23]

The key to understanding Hobbes's influence on modern theories of punishment is the Hobbesian description of civil society's very purpose. Society is artificial. It is created by man to escape the dangers of the state of nature, or the war of all against all that precedes organized civil society. Man agrees to enter civil society—and gives most natural rights to the sovereign—in return for protection from violent death. Accordingly, the purpose of society (and its laws and punishments) is to satisfy the passion for self-preservation of each individual. Hobbes believes that punishment is not justified unless it is inflicted by the sovereign under public authority. The only reason for the laws and the force of punishment that goes with them is self-preservation. Punishment must, then, prevent future threats to preservation; it must deter the offender and others in society from future crimes.[24]

In *On Crimes and Punishments*, Beccaria echoes Hobbes. Man forms society and submits to its laws for no other reason than his own interest. "No man has made a gift of part of his freedom with the common good in mind; that kind of fantasy exists only in novels."[25] No law, then, can seek to punish for any reason other than the satisfaction of society's aggregate self-interest. Law and authority are necessary to prevent the private self-interest of some individuals from breaking down society and forcing a return to the anarchy out of which society was founded. Society has "the necessity of defending the repository of the public well-being from the usurpations of individuals."[26]

The primary basis of society is individual self-interest, not commitment to justice; thus punishments must provide "motives that directly strike at the senses." Punishment must appeal to individual self-interest, so that individuals do not avoid crime because it is "wrong" but because they will be punished if they do not avoid it. Society does not teach us that crime is immoral or unjust but, rather, that it is contrary to our self-interest. Beccaria is blunt about the motivations of human beings; if something is not compatible with their narrow self-interest, they will not do it. Accordingly, Beccaria argues, the only justification for punishment is to create a sufficient disincentive for criminal behavior. Any punishment that goes beyond this purpose (that is, in an attempt to "do justice") is not legitimate.

Understanding Beccaria's Hobbesianism helps to clarify his position on torture. In particular, when torture is used to elicit confessions, this means that the strong will avoid conviction, because they are more able than the weak to resist the pain of torture. Beccaria's general philosophy is to re-dress the imbalance between strong and weak that exists in the state of nature. In Hobbes's state of nature, the strong prey on the weak because there are no laws. Beccaria sees torture as a return to the state of nature, because it gives an advantage to the strong.[27]

Punishment Based on Fear

Beccaria's argument against private tortures brings out another impor-tant point. He asks, "What is the political purpose of punishment?" Then he answers, "[it is] the instilling of terror in other men." He makes it quite clear that this is the only reason for punishment. "A misdeed already committed, and for which there can be no redress, need be punished by a political society only when it influences other people by holding out the lure of impunity." This classic statement of deterrence philosophy reveals the case against tortures out of public view: they serve no legitimate pur-pose. They do not show others in society the consequences of criminal be-havior. Beccaria does not address public tortures, however. One would think that such punishment would certainly go a long way to achieving the Beccarian requirement of instilling fear of disobedience. Beccaria does contend that certain crimes involve a desire for fame and glory, although he does not make it clear how many criminals fall into this category. Such crimes should not be punished by torture, as this would only give the criminal what he wants.[28]

Beccaria's fear-based approach to punishment calls to mind Hobbes's eighth condition of punishment, where Hobbes rejects the retribution view and endorses deterrence: "The aym of Punishment is not a revenge, but terrour."[29] This declares fear to be the most fundamental passion in Hobbes's (and Beccaria's) philosophy: fear of violent death is what leads individuals into civil society in the first place; fear of punishment is what leads them to obey the law. Hobbes states that punishment must be clearly defined in the law, so that men will be aware of the consequences of disobedience and will be deterred by fear of those consequences. Law-abidingness in the modern view is not a matter of virtue, but of fear. One does not strive for high ideals but reacts instead to the basest of human passions—self-preservation. Reason under this teaching is mere calcula-tion in the service of passion. Reason enables man to recognize that his best chance of satisfying his passion is to obey the law.

There are also important, if subtle, differences between the narrow self-interest approach of Hobbes and the utilitarian approach of Beccaria and Bentham. The most significant of these is that the individual natural right to self-preservation remains Hobbes's most fundamental principle. Beccaria, as a utilitarian, does not acknowledge the primacy of individual rights in the way that Hobbes does. For Beccaria and the utilitarians, there may be collective goods that take precedence over individual rights. This difference is illustrated by Beccaria's departure from Hobbes on the question of the death penalty. Beccaria admits that all things are justified by their utility—particularly punishment. So he cannot follow Hobbes and claim that an individual is always justified in resisting the death penalty (even though society is justified in carrying it out).

Instead, Beccaria must show that societal utility can never benefit from the execution of an individual. In utilitarian fashion, Beccaria argues that "if I can go on to prove that such a death is neither necessary nor useful, I shall have won the cause of humanity." This is a difficult case to make, and Beccaria has difficulty making it. In fact, it underscores a fundamental tension in Beccaria's philosophy. Although he remains a utilitarian, Beccaria also at one point asks, "Who has ever willingly given up to others the authority to kill him?"[30]

Although his interpretation of Beccaria is not as strongly utilitarian as the one I present here, Richard Bellamy does admit in the introduction to the most recent and authoritative edition of *On Crimes and Punishments* that the perceived tension between Beccaria's Hobbesianism and his utilitarianism is a central issue. Bellamy argues that the tension needs to be understood as part of "Beccaria's compromise theory"[31] and that Beccaria reflects Hobbes insofar as "fear and the desire for security provided the motivation for uniting to form society." Yet Beccaria, unlike Hobbes, "contended that we give up only the smallest portion of our liberty, i.e. that portion necessary for us to enjoy the remaining part in peace and tranquility." For Bellamy, this constitutes the contractarian element of Beccaria's thought. Bellamy acknowledges, rightly, that the contractarian side of Beccaria ran up against his utilitarian side, but he also contends there may be a coherent philosophy here, since "Beccaria took both the contractarian and the utilitarian aspects of his doctrine seriously and sought to combine them."[32]

Among other issues, Bellamy focuses on Beccaria's treatment of capital punishment. In his view, Beccaria's modification of the utilitarian argument comes from "the utilitarian claim that the death penalty could never have been established because, to give the state the right to kill its members on a regular basis, even subject to numerous limiting conditions, could never be deemed useful or necessary to the protection of their interests."[33] It is in this way that Beccaria's contractarianism moderates his utilitarianism.

Bentham defines the distinction between utilitarianism and Hobbesianism more sharply. Moral laws are those that have the effect of maximizing the utility of society as a whole. By attempting to shape individual action in a manner that will bring about society's aggregate interest, the legislator acts morally.[34] Punishment must be calculated to force individuals to act in accord with the general good. With the proper punishment and legislation, an individual maximizes his own utility by contributing to the maximization of society's utility. The difference between this approach and Hobbesian morality is that Hobbes's teaching is based on the individual. Even though the individual recognizes that it is in his own interest to conform with society, any time the aggregate societal interest comes into competition with his own individual interest (self-preservation), the individual is perfectly justified in resisting.[35] This cannot be the case for utilitarians, because moral action is based on the general good of society. If, for instance, society benefits by killing an individual because the penalty will promote deterrence, then there is no justification for an individual to put up resistance, despite the threat to his own preservation.

In an important phrase, Beccaria makes clear that utility is fundamental, when he states that the object of his penology is "the greatest happiness shared among the greater number."[36] Although Bentham is commonly thought to be the founder of utilitarianism, there is much evidence to suggest he merely carries out the principles laid down by Beccaria. Indeed (as Marcello Maestro has discovered), Bentham once wrote to Beccaria after reading On Crimes and Punishments, "Oh my master, first evangelist of Reason, . . . you have made so many useful excursions into the path of utility, what is there left for us to do?"[37] When discussing the justifications for punishment, Beccaria asks a set of questions: Are punishments useful and necessary? Do they prevent crimes? What is the influence of punishment on customary behavior?

In contrast to retributivist theory, Beccaria and Bentham do not believe there is anything inherently good about punishment. Punishment itself is an evil, because everything comes down to pleasure versus pain. Bentham argues that punishment is a pain, inflicted in order to effect some greater pleasure. Kant states that punishment is justified only insofar as it represents an end in itself, whereas Bentham states that "all punishment is mischief: all punishment in itself is evil. Upon the principle of utility, if it ought at all to be admitted, it ought only to be admitted in as far as it promises to exclude some greater evil." Bentham lays out the conditions under which punishment is not justified: (1) where it is groundless, or there is no evil to prevent; (2) where it is inefficacious; (3) where it is unprofitable, or where the cost-benefit analysis does not tip in favor of the benefit; and (4) where it is needless—that is, where the evil may be prevented without the punishment.[38]

Utilitarians—like retributivists—argue that there must be some sort of proportionality between crimes and punishments; but the reasons for this proportionality are quite distinct. Whereas retributivists argue that punishments must differ based on the extent of the crime's injustice, utilitarians argue that different penalties are required to deter different crimes. Bentham claims that punishment cannot be so severe that it outweighs the benefit gained from deterring the crime.[39] Beccaria also uses this cost-benefit calculus, stating that "the obstacles which repel men from committing crimes ought to be made stronger the more those crimes are against the public good and the more inducements there are for committing them."[40]

Beccaria's formula extends to attempted crimes. Such crimes ought to be punished in order to deter future attempts. Attempted crimes should not be punished, however, as severely as the actual commission of the crime. This is not necessarily because there is a greater injustice when the crime is actually committed, but because society must provide those who have attempted a crime but not yet successfully executed it with some incentive not to follow through. Under Beccaria's conception of human behavior, there would be no reason not to follow through unless it were shown to be against one's self-interest. Beccaria also argues that there is no need to punish criminal behavior any more than is necessary to deter such behavior in the future. "If a punishment is to serve its purpose, it is enough that the harm of punishment should outweigh the good which the criminal can derive from the crime. . . . Anything more than this is superfluous and, therefore, tyrannous."[41]

Punishment Swift and Certain

An important Beccarian concept (echoed in the contemporary debate especially by James Q. Wilson) is the importance to deterrence of consistency, swiftness, and certainty. If, as Beccaria argues, the primary aim of punishment is to demonstrate to others that they do not want to incur the consequences of criminal behavior, then everything must be done to ensure that the potential criminal connects the punishment as closely as possible with the crime. If the potential criminal sees that punishments are applied inconsistently, or there is delay, or there is uncertainty as to whether the crime will actually result in a punishment, he will be much less likely to fear the consequences of the crime. Beccaria says that punishment must be spelled out clearly in the law, so that men can always be aware of the consequences. Since the benefit from the crime is immediate, the longer punishment is delayed the easier it will be for the potential criminal to be undeterred. This is why Beccaria says it is a "misguided love of humanity" that makes people want to delay punishments.[42] The point is that we are all potential criminals, because we all are motivated primarily by self-interest. The less society is able to show us that crime is against our self-interest, the more likely we are to commit it. Swiftness is closely connected to the concept of certainty.

Deterrence does not work without certainty, because a lack of certainty may lead people to believe they can commit crimes with impunity. Beccaria explains that this is why forgiveness can play no role in the criminal justice system. If a victim wants to forgive an offender, this can have no effect on public policy. Potential criminals must be certain that they will be punished for criminal behavior. Beccaria goes so far as to say that certainty of punishment is more important than severity. "The certainty of even a mild punishment will make a bigger impression than the fear of a more awful one which is united to a hope of not being punished at all."[43] This is echoed by Bentham, who makes a detailed argument on the importance of certainty and proximity but contends that there is no way to make the certainty and proximity of punishment equal to that of the crime. This deficiency must be part of the legislator's cost-benefit calculation, and he must compensate with magnitude of punishment. Since "the profit of the offense is commonly more certain than the punishment," Bentham reasons, "the punishment must have its value made up in some other way. . . . Now, there is no other way in which it can receive any addition to its value, but by receiving an addition in point of magnitude."[44] Unlike Beccaria (and Wilson), Bentham does not advocate reforming the criminal justice process so that there is greater certainty. Instead, he is content to leave the process as it is and to compensate by way of severity. Bentham also asserts that we must add more severity into the equation to make up for those offenses that have likely been committed but not detected.

Calculating Deterrence

Bentham goes further than any of his utilitarian brethren in formulating precise equations for legislation based on deterrence. Whereas Beccaria is committed in general terms to fixing penalties to produce a deterrent effect, Bentham actually believes he can calculate the cost-benefit equation for different crimes. Much of his work consists of detailed lists of conditions, which subtract from or add to various pieces of legislation. He states: "Nature has placed mankind under the governance of two sovereign masters, pain and pleasure. It is for them alone to point out what we ought to do."[45] Accordingly, his recommendations for punishments are based on offsetting calculations of pain and pleasure. Bentham comes up with a detailed listing of rules to govern the crafting of criminal punishments. He says, first, that "the strength of the temptation . . . is as the profit of the offense: the quantum of the punishment must rise with the profit of the offense. . . . It must therefore rise with the strength of the temptation." Bentham also claims that the greater the pain caused by the offense, the greater the amount of expense that rightly goes to preventing it. In order to prevent the offense as cheaply as possible, however, the punishment ought to be no more than is necessary to deter. Since punishment itself is an evil—or a cost—it is wrong to expend any more of it than necessary to achieve the benefit.[46]

If one is to go about providing formulas that determine the amount of punishment necessary to achieve utility, the ambiguity lies in determining what, exactly, constitutes "utility." If one follows Bentham's strict formula for justifying punishment (that penalties are justified by the extent to which they prevent future crimes), one can make a good argument as to the utility of severe incapacitation. In other words, if perpetual imprisonment or death prevents the offender from committing future crimes, and other methods might not be as effective, would not such punishments be justified from Bentham's perspective? Bentham's response is that, despite his utilitarian formula, such punishment is simply too rigorous.[47] The benefit does not outweigh the cost. It is interesting that although Bentham condemns severe punishments because they do not fit the principles of utility, when it can be shown that severe punishments do indeed reduce crime where other punishments do not, he retreats to claiming that such punishments are too costly or that they provide more pain than benefit. The reasoning is that some punishments are too severe even though they contribute to deterrence, on the grounds that the marginal deterrent value is too low to justify the increase in severity. It is in this way that utilitarianism seeks to place limits on the severity of punishment without resorting to arguments about justice.

Enlightenment and Milder Penalties

Whereas Bentham's particular emphasis is on developing a strict equation for the formulation of legislation, Beccaria's emphasis is on enlightenment. There is an exchange of letters between Beccaria and various Enlightenment philosophers that indicates Beccaria's connection to the movement. In particular, there is a letter to André Morellet, who, at the encouragement of d'Alembert, translated *On Crimes and Punishments* into French. Remarking on the translation, Beccaria wrote to Morellet, "how honoured I felt on hearing my work had been translated into your language—the language of the nation that enlightens and instructs all Europe. I myself owe everything to French books. They developed in my soul the sentiments of humanity which had been stifled by eight years of fanatical and servile education." Beccaria refers here to his eight years of education under the Jesuit order.

In sending his French translation, Morellet passed along praise from Diderot, Helvétius, Buffon, and Hume. In response, Beccaria wrote that he was "abashed by the obliging things which you pass on to me from those matchless philosophers who do honour to humankind, Europe and their nations. . . . Your immortal works are my constant reading, the object of my studies during the day and of my meditations at night." He went on to praise the various Enlightenment philosophers from whom he had learned so much: "I set the date of my conversion to philosophy as five years ago, and I owe it to the reading of [Montesquieu's] *Persian Letters*."[48] He also discusses the influence of Helvétius's *Esprit* and of Diderot and Hume.

Beccaria thought that the Italian authorities of his day were reactionary; he believed they were attempting to retard human progress. In explaining to Morellet some of the more obscure passages of his work, he admits he was trying to hide certain teachings out of fear of persecution. He attributes this method of writing to having "had before me the examples of Machiavelli, Galileo and Giannone," and he continues, "This country is still buried under the prejudices which its ancient masters left it. The Milanese do not forgive those who wish them to live in the eighteenth century."[49] By the "ancient masters" of Milan, Beccaria is probably referring to the Inquisition of the Roman Church in Lombardy; although this Inquisition had been dismantled, Beccaria still feared the power of the "intolerant" rulers in Milan. He shows his fear of the Milanese government by his flattery of its leaders in the introduction to *On Crimes and Punishments*. Even in this part of the work, Beccaria's reliance on Enlightenment principles is evident. He writes that the government will be pleased to hear his truths, which he posits to combat those who are "eschewing reason." He expresses confidence that the government will appreciate his work, "if persuasion is more efficacious than force with men." Finally, he contends that his book is an "address to enlightened readers."[50]

Beccaria believes Enlightenment principles are important because his deterrence theory rests on them. He believes individuals will be able to understand the law clearly and be aware that incurring the consequences of criminal behavior is not in their self-interest. They will be able to make informed, rational choices about their own behavior. Enlightenment, as Beccaria understands it, means *enlightened self-interest*. Man's growing rationality allows him to become increasingly aware of what is in his self-interest. Increasingly enlightened individuals will better recognize that crime does not pay. Much as Hobbes teaches that reason serves passion, so Beccaria teaches that enlightenment—or knowledge—serves individual self-interest. Throughout the penal reform movement, there is the premise that one does not obey the law because it is right to do so, but because one becomes increasingly aware that doing so is in one's self-interest.

Beccaria's advocacy of milder punishments is based squarely on his faith in enlightenment. Since society has become more enlightened, the severity of punishment can decrease while the level of deterrence will remain consistent:

> The severity of punishments ought to be relative to the state of the nation itself. Stronger and more easily felt impressions have to be made on people only just out of the savage state. . . . But as souls become softened by society, sensitivity grows. And as it does so, the severity of punishments ought to diminish, if the relation between the object and the sensation is to remain constant.[51]

Beccaria goes beyond Hobbes in contending that there is progress once individuals escape from the state of nature. This progress is reflected in the ability to reform the penal system and to maintain adequate levels of deterrence. Accordingly, in one of his best-known phrases, Beccaria asks: "Do you want to prevent crimes? Then see to it that enlightenment and freedom go hand in hand."[52]

Locke and Montesquieu

Many early American statesmen had read Beccaria, and some of them were significantly influenced by him. On the whole, however, the founders were not nearly as familiar with Beccaria as they were with Locke and Montesquieu. It is necessary to examine what Locke and Montesquieu wrote about criminal punishment, although Beccaria was the one responsible for developing the more comprehensive theory of punishment that arose during the founding period. The examination of Locke and Montesquieu reveals that their politics of punishment is quite compatible with the utilitarian approach of Hobbes, Beccaria, and Bentham.

If one wants to discover in Locke the foundation of society's right to punish, one must determine where such a right exists in man's natural condition, before he founds civil society. Since civil society is an artificial construction designed to aid man's escape from the dangers of his natural condition, society can have no right to punish unless such a right existed in man's natural or prepolitical state. In his discussion of the state of nature in chapter 2 of the *Second Treatise*, Locke asserts that the natural right to punish comes out of the law of nature, which exists apart from government and aims at "the Peace and Preservation of all Mankind." For the purposes of his preservation, each individual has the "Power to Execute" the law of nature. This power to enforce the law of nature allows each individual to "preserve the innocent and restrain offenders."[53]

Without civil society every individual is on his own to keep the peace and to preserve himself, and therefore "every Man hath a Right to punish the Offender, and be Executioner of the Law of Nature." Why does every individual have the right to punish criminal behavior in the state of nature? Locke says it is "to prevent its being committed again." An individual seeks to prevent future crime both in order to protect himself and because of "the Right he has of Preserving all Mankind." Locke makes this clearer when he discusses why every man in the state of nature has the right to kill a murderer. There are two reasons for this right: (1) "to deter others from doing the like Injury," and (2) "to secure Men" from becoming victims of the same criminal in the future.[54] This formulation has a direct connection to contemporary utilitarian language, where these reasons are called "general deterrence" and "incapacitation."[55] Both are utilitarian: the latter aims at preventing the particular offender in question from offending again, while the former seeks to convince others not to engage in criminal behavior.

Locke does mention the purpose of "Reparation" along with "Restraint," but even his notion of reparation is utilitarian, not retributive. Reparation is intended to restore the "peace and safety" of man's natural state. When Locke takes up the idea of reparation in a later paragraph, he makes clear that it pertains to "recovering from the Offender" any loss that the victim has suffered from the "injury."[56] There is no mention of ensuring that the offender receives the penalty he justly deserves for having committed the crime.[57] In fact, other than the brief discussion of reparation, Locke's emphasis is almost entirely on prevention. The purpose of punishment is to "deter" the offender and "by his Example others, from doing the like mischief." When Locke discusses the punishment of crimes "lesser" than murder, the purpose remains deterrence. Locke says (as Beccaria does) that these lesser crimes should be punished "with so much Severity as will suffice to make it an ill bargain to the Offender."[58]

Up to this point Locke's discussion of punishment is based on a peaceful state of nature; but it is his discussion of the state of war that brings him even closer to the narrow utilitarian view of punishment. Locke makes a clear distinction between these two extrapolitical states, and we need to ask where society's right to punish originates: in the state of nature or in the state of war? It is in the state of war where each individual may justly exercise the natural right to punish. In fact, criminal behavior is precisely what compels man out of the state of nature and into the state of war, where there is a Hobbesian competition for preservation. Locke says that he who commits a crime, or "attempts to get another Man into his Absolute Power, does thereby put himself into a State of War with him." By *definition*, there is no crime in the state of nature, because that is the state where men live at peace with each other even though there is no civil government. Crime marks the transition from the state of nature to the state of war. The right to punish crime, although it may exist abstractly in the state of nature, can only be legitimately exercised in the state of war. "Force, or a declared design of force, upon the Person of another" compels man into a State of War, and in that state each man has the "Right of War."[59] This right of war is nothing other than the natural right to punish, because war is an extrapolitical state where each man has the right to punish in defense of his own life.[60]

This last point is worthy of emphasis. Preservation is the *sole* purpose of the right to punish in the state of war. Locke says that the criminal must be considered "an Enemy to my Preservation." In Locke's discussion of the state of war, in chapter 3, there is no emphasis on retribution or just deserts. The very foundation of the state of war is the right to do whatever is necessary to preserve oneself; this right constitutes Locke's natural right to punish. The natural right to punish justifies killing not only a murderer but any person who one believes *might* threaten one's life. Locke uses the example of a thief. Even though a thief might not initially attempt to kill his victim, the victim has no way of knowing that he will not try to do so later. By then it will be too late, so the victim is entitled in the state of war to kill (punish) the thief in the interest of his own preservation.[61] Once man forms civil society for the very purpose of escaping the state of war, he gives up his natural right to punish insofar as civil government is able to protect him and his property.

Although a comprehensive discussion of Locke's philosophy of punishment is beyond the scope of this book, we can at least see that the foundation of society's right to punish in Locke makes his approach essentially utilitarian. What remains to be determined is how closely the American founders adhered to this utilitarian view (a question that is taken up in part three). For now, turning to an examination of Montesquieu's brief discussion of punishment, we can see that he, too, shares a close kinship with the utilitarians.

Whereas Locke bears much resemblance to Hobbes, Montesquieu more directly foreshadows Beccaria. It may not be too gross an exaggeration to suggest that Beccaria, having been influenced by earlier Enlightenment writers, represents an extensive working out of Montesquieu's few paragraphs on criminal punishment. It is first necessary to clear up an apparent tension between the writings of these two authors. Whereas Beccaria spends much energy advocating simple criminal laws, Montesquieu at one point makes the opposite argument by criticizing "simplicity" in the criminal law. But Montesquieu makes this criticism from the standpoint of criminal procedure. Simple laws make it easier for a despot to succeed. Montesquieu says that "when a man makes himself more absolute, his first thought is to simplify the laws." Montesquieu does not oppose the simplicity of the criminal laws in the way that Beccaria means it. Beccaria wants simple and clear laws so that each individual will be well aware of the negative consequences pertaining to criminal behavior. In the *Spirit of the Laws* Montesquieu even urges a more uniform enforcement of the criminal law, which is consistent with Beccaria's argument that deterrence will best be served if the laws are always enforced in the same manner.[62]

Montesquieu contends that terror and severe punishments are only necessary in "despotic government." In "moderate states," severe punishment is unnecessary. "Civil laws will make corrections more easily and will not need as much force." This is consistent with Beccaria's understanding of enlightenment, where the more enlightened state will require milder punishment because it will not take as much threatened force to deter crime. Citizens will more readily recognize that criminal behavior is not in their best interest. Montesquieu pushes his argument for mild punishment even further, implying that it would be difficult to show that harsh punishments are *ever* necessary or effective. He reasons that severe penalties are not necessarily stronger deterrents, at least over the long run, because "the imagination becomes inured to this heavier penalty as it had to the lesser." Montesquieu cites the example of punishing highway robbery during his time. He notes that severe penalties were implemented in order to deter the practice, but they were effective for only a brief period. After the citizens became accustomed to the more severe penalties, incidences of highway robbery returned to the normal level. Montesquieu employs the utilitarian line of thought, contending that the increased penalties were unjust because they were neither necessary nor effective at reducing crime.[63]

The Root Social Causes of Crime and the Modern Rehabilitation Argument

The question of enlightened self-interest assumes that once one recognizes what is in one's own interest, one actually possesses the requisite freedom to make the logical choice. The Beccarian reform approach to punishment believes that men exist first in a state of natural freedom where they make rational decisions. Individuals decide to leave the state of nature for civil society because they recognize that it suits their own interest; once in society, individuals decide to obey the law because the punishments for disobedience are contrary to their own interest. The rehabilitation approach that became such an important part of the American politics of punishment during the 1960s and 1970s denies that this very freedom of choice exists.

The idea of rehabilitating offenders is certainly nothing new. It was as important a part of the philosophy of punishment for the ancients and medievals as it was for the moderns. But, like both the retributive and the utilitarian arguments, rehabilitation is pushed to its extreme in the modern tradition. Instead of playing an important part in a more comprehensive understanding of criminal justice, rehabilitation in the modern era focuses narrowly on the "root social causes" of crime. In the rehabilitation literature of the 1960s and 1970s (of which Ramsey Clark's and Karl Menninger's writings are prime examples), the focus becomes almost exclusively root social causes.[64] Rehabilitation has more recently started to show up in some broadly focused utilitarian arguments (for example, that rehabilitating criminals is cost effective), but for decades the dominant strain of rehabilitation theory has been directly at odds with the rational, cost-benefit calculus of utilitarianism. According to the rehabilitation view, potential criminals are not free to make rational decisions based on a set of options provided by the criminal law, because there really are no options. Instead of being able to choose between the options of criminality or law-abidingness, this approach assumes that one is forced into a particular course of action. There can be no deliberation or choice.

Although the general concept of rehabilitation can be traced back to the view of the ancient and medieval traditions, the root social causes strain of it that became so dominant in America has origins in the eighteenth century. The determinism or dialectical materialism that governs this view of human behavior, although fully developed into a general teaching by Marx, can first be found in the criminal justice writings of William Godwin.[65] Godwin, a British thinker, published *An Enquiry Concerning Political Justice and Its Influence on General Virtue and Happiness* in 1793. The book addresses the fundamental issues surrounding criminal punishment in a manner that lays the groundwork for contemporary root social causes arguments. Godwin contends that the human mind is not free. Rather, the mind is molded by one's circumstances and environment. Accordingly, crime is caused by man's economic condition. "A numerous class of mankind are held down in a state of abject penury and are continually prompted by disappointment and distress to commit violence upon their more fortunate neighbours." Punishment is an ineffective means of dealing with crime because punishment does not address the forces that propel men into criminal behavior. While "hundreds of victims are annually sacrificed at the shrine of positive law and political institution," Godwin says, society does nothing to improve the poor economic conditions that cause criminal behavior.[66]

Central to this approach is the notion that not only is modern society not based on just or rational principles, but society itself is to blame for individual criminal behavior. The most important thinker in the Western tradition who contends that society itself is corrupt is, of course, Jean-Jacques Rousseau. His *Discourse on the Origin and Foundations of Inequality among Men*—the *Second Discourse*—lays the blame squarely on modern bourgeois society. It is modern society with which Rousseau answers the question implicit in the title to his discourse; modern society is the cause of inequality. Fundamental to Rousseau's thought is the notion that men are fundamentally good by nature. Unlike Hobbes, Rousseau does not believe that society is an improvement on man's natural state. Instead, the focus of modern society on private property has led man away from his good nature. Hence, man is miserable in modern society, and his criminality is evidence of society's corrupting influence.

Rousseau's view of natural man gets us only halfway through the rehabilitationist argument, however. What can be done to improve man's wretched condition? Even though man is content in his natural state, he is not necessarily moral. Rousseau's *Social Contract* teaches that the right kind of society can rehabilitate the miserable, bourgeois man.[67] Like many rehabilitationists who believe that social science can somehow make men moral, Rousseau claims that his society of the social contract will be able to engender the appropriate communitarian spirit.

Looking more closely at Rousseau's teaching in the *Second Discourse*, we see that man is unhappy because society has created a state of inequality, which Rousseau compares to slavery. "Moral or political inequality," he says, "depends upon a sort of convention and is established, or at least authorized by the consent of men." Man's natural state does not contain the "lies" of modern society but the truth about man's real nature.[68] The lies Rousseau mentions partly concern private property; he believes that man's true nature reveals the artificiality of private property. As man seeks—or accidentally stumbles into—the material comforts of modern society, he takes the steps that lead to his own enslavement.

> The first person who, having fenced off a plot of ground, took it into his head to say this is mine and found people simple enough to believe him, was the true founder of civil society. What crimes, wars, murders, what miseries and horrors would the human race have been spared by someone who, uprooting the stakes or filling in the ditch, had shouted to his fellow-men: Beware of listening to this impostor; you are lost if you forget that the fruits belong to all and the earth to no one![69]

"Crimes" and "murders" would have been avoided if the concept of private property had never been introduced. The real source of these crimes is the inequality of property and wealth—or, as Ramsey Clark has written, poverty is the "mother of crime." Of the founding of modern society, Rousseau says, "Such was, or must have been, the origin of society and laws, which gave new fetters to the weak and new forces to the rich, [and] destroyed natural freedom for all time."[70] Like Godwin's and Clark's, Rousseau's idea is to remove the "fetters" of the weak, so that the crimes, murders, and miseries caused by society will be eliminated.

Since the weak are in fetters and have little or no control over their own behavior, punishments based on a utilitarian or retributive approach are not permissible. Both of these approaches imply that the offender has free will, which the rehabilitationists deny. Godwin argues that punishment is only justified if the individual is in some way guilty of the crime. The individual cannot, however, be guilty because he does not freely choose to commit the act. "The justice of punishment therefore . . . can only be a deduction from the hypothesis of freewill, and must be false if human actions be necessary."[71] Since human action is determined by the external conditions imposed by society, criminal justice should focus on eliminating those conditions. Godwin states: "I should obtain little success by the abolition of punishment unless I could at the same time abolish those causes that generate temptation and make punishment necessary."[72] Society must focus on economic improvement.

Consequently, Godwin rejects both deterrence and retribution arguments. His rejection of deterrence is based on the same principles as Kant's: that no individual should suffer for the sake of some other end. "He that suffers, not for his own correction, but for the advantage of others, stands, so far as relates to that suffering, in the situation of an innocent person." Unlike Kant, however, Godwin believes that the punishment cannot reflect retribution for the crime committed. Punishment "cannot have relation to him as to the past, for that is concluded and beyond the reach of alteration or remedy." Man cannot "deserve" punishment. The only justification, then, for the sanctions of the criminal justice system is the extent to which they are directed toward the good of the offender. If man is not at fault, he cannot be held accountable and cannot serve as an example to others. Indeed, society owes a debt to the offender; it is not the offender who must repay a debt to society. "The only true end of punishment is correction."[73]

The way to provide this correction is not through force but through reason. Godwin contends that since society owes it to offenders to do them some good, and since that good cannot be accomplished with force, all punishment should attempt to "reason" with offenders. The conflict between offender and society is a difference of opinion. There must be a reasonable discussion between the offender and society—this is the only justification for the criminal justice system. "An appeal to force must appear to both parties, in proportion to the soundness of their understanding, to be a confession of imbecility." This is why Godwin suggests that jurisdiction over criminal justice matters should be limited to very small communities. In this way, an offender's neighbors can undertake to reason with him and convince him that he has behaved inappropriately. If political communities, Godwin reasons, "were contented with a small district," then every person would "live under the public eye, and the disapprobation of his neighbours, a species of coercion not derived from the caprice of men, but from the system of the universe, would inevitably oblige him either to reform or to emigrate."[74] Society commits an injustice when it tries to use anything other than the force of its reason to change individual behavior. Punishment through brute force is simply an admission, Godwin argues, that society's argument against the offender is weak.

Godwin contends that punishment cannot use coercion, whereas Rousseau argues that it cannot be based on any notion of nature or natural principles of justice. Man knows too little about nature. In the *Second Discourse*, Rousseau criticizes earlier natural rights philosophers for ascribing to "natural man" qualities that must truly have been the products of civilization. Although these previous thinkers attempt to understand nature, Rousseau contends that "none of them has reached it."[75] This is why we need civil punishment based on convention alone; divine and natural justice do exist, but their principles are not readily accessible to the human mind.[76]

Man's criminal justice system—and society in general—must be designed to free man from the bonds of determinism. This is implied in the famous phrase from the *Social Contract*: "Man was born free, and everywhere he is in chains."[77] The goal for Rousseau is to find a way for man to be truly free from his fetters, even though it is impossible to return to the natural state. Rousseau's objective is to

> find a form of association that defends and protects the person and goods of each associate with all the common force, and by means of which each one, by uniting with all, nevertheless obeys only himself and remains as free as before. This is the fundamental problem which is solved by the social contract.[78]

Like Clark's, Rousseau's solution is for individuals to stop focusing on their own narrow interests and to give themselves totally to the community. The question is, of course, how can society condition men into this communitarian spirit? Both Clark and Menninger think it can be accom-

plished with social or medical science and rehabilitation. Rousseau believes that those who still want to pursue their own private interests instead of the general will must be coerced by the state; they must "be
forced to be free."[79]

The interesting part of Rousseau's approach for our purposes is that,
when it comes to discussing the power of punishment *within* his society of
the social contract, he sounds very much like a utilitarian. Once individuals have been freed from the fetters of bourgeois society by entering the
society of the social contract, punishment can be based on the assumption
that individuals may rationally choose among alternative courses of behavior. Once the fetters of bourgeois society have been shed for the freedom of the social contract (even though this freedom might have to be
coerced), the goal of civil society is "the preservation of the contracting
parties." If, as a contracting party, one is part of the general will (whose
aim is the preservation of society), one necessarily wills the means to that
goal. The means to this preservation is the power of the sovereign authority to punish, even by death, anyone who becomes a threat to society.

> The social treaty has the preservation of the contracting parties as its end.
> Whoever wants the end also wants the means, and these means are insepa-
> rable from some risks, even from some losses. . . . The death penalty in-
> flicted on criminals can be considered from approximately the same point
> of view: it is in order not to be the victim of a murderer that a person con-
> sents to die if he becomes one.[80]

Although much of the contemporary rehabilitation theory certainly rests
on Rousseau's assumptions and his overall goals, Rousseau's ultimate solution—the social contract—takes him in a very different direction.

CHAPTER FIVE

Answering the Enlightenment

Moral Idealism and Punishment as Power

THE ENLIGHTENMENT APPROACH of reform and deterrence is only one of the punishment philosophies with origins in modernity. As the previous chapter demonstrated, utilitarianism and rehabilitationism are pushed to their extremes in the Enlightenment. The idea of just deserts is also pushed to its extreme by writers such as Kant and Hegel. Indeed, this polarization in the modern era culminates in Michel Foucault's criticism of all punishment systems. The present chapter addresses these other extremes in the modern political tradition on punishment.

The earliest roots of the retributive approach preceded any systematic philosophical defense. Before political society became involved in criminal justice most crimes were private matters. It was up to the aggrieved party to exact retribution on the offending party; the state, for example, would take no part in the punishment of a murderer. Instead, as Egon Bittner and Anthony Platt explain, the victim's family would seek vengeance by killing the murderer. Vengeance by the aggrieved party was based upon the "eye for an eye" principle expressed in the Old Testament. The role of society in such cases was primarily to define the principles of justice, based on the idea that the punishment ought to fit the crime as closely as possible.

When society increased its involvement in the actual criminal justice process, it was more to prevent chaos and feuding than anything else. The aggrieved party retained the responsibility for bringing a complaint against the criminal and for carrying out the punishment. To ensure some modicum of due process, the state might play a role in ascertaining and judging the facts. The purpose of society's role in this sort of system was merely to regulate private retribution—to prevent *unjustified* violence. That is, society certified that violence—or punishment—was *justified* on the basis of the facts and the principles of justice upon which the laws of society were founded. Bittner and Platt show that one of the first significant instances of systematic public prosecution and punishment came in the form of the sixteenth-century *Constitutio Criminalis Carolina,* which was the uniform criminal code for the German nation under the Holy Roman Empire. They also mention England under Henry VIII, where there were large numbers of public executions in an effort to suppress the private administration of justice by the various princes.[1]

EXTREME RETRIBUTION

Kant

Kantian moral idealism provides perhaps the clearest philosophical defense of extreme retribution. By definition, Kant's moral idealism rejects any and all considerations of utility; Kantian thought is the natural antithesis to utilitarian theories of punishment. For Kant, morality is a priori, that is, from first principles without consideration of experience. In Kant's *Groundwork of the Metaphysic of Morals,* we discover that one is compelled to behave morally not because of any benefit such behavior might produce (such as salvation or the avoidance of punishment) but only because one intends to obey the moral law. Any action that considers the potential consequences cannot be moral; morality must not be diluted by considerations of experience or self-interest. Kant believes it is a "matter of the utmost necessity to work out for once a pure moral philosophy completely cleansed of everything that can only be empirical"—completely cleansed, in other words, of utilitarian considerations such as what sorts of punishment will prevent crime. Kant argues that moral action cannot consider society's "circumstances" but must instead originate "solely *a priori* in the concepts of pure reason."[2]

Unlike Plato or Aquinas, for whom the moral law is also central, Kant does not allow consideration of the offender's happiness or salvation. Indeed, to be motivated by such considerations would deny true freedom, because action would be confined and restricted by teleological concerns. This a priori morality also explains why Kant rejects the political thought of Hobbes and other Enlightenment writers. Hobbes's politics could not be moral because it made the pursuit of self-interest the most important aim of political life. Kant's departure from Hobbes demonstrates why narrow forms of retributive and utilitarian approaches to punishment are incompatible: whereas one approach considers self-interest or utility, narrowly understood, to be the driving force of moral and political life, the other argues that a politics driven by any consideration of self-interest or utility cannot be moral.

A priori morality comes from what Kant calls the Good Will. The Good Will is pure—it "is not good because of what it effects or accomplishes." Instead, it merely wills something for its own sake; the Good Will is "good in itself."[3] Punishment, according to this Kantian reasoning, must be justified for its own sake, not for any way it might serve society's interests.[4] Kant's theory of the Good Will leads to the centrality of duty in his political thought. He is careful to distinguish duty from calculation. Utilitarian punishments are based upon calculation, because they try to determine how best to serve society's interests. Duty does not consider such factors, and this understanding of duty is the basis of Kant's "categorical imperative." To will the moral law, he argues, one must intend to obey the categorical imperative—the duty to do that which is universalizable. Only those actions that would properly be the will of all reasonable men can be the object of the categorical imperative.[5]

Everyone wills that criminals ought to be punished. That criminals suffer the pain of punishment is a universalizable maxim. Kant's theory of punishment cannot allow a practical consideration of the circumstances or the potential benefits to particular societies or offenders. Because "the law concerning punishment is a categorical imperative," considerations of interest, happiness, or any other beneficial consequence cannot interfere with the primarily retributive aim of punishment.[6] Society's circumstances change, and what constitutes its interest and happiness may also change; but for Kant, one's will must be universalizable, which means that any just punishment must be just in all circumstances.[7]

Prudence—the most important principle for statesmen, according to the ancient political tradition—has a much diminished role in Kantian penal theory. Prudence is the skill of properly applying right principles to particular circumstances. For Kant, however, the particular content of the law is secondary; that we obey the human law is the important consideration. Reverence for the law must be a universalizable maxim. "Nothing but the idea of the law in itself . . . can constitute that pre-eminent good which we call moral, a good which is already present in the person acting on this idea and has not to be awaited merely from the result."[8] In fact, on some of the most fundamental political questions, Kant does not allow for any differences in legislative prudence from one nation to another. For example, Kant asserts that the *only* justifiable punishment for a murderer is the death penalty (see below).

Whereas utilitarians—particularly Bentham—favor deterrence because they believe individuals act in response to stimuli of pleasure and pain, Kant argues that good and evil must be distinguished from the pleasant and the painful. To know whether something provides pleasure or pain requires experience; it requires one to consider the consequences of an action. But Kantian morality rejects all such a posteriori considerations. The standard for morality is simply one's will, without consideration of whether an action will bring pleasure or pain. Accordingly, good and evil are determined by the content of will; pleasure and pain are merely sensations. Punishment is based upon good and evil, not pleasure and pain. Kant says that "if something is to be, or is held to be, absolutely good or evil in all respects and without qualification, it could not be a thing but only the manner of acting, i.e., it could be only the maxim of the will." This is why punishment, although painful, is not an evil. Indeed, since punishment for crimes is part of the universalizable will, it is a good. Kant, for example, describes a person crying out in pain from gout. The pain does not represent anything morally evil. "The pain did not in the least diminish the worth of his person but only the worth of his condition."[9]

Kantian philosophy considers deterrence theory particularly untenable. Deterrence requires that one person be punished for the purposes of achieving some other good, namely, the prevention of future crime by demonstrating to others the consequences of criminal behavior. As such, the punishment is merely a means to an end, not an end in itself. But Kant's a priori morality—with the requirement of the categorical imperative that we will only that which is universalizable—does not allow us to consider other ends. When we treat a person as a means only, that person cannot share our will. As Kant states: "the man whom I seek to use for my own purposes cannot possibly agree with my way of behaving to him, and so cannot himself share the end of the action."[10] This is precisely why, in Kantian morality, crime is wrong in the first place. By committing a crime, one treats another person as a means to an end that the victim cannot possibly share. Kant confirms this in *The Metaphysical Elements of Justice:* "judicial punishment can never be used merely as a means to promote some other good for the criminal himself or for civil society, but instead it must in all cases be imposed on him only on the ground that he has committed a crime." Kant reasons that "a human being can never be manipulated merely as a means to the purposes of someone else."[11]

In the *Critique of Practical Reason*, Kant emphasizes that punishment is good for its own sake. He argues that punishment is certainly painful, but this is not to say it is an evil. "Whoever submits to a surgical operation feels it without doubt as an ill," Kant says, "but by reason he and everyone else will describe it as good." While Kant echoes early just deserts theorists when he claims that justice requires punishment and that punishment must fit the crime, he goes even further to make it clear that the effects of punishment on the offender are irrelevant. Even if the punishment is to the detriment of the offender's soul, Kant considers the punishment justified:

> When . . . someone who delights in annoying and vexing peace-loving folk receives at last a right good beating, it is certainly an ill, but everyone approves of it and considers it as good in itself even if nothing further results from it; nay, even he who gets the beating must acknowledge, in his reason, that justice has been done to him because he sees the proportion between welfare and well-doing, which reason inevitably holds before him, here put into practice.[12]

That an offender has committed a crime is the sole justification for punishing him; there need not be any proof that the punishment will benefit society by reducing crime in the future or that the punishment will benefit the offender by removing evil from his soul. Society punishes "in consequence of [the offender] having committed a crime."[13]

Since Kantian morality requires freedom to will the categorical imperative, criminal behavior presents a problem; it hinders the freedom necessary for the Good Will. Everyone in Kant's society must be equally free. Criminal behavior is an attempt to upset that balance, and punishment is required to restore the proper relationship among individuals in society. To demonstrate the necessity of understanding punishment in this manner, Kant brings in the idea of just desert, a central tenet of the retributive approach. When an offender commits a crime, he does so to someone who does not deserve it. In order to remedy the situation, punishment must be inflicted on the person who does deserve it—the criminal. This is why the punishment must be directly proportionate to the offense:

> What kind and what degree of punishment does legal justice adopt as its principle and standard? None other than the principle of equality (illustrated by the pointer on the scales of justice), that is, the principle of not treating one side more favorably than the other. Accordingly, any undeserved evil that you inflict on someone else among the people is one that you do to yourself. . . . Only the Law of retribution can determine exactly the kind and degree of punishment.[14]

Kant applies this balancing principle to the crime of murder as an example. Since punishment must be in direct proportion to the crime, all murderers must receive the death penalty. Kant argues that "there is no sameness of kind between death and remaining alive even under the most miserable conditions, and consequently there is also no equality between the crime and the retribution unless the criminal is judicially condemned and put to death."[15]

Continuing his discussion of the death penalty, Kant emphasizes the differences between his retributive approach and the utilitarian approach of Enlightenment penal reformers. In fact, he attacks Beccaria by name. Kant asserts that Beccaria was "moved by sympathetic sentimentality and an affectation of humanitarianism" in his opposition to the death penalty. While Beccaria says that he cannot see how a party to the social contract would give to the state the right to take his life, Kant calls this "sophistry" because Beccaria fails to make a critical distinction. Kant argues that there is a difference between the principle that all criminals must forfeit their life if they commit murder (which is part of the universalizable will and also the social contract) and each criminal's own judgment (which prevents him from volunteering his own life). Simply because it is not natural for an individual to relinquish willingly his own life does not mean that society cannot agree that all those guilty of murder *should* forfeit their lives.[16]

Hegel

Like Kant's, Hegel's moral idealism leads to a retributive theory of punishment; but for Hegel, the will can only be universalized—or objectified—in the rational state. Hegel does not believe that a universal morality can exist without an overarching political structure. True morality, for Hegel, is only possible through the laws of the state. It is only in Hegel's ideal state, which comes at the culmination of an evolving historical process, that each individual's subjective will is "objectified." In other words, it is the function of the state to ensure that each individual's will is moral. The state represents "the union of the *subjective* with the *rational* Will."[17] In this way, the laws of the rational state—including the criminal law—represent the perfect expression of each citizen's will.

There is a sharp distinction here with the utilitarian argument. While utilitarians consider punishment an evil outweighed by a greater societal good, Hegel believes that punishment is good in itself because righting wrongs through the criminal law of the rational state is an inherent part of the objective will; therefore, punishment can never be considered evil. Hegel admits there may be other considerations that are "relevant to punishment," such as deterrence and reformation, "but all these considerations presuppose as their foundation the fact that punishment is inherently and actually just." Considerations other than objective will are merely subjective and secondary. "If you adopt that superficial attitude to punishment," Hegel says, "you brush aside the objective treatment of righting the wrong." Not understanding the inherent goodness of punishment leads, in part, to "trivial psychological ideas of stimuli."[18] Hegel is referring to the strict utilitarian calculus of punishment, where laws are designed to prevent crime by demonstrating to potential criminals that they will receive more pain than pleasure from criminal behavior.

Idealism is as complex as it is influential, particularly with regard to criminal behavior. Considering criminal punishment as a matter of objective will means that the criminal himself actually wills to be punished. Rejecting the social contract argument of Beccaria (that no rational individual could freely enter into a contract whereby the sovereign would gain the right to execute the individual), Hegel contends that the state has nothing to do with a contract. The state is the ultimate and perfectly rational expression of human will. Accordingly, all individuals acknowledge the right of the state to take life and property. They will this because their will is consistent with the will of the state. This explains how the criminal wills his own punishment by committing a crime (Hegel says that the criminal claims his right to punishment). Hegel argues that "the injury [penalty] which falls on the criminal is not merely implicitly just—as just, it is *eo ipso* his implicit will, an embodiment of his freedom, his right; on the contrary, it is also a right established within the criminal himself."[19]

Like other retributivists, Hegel believes that punishment should be in direct proportion to the crime. "The annulment of crime is retribution." Punishment is justified solely by the crime because the punishment is simply an extension of the crime. In committing the crime, the criminal implicitly wills the punishment. The criminal act and the objective will that such an act be punished are inseparable. Hegel says that "crime, as the will which is implicitly null, *eo ipso* contains its negation in itself and this negation is manifested as punishment."[20]

The objective will embodied in the rational state requires that the precise nature of the punishment be derived from the criminal's own act. Crime represents a situation in which the subjective will of the criminal runs contrary to the objective will of all individuals in the rational state. Punishment "annuls" the contrary subjective will.[21] Both crime and punishment are acts of coercion; but crime is the initial act of coercion that denies another's freedom of will. The coercion of punishment is justified by the coercion of crime. "Abstract right is a right to coerce, because the wrong which transgresses it is an exercise of force against the existence of my freedom in an external thing."[22]

Kant, Hegel, and the Problem of Crime

While it is not the purpose of this section to explore fully the many important issues inherent in German idealism, there are some difficulties pertaining to criminal punishment that must be addressed. In particular, the idealistic view that the criminal wills his own punishment certainly raises some questions. There is the familiar example, for instance, of a man who walks in the sun on a hot day. Such a man chooses to sweat; he accepts the consequences of his act and, knowing the consequences, "wills" them as necessary to that which he wills primarily, that is, his walking. This does not mean that the man "wills" the perspiration per se. He would avoid perspiring if he could but accepts that he cannot. This scenario presupposes a rational actor for whom the incidental consequence (sweating) is tolerable in the service of his greater aim. But Kant and Hegel apply this same reasoning to the criminal, which is cause for question. The criminal, unlike the sweaty stroller in the example, precisely seeks to sever the good of his aim (the fruits of his crime) from the adverse consequences (detection and punishment). Unlike the stroller, the criminal's decision to commit the crime is (almost) never undertaken unless he thinks that he can avoid the consequence.

In order to achieve a universality of wills, both Kant and Hegel deny that the criminal wills this severability. For them, consent to the universal will (that is, the imperative that criminals be punished) bars the severability that the criminal, according to common sense, desires. Kant's and Hegel's idea of consent, therefore, must be understood as radically different from the principle of consent with which we are familiar in modern republicanism. Republicanism holds that one consents (wills) to the "adverse" consequences of an election in which one's candidate or party has lost, because one really consents to the higher aim of equal representation and majority rule. We must accept sometimes or even always losing an election (sweating, to use the example above) because we recognize that a greater good may have certain downsides. The man who challenges the elections because he does not like the results has withdrawn his consent from the regime.

Kant and Hegel, however, envision a universal will, and thus want to eliminate the possibility of individuals' withdrawing their consent and to preclude rebellion from the universal will. Therefore, the undeniable phenomenon of criminal behavior poses a difficulty. The universal will says that criminals must be punished, but does it not say first that the law shall be obeyed? Having withdrawn from or rebelled against the universal will by violating the latter imperative, how can the criminal be said to will the former?

All of this discussion perhaps raises more questions than it answers, but it also serves to highlight the complexities of an influential approach to punishment. One final task is to note an important distinction between Kant and Hegel. Like Kant, Hegel rejects Beccaria's argument against the power of the sovereign to execute criminals. Hegel criticizes the contention that the right to execute criminals is not part of the social contract. But Hegel parts company with Kant on the question of the state. Whereas Kant disputes Beccaria's understanding of the social contract, Hegel attacks Beccaria because Hegel believes there is no such thing as a social contract; the state is a "higher entity" than individuals.[23]

It is along these lines that Hegel criticizes Kant's individualistic morality. Hegel contends that one cannot will a universal good from an individual perspective. He says that "such an abstraction as 'good for its own sake,' has no place in living reality." Instead, moral action is determined "by the laws and customs of a State."[24] This is why, for Hegel, each criminal act is really an expression of the criminal's will to be punished. Since each individual will is, in truth, the will of the state, then just as the state wills criminals to be punished, so too does the criminal himself will to be punished. In the *Philosophy of Right*, Hegel admits that there might be a gap between the subjective will of some individuals and the objective will of the state. These individuals have not quite reached the end of the historical process. Hegel's goal is to demonstrate to the "experts" charged with running the rational state how they might bring such people up to the level of objective will. The "annulment" of subjective will with criminal punishment is an essential part of this scheme.

PUNISHMENT AS POWER: FOUCAULT

Modern political thought contains a fragmenting of approaches to punishment, where utilitarian, rehabilitative, and retributive arguments become narrow and exclusive. In the face of such polarization, Michel Foucault's book on punishment, *Discipline and Punish*, lays out an approach to the issue that challenges the traditional philosophical justifications for the criminal law. Perhaps the best way to describe Foucault is to say that he questions *any* criminal justice system's claim on justice or effectiveness. Whether the theory is just deserts, deterrence, or rehabilitation, Foucault contends that the law and the political authority from which punishment derives are merely expressions of power. He looks at the historical changes in punishment as part of his overall thesis.

Foucault contrasts punishment by torture in the eighteenth century to punishment by imprisonment in the nineteenth century in order to demonstrate the "reform" movement. Describing the reform, Foucault argues that the body ceased to be the receptacle for punishment when regimes began to understand that the "savagery" of the penalty exceeded the injustice of the crime. He interprets the decline of the public spectacle of punishment as an admission by "justice" that it could not account for punishment. In other words, the justice approach became ashamed of punishment so it moved to hide it from public view.[25] As the justice view was replaced by the reform view, the emphasis of the criminal justice system shifted from the carrying out of the punishment to the conviction of the offender. "The execution itself is like an additional shame that justice is ashamed to impose on the condemned man; so it keeps its distance from the act, tending always to entrust it to others, under the seal of secrecy."[26]

Under the reform movement, the body was no longer the direct recipient of punishment. While it is true that imprisonment—unlike fines—affects the body, the connection is indirect in that the body serves as a conduit for depriving the human of his freedom. Even executions after the reform movement reflected this change; the penal system always searched for the most painless method, and the offender was administered tranquilizers. In this way, the execution more directly emphasizes the deprivation of life and liberty than it does bodily suffering. Foucault views the use of the guillotine as a reform along these lines. The guillotine reduced physical pain to a minimum; the bodily contact lasted only for an instant. Foucault points to the example of reform in France, where the guillotine had previously been reserved for the nobility but was extended as the method of execution for all condemned. "The guillotine takes life almost without touching the body, just as prison deprives liberty or a fine reduces wealth."[27] In France, the condemned wore a black veil to further reduce the public spectacle.

Moving from the Enlightenment reforms to modern rehabilitation, Foucault asserts that the new methods are no better than the old. Rehabilitation does not restrict punishment but expands it. Allowing psychiatrists into the punishment phase of the criminal justice system exposes the individual's "penal soul" to punishment[28]:

> [Psychiatrists] provide the mechanisms of legal punishment with a justifiable hold not only on the offenses, but on individuals; not only on what they do, but also on what they are, will be, may be. The additional factor of the offender's soul, which the legal system has laid hold of, is only apparently explanatory and limitative, and is in fact expansionist.[29]

Foucault writes that punishment no longer fits the crime but, instead, fits the individual. Consequently, the power to punish has become fragmented; the judge is not alone. Rather, there is a punishment bureaucracy of psychiatrists, parole boards, and other corrections officials. All of this serves to alienate punishment from the criminal justice system—to move it into the realm of science and bureaucracy.

Although Foucault clearly abhors what he sees as the excesses of the old understanding of punishment, he is no less opposed to modern punishment. Modern punishment simply reflects a new form of oppression and subjugation—a new power relationship. Foucault describes the modern punishment bureaucracy as exercising a "technology of power."[30] While the old system was an expression of power in that it marked its victims to demonstrate its strength, the new system marks the individual in equally damaging ways.

Through power, which is exerted by the one who inflicts the punishment, the political regime makes its will universal. While the reformers attacked the old power structure, they erected a new one in its place. "The true objective of the reform movement . . . was not so much to establish a new right to punish based on more equitable principles, as to set up a new 'economy' of the power to punish." Foucault contends that the reformers' interest in redefining crime represented a reorganization of the power distribution of the old approach to punishment. The reform movement is characterized by what Foucault calls "generalized punishment. It is an unequal struggle: on one side are all the forces, all the power, all the rights."[31] Society resorts to exerting its will by the force of numbers, and punishment represents this force. Foucault is not concerned primarily with retribution, or with the crime rate, or with the societal rehabilitation of offenders. Instead, he questions the legitimacy of the authority to punish, and he considers different approaches to punishment to be mere variations on this questionable authority.

Connecting Foucault's argument to a foundation in the philosophic tradition on punishment is difficult, precisely because Foucault's work questions the notion that there can, in fact, be a rational, philosophic grounding for criminal penalties. It is no accident that Foucault's argument, instead of developing out of one of the traditional philosophic approaches to punishment, resembles the argument of the pre-Socratic tradition. This pre-Socratic approach to the law, perhaps best represented by Heraclitus and fully developed after Socrates by Epicurus, is made most familiar by Thrasymachus, one of Socrates' interlocutors in the *Republic*. Thrasymachus, like Foucault, denies that there can be any objective standard, abstracted from conventional politics, that serves as a means of judging the extent to which the regime and its laws are just or unjust.

Whereas Foucault sees the various approaches to criminal punishment within the tradition as different "economies" of the power to punish, each using the "technology of power . . . as a tool for its ends," Thrasymachus asserts that justice itself is a function of power. He defines justice as "the advantage of the stronger,"[32] or the advantage of the person or persons who have the strength to assert their control over a regime. Punishment, Thrasymachus explains, is merely the means by which a regime—whether democratic, aristocratic, or tyrannical—maintains its authority. Accordingly, to "punish" a person "as a breaker of the law"[33] is, as Foucault says, to use the system of laws as a technology of power in order to achieve the ends of those in authority. Foucault's work, the most important of several reexaminations of punishment during the 1970s, is thus the classic postmodern treatment of the criminal law. It returns the debate to its roots, questioning the philosophic foundations of the contemporary politics of punishment.

CHAPTER SIX

A More Comprehensive Approach

Ancient and Medieval Political Thought

THE APPROACHES DISCUSSED so far represent rather extreme arguments. Retribution is embraced by the moral idealists precisely because it does not consider *any* utilitarian concerns in the formation of punishments. Similarly, Enlightenment penal reform is predicated upon dissolving the ties between the criminal law and any notion of just deserts that is informed by a higher moral authority. Consequently, public safety and preservation must be the *only* aim of punishment. Also, the causal version of rehabilitation rejects both retributive and utilitarian approaches because it denies the moral autonomy upon which those other theories are founded. None of these more narrow philosophies of punishment is satisfactory in attempting to trace the roots of the American founding debate or, for that matter, in attempting to discern a coherent public consensus in the contemporary policy debate about crime and punishment.

The view of punishment during the founding era was a complex synthesis of the various approaches, where concerns for public safety and the reform of offenders proceeded from an understanding that punishment—appropriately applied—is inherently just and deserved. Although each of the narrow approaches from the philosophic tradition has its influence, it is a mistake to point to any one of these more narrow views and impute it to the founders as their philosophy of punishment. Instead, if one looks to the older political ideas of many ancient and medieval writers, one finds a comprehensive understanding of the criminal law that serves as a truer reflection of the complex punishment philosophy during the founding era. Four justifications for punishment played important and complementary roles in this older tradition: (1) just deserts and the understanding that the criminal law must approximate the higher moral law; (2) reform of the offender; (3) achieving the public good through the satisfaction of moral indignation; and (4) public safety.

JUST DESERTS AND THE MORAL LAW

St. Thomas Aquinas establishes just vengeance as the basis of punishment in the *Summa Theologiae*. He says that "to work evil is to sin. Therefore sin incurs a punishment which is signified by the words tribulation and anguish." Describing punishment as "tribulation and anguish," Aquinas refers to a passage from Romans 2:9: "Tribulation and anguish upon every soul of man that worketh evil." Aquinas contends that punishment is natural and is consistent with the natural order upon which just societies are based. "The natural inclination of man is to repress those who rise up against him. . . . Consequently, whatever rises up against an order, is put down by that order or by the principle thereof." He reasons that "whoever sins, commits an offense against an order: wherefore he is put down, in consequence, by that same order, which repression is punishment." Since man is part of three orders, Aquinas says, there are three forms of just punishment. Man belongs to the order of his own reason, to the order of another man who governs him in either spiritual or temporal matters, and to the universal order of divine government. The punishments for violating the principles of these orders are, respectively, remorse of conscience, man-inflicted punishment, and God-inflicted punishment.[1] Since all three orders are consistent with one another, so too are all three punishments. In other words, the existence of God-inflicted punishment for a violation of the universal order of divine government does not preclude man-inflicted punishment for violations of the temporal order.

Like other retributivists, Aquinas contends that the kind or amount of punishment must be determined directly by the seriousness of the offense. "Punishment is proportionate to sin," he says, and "in so far as sin turns inordinately to something, its corresponding punishment is the pain of sense." Sin is both finite and infinite. The infinite part of sin is the offense against God, and the corresponding infinite punishment is the "loss of the infinite good, i.e. God."[2] The finite part of sin allows man to determine the appropriate severity of punishment. Man's judgment of sin and his determination of the appropriate punishment must be in line with the principles of justice in order to be legitimate. Aquinas states: "a judge is so called because he asserts the right and right is the object of justice." Citing Aristotle's *Nicomachean Ethics* (V.4), Aquinas contends that "men have recourse to a judge as to one who is the personification of justice."[3] Punishment reflects the just foundations of a society and its revulsion to the injustice of crime. Emphasizing the need for a proportionate societal response to crime, Aquinas reminds the reader that restitution is necessary for salvation. "Restitution denotes the return of the thing unjustly taken; since it is by giving it back that equality is re-established." Salvation requires the "safeguarding of justice."[4]

More recently, Pope Pius XII used the Thomistic framework in his discussions of criminal punishment. In a retributivist mode, Pius writes that "punishment is the reaction, required by law and justice, to the crime." Echoing Aquinas's *Treatise on Law,* Pius points out that crime can only be understood as an act against a just human law. This demonstrates the dependence of crime and punishment on the higher principles of justice. Because just law is based upon a harmonious relationship between the universal principles of justice and the political community, the aggrieved party in any criminal act is both God Himself and the legally established community. The purpose of punishment, therefore, is to return the individual and the principles of justice to a harmonious relationship. In both a retributive and a reformative mode, Pius asserts, "punishment . . . cannot therefore have any other meaning and purpose than . . . to bring back again into the order of duty the violator of the law, who had withdrawn from it." Civil society plays a crucial role in the link between individuals and natural justice. Indeed, criminal punishment is a vital element of this link. "Sacred Scripture (Romans 13:2–4) teaches that human authority, within its own limits, is, when there is a question of inflicting punishment, nothing else than the minister of divine justice."[5] Although the human judge cannot have the infallible certainty of God, this does not mean that humans cannot have the necessary moral certainty to impose legal punishment. Pius claims that "in every case where human judges have erred, the Supreme Judge will re-establish the equilibrium."[6] This does not absolve the human judge of his accountability but ensures that there will be a final equating of guilt and punishment that will be absolutely perfect. It also underscores the idea that the very basis of punishment is the violation of justice effected by the crime.

We know from the *Republic* that Plato shares with Aquinas a very similar understanding of the relationship between the political community and the natural principles of justice—without, of course, Aquinas's specific teaching on divinity and salvation. It is clear that Plato's idea of society involves the use of political authority to implement "justice." In the *Gorgias*—a dialogue on rhetoric—Plato gives us a more concise and focused teaching on the role of criminal punishment in a just society.[7] The legitimate definition of power, Plato contends, centers upon the infliction of punishment in accord with the principles of justice.[8] The man who executes and punishes, without regard to justice or injustice, cannot be said to act with power properly understood. Since power can only be a "good," the man who punishes others unjustly cannot be said to have power. The justification for punishment does not come initially from its utility but from a standard that defines happiness. This standard applies to all men. Socrates undertakes a discussion of punishment in order to make a point about rhetoric: that it is good only insofar as it argues for justice and that it is not good when it argues for injustice. Polus—Socrates' main interlocutor in the dialogue—claims that rhetoric is always good, regardless of its purpose. Socrates responds: "For speaking in defense of one's own injustice, therefore, or that of parents or comrades or children or fatherland when it does injustice, rhetoric will be of no use to us, Polus."[9] Socrates contends that injustice is the greatest evil, and men must seek to have it corrected if it finds its way into their souls.

REFORM OF THE OFFENDER

Unlike the narrowly retributive approach within modern political thought, the ancient and medieval view held that, although punishment must be understood from the perspective of just vengeance, the idea of justice obligates society to attempt to reform offenders. Contrary to the modern view, this reform was to be spiritual, requiring society to aim at amending offenders' souls. The more comprehensive approach to punishment is expressed nicely in Aquinas's question on vengeance in the *Summa Theologiae*. He defines vengeance as "the infliction of a penal evil on one who has sinned." The first consideration—the initial justification for punishment—is the commission of a crime by the individual in question. Sin is the basis of punishment, reflecting a violation of the higher principles upon which the law is based; but although the offender's guilt is a necessary condition for just punishment, it is not sufficient. To decide whether a punishment is just, "we must consider the mind of the avenger." If the *intention* of one who punishes "is directed chiefly to the evil of the person on whom he takes vengeance, and rests there, then his vengeance is altogether unlawful."[10] In such a case, the avenger merely takes pleasure in doing evil to another; Aquinas defines this as hatred, which is contrary to the principle of charity. To be lawful, vengeance must have the intention of doing the offender some good. The idea is that, by suffering punishment, the soul of the offender becomes clean by paying the penalty required by justice. The "good" that must be the object of lawful vengeance must be the moral amendment of the offender's soul.

Reforming offenders is also a central part of Plato's understanding of criminal justice. Reflecting Plato's argument in the *Republic*, Socrates demonstrates the importance of a properly ordered soul. Justice requires one's soul to be in proper order. Punishment must be understood from the perspective of justice because it is designed to return the soul to its proper order. "The soul's arrangements and orderings . . . have . . . the name 'lawful' and 'law,' whence they become both lawful and orderly; and these things are justice and moderation."[11] Criminality, according to this understanding, is the antithesis of a just and orderly soul. Aristotle makes a similar argument.[12] He explains that the judge, or the law, represents justice. Punishment is based upon justice: "The judge is intended to be a sort of living embodiment of what is just."[13] In one respect, Aristotle claims, justice is law-abidingness. This is because, in a decent regime, the laws aim at making citizens virtuous. Accordingly,

> the law instructs us to do the actions of a brave person, . . . of a temperate person, . . . of a mild person, . . . and similarly requires actions that express the other virtues, and prohibits those that express vices. The correctly established law does this correctly, and the less carefully framed one does this worse.[14]

An important distinction between Thomistic or Platonic retribution theory and Kantian or Hegelian retribution theory is that the *intent* of the punishment in the former is to remove evil from the offender's soul and thereby benefit or improve him. Aquinas defines sin as a "sickness of the soul."[15] Vengeance—aimed at restoring the offender's soul to goodness—is a special virtue. Justice requires punishment, because there is a "special inclination of nature to remove harm." Man can fulfill this natural inclination if he "avenges those [harms] which have already been inflicted on him, with the intention, not of harming, but of removing the harm done."[16] Punishment motivated by lawful vengeance is defined as following a natural inclination in accord with natural right. Since crime creates a debt in the soul, punishment relates to paying for the debt. Aquinas addresses this teaching in his discussion of Purgatory. The general idea of Purgatory is itself an excellent illustration of Thomistic punishment theory. Justice requires that those who have sinned must have their souls cleansed before entering God's kingdom. The pain of Purgatory is for the good of the sinner, because it prepares his soul for its proper destiny. "Since the obligation incurred by guilt is nothing else than the debt of punishment, a person is freed from that obligation by undergoing the punishment which he owed. Accordingly the punishment of Purgatory cleanses the debt of punishment."[17]

In contrast to narrowly utilitarian theories, the comprehensive theories of Plato and Aquinas hold the status of the human soul as the central question in matters of punishment. Justice requires that the criminal suffer for his crimes; this is the only way for the criminal to change his evil state and, where Aquinas is concerned, to earn salvation. Pius XII describes this approach as expiation. Legitimate punishment must be designed to make the criminal suffer. "Suffering," Pius explains, "has great moral value. . . . Suffering can reach moral heroism, heroic patience and expiation."[18] Even in the *Republic*, Plato emphasizes that punishment and judgment are based upon the importance of the soul. Socrates illustrates this when he explains the difference between doctors and judges. It is best for doctors to have suffered the various diseases they must treat in order to better understand effective treatment. This is not a problem, Socrates says, because it only requires doctors to become diseased in body, while their souls remain healthy. But judges are different. Since crime is a disease of the soul, we cannot ask that judges become criminals in order to know best how to treat crime—it is unacceptable for them to have injustice in their souls.[19]

The teaching is even more explicit in the *Gorgias*. We learn here that it is worse to be unjust and to go unpunished than to be unjust and punished for your deed. This is because the criminal himself is unhappy when his soul is not in proper order. In one way, this approach to punishment is teleological because punishment is seen as a means to effecting the offender's happiness. Unlike many contemporary rehabilitative theories, this approach also aims to make just vengeance and the good of the offender the same thing. In the *Gorgias*, Socrates teaches that the soul is superior to the body, because only the soul can distinguish between true and untrue, or between flattery and justice.[20] In response to Polus, who envies the unpunished tyrant and contends that such a man must be happy, Socrates argues that punishment is necessary for the unjust man.

> Socrates: The doer of injustice, then, will be happy; will this be so, then, if he meets with just judgment and retribution?
>
> Polus: Not in the least, since thus he would be most wretched.
>
> Socrates: But if, then, the doer of injustice does not meet with just judgment, according to your argument he will be happy.
>
> Polus: So I assert.
>
> Socrates: But according to my opinion, at least, Polus, the one who does injustice and is unjust is altogether wretched, but more wretched if he does not pay the just penalty nor meet with retribution when he does injustice, and less wretched if he pays the just penalty and meets with just judgment from gods and human beings.[21]

For strict deterrence theorists, the goal of the criminal is to escape punishment. For Plato, the criminal ought to *seek* punishment, although the criminal may not ordinarily understand what is good for him. In the Platonic teaching, the difference is that the laws are based upon justice and are designed to improve the soul.

> Polus: If someone is caught doing injustice, plotting to attain tyranny, and having been caught is tortured on the rack and castrated and has his eyes burned out, and having suffered many great mutilations of all kinds himself and having beheld his children and wife suffer them, at the end is impaled or tarred and burned this man will be happier than if, getting away, he is established as tyrant, rules in the city, and passes his whole life doing whatever he wishes, being enviable and accounted happy by the citizens and by others who are foreigners? These are the things you say it is impossible to refute?
>
> Socrates: The one who gets away and becomes tyrant is nevertheless more wretched.[22]

Socrates even argues that it is better to suffer wrong than to do wrong. He explains that at least the just man who is unjustly tortured or killed has his soul in order. He who does wrong has a disordered soul and is, consequently, unhappy. Plato's *Laws*—which might superficially be interpreted as backpedaling from the more retributive approaches to punishment—reaffirms that the soul is the critical focus.[23] The Athenian Stranger contends that the city must "honor" the soul. He defines the task of the legislator as deciding which things honor and which things dishonor the soul. This legislative judgment forms the basis of the penal code.[24]

THE SATISFACTION OF MORAL INDIGNATION

Punishment in the ancient and medieval traditions is also an expression of the public's moral indignation. The public becomes angry about crime. Whereas many critics of the just deserts argument in the contemporary debate decry this anger and any punishment policy that derives from it as a sort of irrational bloodthirstiness, others defend anger as the appropriate expression of the outrage of a moral people. In this sense, public anger represents a moral judgment and condemnation that is most accurately characterized as moral indignation. Indignation of this sort plays an important part in the comprehensive approach to punishment of the older political tradition. Punishment was also understood in this tradition as serving the public good by acting as an outlet for the satisfaction of rightful public indignation about crime. In this way, public indignation is channeled through the appropriate procedural safeguards of the criminal law, which takes the place of the chaos of private vengeance seeking.

Those contemporary retributivists who discuss the importance and propriety of anger closely reflect the teaching of Aquinas. Aquinas observes that anger is often a central element in the infliction of punishment. Since punishment is the correction of evil, anger is proper; punishment represents anger at injustice. Citing St. Augustine (*Confessions* II.6), Aquinas says, "Anger craves for revenge. But the desire for revenge is the desire for something good; since revenge belongs to justice. Therefore the object of anger is good." While many critics of retributivism characterize the approach as hatred or anger, Aquinas makes a careful distinction between the two terms. Anger is a two-part concept. One part wishes vengeance that is good and lawful; the other part of anger wishes harm to another. The concept of hatred, on the other hand, is one-dimensional; it only wishes harm. Thus anger is acceptable and hatred is not; anger reflects the justice that is part of vengeance.[25] Aquinas explains that hatred is "far worse and graver than anger":

> The object of anger is the same in substance as the object of hatred; since, just as the hater wishes evil to him whom he hates, so does the angry man wish evil to him with whom he is angry. But there is a difference of aspect: for the hater wishes evil to his enemy, as evil, whereas the angry man wishes evil to him with whom he is angry, not as evil but in so far as it has an aspect of good, that is, in so far as he reckons it as just, since it is a means of vengeance.[26]

This is a distinction not made by modern utilitarians—especially Bentham. For Bentham, punishment is always pain, or a "cost." In justifying it, we must simply consider whether it is outweighed by other benefits. Kant's approach is equally one-dimensional. He argues that the pain of punishment itself is a good, regardless of anything else that might come from it. For Aquinas, Kant would fit perfectly the definition of a "hater" and would thus merit condemnation. Aquinas also rejects the utilitarian idea that punishment itself is an evil. Citing Dionysius, he says, "Punishment is not an evil, but to deserve punishment, is."[27]

The key to understanding Aquinas's teaching on anger is the role of reason. Although partly a passion, anger also reflects reason because there is a judgment about the appropriateness of the punishment for the crime. In other words, there needs to be a determination of moral culpability, which depends upon reasoned judgment. Reason is a critical element of anger because it tells us that our anger ought to be directed at a wrongdoer. Citing Aristotle (*Nicomachean Ethics* VII.6), Aquinas explains that "anger, as if it had drawn the inference that it ought to quarrel with such a person, is therefore immediately exasperated." In order to draw this proper inference, anger "listens to reason somewhat." Aquinas is careful to say that anger identifies the proper object, but it does not use reason when determining the measure of vengeance. Anger, although good, must be kept in its proper place, so that vengeance is only what is deserved and no more. Legal punishment, in this way, ensures that anger is kept at a level commensurate with the crime. Again referring to Aristotle (*Nicomachean Ethics* VII.6), Aquinas puts it this way: "Anger listens somewhat to reason insofar as reason denounces the injury inflicted, but listens not perfectly, because it does not observe the rule of reason as to the *measure* of vengeance." In another indication of the centrality of the moral law, Aquinas is also careful to say that anger is directed only at those with whom we have relations of justice. Human beings have common moral relations; punishment is based upon such common moral principles. This explains the centrality of anger in punishment. Using Aristotle's explanation (*Rhetoric* II.4), Aquinas says: "one difference between hatred and anger [is] that hatred may be felt towards a class, as we hate the entire class of thieves, whereas anger is directed only towards an individual."[28]

PUBLIC SAFETY

In addition to retributive and reformative concerns, the older view of justice incorporates utility. Just as Aristotle acknowledges that the polis has two ends (to secure mere life and to secure the good life), the older approach to punishment recognizes that public safety is an important part of justice—*criminal* justice in particular. Unlike the modern utilitarian view, however, the goal of public safety exists in coordination with, not as a substitute for, the moral law.

In the *Laws*, Plato makes allowance for the differences between the ideal state and a good constitution. The discussants in the dialogue agree that the ideal state would be one in which there would be no laws but rather the rule of philosophers. Under the laws of a good constitution, when a person does evil, continues to associate himself with evil persons, and continues to commit evil acts, such a person must be punished by execution in order to protect the state. It is agreed that, when punishment is done for this purpose, it is not appropriate to call it a good; instead, it is a "miserable" consequence.[29] Throughout the *Laws*, Plato makes allowances for utility. Such punishments are the practical consequences of his philosophy and reflect a broader understanding of political justice.

The concession made in the *Laws*, which is not present in the *Gorgias*, is that there are some offenders on whom it is impossible for punishment to have a beneficial effect. The goal of Platonic punishment is consistent: to restore the offender's soul to a just order. For those offenders whose souls are not capable of being restored, however, the Platonic teaching in the *Laws* states that there must be a consideration of society's safety. While society must seek to help an "unjust" man "when his illness is curable," anger must have "free rein" against the "purely evil, perverted man who cannot be corrected." The Athenian explains that this is why it is best for men to be both "spirited" and "gentle," depending upon the situation.[30] The teaching on punishment in the *Laws* represents the classic synthesis of nature and convention in the ancient political tradition. While we learn in both the *Gorgias* and the *Laws* that the only just punishment is that which is based upon natural principles of right and which seeks to improve the soul of the offender, we also learn in the *Laws* that political society—which is always less than ideal—must make certain compromises with convention and necessity. Hence, the Athenian of the *Laws* is willing to admit that, where the ideal motivation for punishment is not possible, the secondary consideration of utility has an important role to play.

There will always be those who cannot be improved by the laws, and the legislator must seek to purge society of such evil elements. Society cannot allow bad men to remain because they will poison other citizens. The Athenian says that there is a range of punishments that can protect society—from the extreme of banishment or execution to the milder punishment of colonization. The Athenian compares the legislator who punishes in this manner to a herder who separates the diseased animals from the good, in order to prevent the disease from spreading. Where reformative punishment fails, this secondary approach is the most prudent option. For those who cannot be reformed, "it isn't better for them if they go on living." In fact, "by departing life they would confer a double benefit on the others (becoming examples to the others of why not to do injustice, and emptying the city of bad men)." The Athenian concludes that "the lawgiver must necessarily assign to such men the punishment of death for their faults." He even contends that, where homicides are committed out of passion, society should send the offender into exile so that he can learn to control his passion; ultimately, the offender should be allowed back into society if he has changed. There is a description of what we might call a parole board. The Athenian suggests that a board of citizens should go to the place of exile and deliberate on the offender's behavior during his exile. If there is improvement, the board should allow the offender to return to the city. If the offender recidivates after being allowed to return, the primary goal of punishment has failed and the person should be executed or permanently exiled.[31]

The Athenian reminds everyone that the first obligation ought to be the ideal punishment: the reform of the offender by reordering his soul in accord with natural justice. He admits that "the best method is painful"; it is like a "medicine." This ideal method "involves punishing with justice and retribution, and completes the retribution by means of death and exile."[32]

The discussants in the *Laws* agree that the criminal statutes should attempt to have a morally educative effect. By portraying punishment as a form of moral condemnation, society may cultivate the habit of law-abidingness. The Athenian suggests that "praise and blame can educate" the citizens, so that they become "more obedient and well disposed to the laws," contending that no rational man can ever intentionally do wrong. While the damage caused by a wrong may be either voluntary or involuntary, the wrong itself must always be unintentional. The goal of legislation, then, is to make citizens realize that causing damage is a wrong; the legislator must make citizens hate the iniquity that is caused by the damage. Punishment may also be a useful tool in inculcating law-abidingness. The Athenian argues that "pleasures or pains" might be employed to "compel" an offender "never again to dare voluntarily to do such an [injustice], or to do it very much less."[33]

Even Aquinas acknowledges the importance of utilitarian motivations in punishment. He recognizes that deterrence may have a role to play. Aquinas says that "laws were made that in fear thereof human audacity might be held in check, that innocence might be safeguarded in the midst of wickedness, and that the dread of punishment might prevent the wicked from doing harm."[34] In outlining the different types of punishment, Aquinas argues that, in addition to its need of being directly proportionate to the crime and reflecting the injustice done by the criminal act, punishment also has the advantage of deterrence by threatening the removal of things that men love most. Death deprives a man of his life, stripes or retaliation deprive a man of his bodily safety, slavery or imprisonment deprive a man of his freedom, exile his country, fines his riches, and ignominy his good name. In all of these punishments, man is deprived of something he loves; this deprivation ought to deter potential criminals.[35]

In addition to deterrence, Aquinas echoes Plato's *Laws* in suggesting that those offenders who are incapable of amendment ought to be permanently incapacitated in the interest of public safety. When "the health of the whole body demands the excision of a member," he argues, it is "praiseworthy and advantageous" that the offender "be killed in order to safeguard the common good."[36] This argument ought to be contrasted with the narrowly retributive view of Kant, in which public safety cannot be taken into account; to do so would, in Kant's thinking, treat the offender as a means to an end and not an end in himself.

Part Three

Just Punishment and the Founding Debate

CHAPTER SEVEN

Reevaluating the Reform Movement

MANY ACCOUNTS OF THE CRIMINAL LAW in early American politics overemphasize the role of Beccaria and Enlightenment political thought. Above all, Enlightenment penal reform was a movement of ideas. During the early days of the republic, there certainly was a commitment—in some states more than in others—to reducing the severity of criminal penalties. We must, however, distinguish between the practical recommendations of those involved in drafting the criminal law on the one hand and their commitment to the Beccarian philosophy of punishment on the other.

The core of Beccaria's reforms rested upon a move away from the moral law or natural justice perspective to an emphasis on utility or self-interest. How important was this central Beccarian principle to those who were implementing changes in our criminal laws? There was a great variety of ideas about punishment during the founding period, and although Beccaria's penal reform philosophy was significant and influential, it was not necessarily the dominant principle underlying the development of early American criminal law.

Many writers who see Enlightenment penal reform as the dominant principle of the early American criminal law make two assumptions. First, they presuppose that a reduction in the severity of criminal penalties implies an acceptance of Beccaria's utilitarian principles. Second, the focus on reform in Pennsylvania makes an implicit assertion that the changes there represent a larger movement in the nation as a whole. With regard to the first assumption, little evidence suggests that the reductions in severe penalties were not at least equally based upon principles of just deserts. One of the most frequent expressions of even the most ardent reformers was that penalties should be proportioned to the gravity of crimes. Many state laws that reduced the severity of criminal penalties announced in their titles that their purpose was to proportion more equitably crimes and punishments. One must consider the argument that states abolishing the death penalty for crimes other than murder and treason acted on the basis of just deserts and proportionality. By enacting death penalty statutes only for the crimes of murder and treason, founding statesmen may well have been striving for just deserts, not simply rejecting this approach in favor of utilitarianism.

With regard to the second assumption, such reform efforts as Pennsylvania's tended to be more the exception than the rule during the founding period. When America declared its independence, most states transferred the English common law to their citizens. The federal government expressed its belief that U.S. citizens were "entitled to the common law."[1] Whereas Pennsylvania was fairly quick to reject the severe criminal punishments of the common law (partly because the Quakers resented English persecution), even states such as Virginia accepted the common law approach to punishment. In 1776 Virginia adopted the "rule of decision," which declared that all laws existing under British rule were valid in the state unless and until they were changed.[2] Between 1776 and 1784, eleven of the thirteen states adopted statutes accepting the principles of the common law.[3] Other than Pennsylvania, no state acted to reduce the severe penalties of the common law until 1796. Even then, only Virginia, New York, and New Jersey adopted new penal codes, and the new codes themselves reflected the principles of just deserts and proportionality at least as much as utility and reformation. Even Jefferson's code, though known for its softening of colonial penalties, was much concerned with proportionality and desert (his proposed code for Virginia was entitled "A Bill for proportioning Crimes and Punishments"). The revised New York law was certainly not the ideal of Beccaria's followers, as it called for life in prison for all felonies not punished by death. The New Jersey reform of 1796 mandated death for murder and treason, as well as for most other felonies on the second offense.[4]

Significant reform efforts were more gradual in other states. Bradley Chapin concedes that most states proceeded slowly and admits that many did indeed keep their sanguinary penalties well into the nineteenth century. He admits that most of his argument regarding the influence of penal reform is taken from those few states where the movement was successful. Claiming that evidence from those states maintaining severe criminal codes was difficult to gather, he reasons that "it seems fair to conclude that voters and legislators in those states could not be influenced by rational or humane arguments."[5]

In the New England states, especially, the criminal codes were severe. Significant reform did take place but not until several decades after the founding period. Colonies in the region had strict penalties intended to correspond to the Bible. In the 1641 Massachusetts Body of Liberties, a list of capital offenses is provided, and next to each offense is a citation from Scripture, which shows the source of each provision. Capital crimes listed include worshiping false gods, witchcraft, blaspheming the Holy Trinity, murder, manslaughter, bestiality, sodomy, adultery, kidnapping, rebellion, and perjury in a capital case.[6] David Flaherty explains that "the equation of sin and crime" was a central component of New England's colonial codes and that "the enforcement of the moral law became one of the primary obligations of colonial governments."[7] Colonial laws from Massachusetts, Connecticut, Rhode Island, and New Hampshire all had long lists of capital crimes.[8] Although strict penal codes were not unique among the colonies, Chapin notes, a key difference between New England and elsewhere was the greater severity with which New England laws treated sex crimes.[9]

Like other states, New England states did eventually moderate their criminal penalties and provide for the building and maintenance of penitentiaries but not until well into the nineteenth century, with the advent of Jacksonian democracy. This is why several of the important historical works on penal reform and the development of the penitentiary in America focus on the Jacksonian era. Adam J. Hirsch explains, for example, that "the move from pillory to penitentiary" in Massachusetts did not take place as a formal matter of law until 1813, at the earliest. Incarceration then became a statutorily authorized substitute for all crimes that had previously been treated with corporal punishment. Corporal punishment was not abolished in the law until 1826, and bonded servitude was not abolished until 1836. Although Massachusetts did take some early first steps toward reform, Hirsch notes, it was Pennsylvania and New York that took the lead in implementing incarceration as a regular criminal penalty.[10]

Pennsylvania was certainly the leader in moderating its criminal penalties, but even Barnes admits that "real reform" did not come to the state until at least the 1830s. He concedes that even though Pennsylvania's founding-era revisions reduced criminal penalties and recognized for the first time the aims of deterrence and reformation, the prevailing attitude was still based largely upon just deserts. He also concedes that, to the extent Pennsylvania did undertake penal reform, it was the exception among states during the founding period.[11]

Just deserts was not the exclusive approach to punishment in early America. Utilitarianism and reformation were important considerations in the formation of America's earliest criminal laws. The examination of the early American politics of punishment does suggest, however, that just deserts was a fundamental element in an approach to punishment that was far more comprehensive than Beccaria's narrow utilitarianism. Perhaps the most important evidence for this comprehensive approach is the unmistakable understanding of the founding's most influential leaders that positive law must be founded upon a higher moral law. This understanding is evident in their writings, as well as in the key documents of the founding era. Along with an increased appreciation for utilitarian and reformative aims of the criminal law, this understanding informs the early American politics of punishment.

PENNSYLVANIA REVISITED

Pennsylvania was certainly the most reform-minded state during the founding period, but its reform movement embodied many ideas. In order to comprehend the principles at the root of Pennsylvania's relatively mild criminal statutes, one must appreciate not only the obvious influence of Beccarian utilitarianism but also the religious and reformative approaches. Particularly with regard to Benjamin Rush (probably Philadelphia's foremost reformer), there are important departures from Beccaria's utilitarianism. Michael Meranze describes Philadelphia's reforms as "laboratories of virtue," because Rush and others combined a utilitarian call for milder penalties with an emphasis on reforming offenders through the penitentiary system. Philadelphia's reformers also contradicted some of Beccaria's central teachings, such as in their call for an end to public punishments. Beccaria approved of public punishments (not tortures) whereas Philadelphia's reformers fought them with great vigor.[12] Reformers like Bradford adhered more strictly to utilitarian arguments, whereas the Quaker tradition of mild penalties derived largely from nonutilitarian religious principles.[13]

Religious Influences

Quaker religious principles are consistent with moderating the power of the civil government. William Penn's primary purpose in seeking a charter from Charles II was to escape the persecution of Quakers in England. Since the king owed a debt to Penn's father, he granted Penn the charter.[14] Although many communities at the time justified their severe criminal penalties by the Mosaic law of the Old Testament, the Quakers were dubious about the manner in which the Mosaic law had been applied to contemporary circumstances. Early Quaker reformers George Fox and his disciple John Bellers emphasized the importance of considering the Old Testament in light of the New Testament. Fox wrote that we must understand the full and true spirit of the Mosaic law, since "none could read Moses aright without Moses's Spirit." The coming of Christ had made repentance possible.[15] The death penalty, therefore, ought to give way in certain circumstances to an effort to reform offenders.

Neither Fox nor Bellers rejected the Mosaic law. Instead, they quite rightly pointed out that the severe criminal codes of the time were themselves more punitive than the Old Testament Scripture upon which they were supposedly based. Nor did Fox or Bellers call for the complete abolition of the death penalty. They argued that the death penalty should be limited to those crimes for which it is prescribed in the Old Testament. Fox pointed out that, under the Mosaic law, theft was not punished by death but by making the offender pay restitution.[16] The common law stipulated death for all felons. Bellers admitted the biblical foundation for punishing murder with death, conceding that "he that spills Man's Blood, by Man was his Blood to be spilt," yet he reminded us that "the Thief was to restore but four or five fold, by the Ancient Law of God."[17]

Some historians, such as Herbert William Keith Fitzroy, have equated the Quaker emphasis on milder punishments with Beccarian principles, but there is much evidence to suggest that the Quaker reform was based more on religion than on utilitarianism.[18] The religious argument forwarded by Fox and Bellers rests largely on proportionality between the severity of crimes and punishments. Bellers wrote: "to make no difference between the Punishment of Theft and Murder, seem a great deficiency in our present Law."[19] Fox and Bellers also made clear that the law of God must be the foundation for the criminal law—a principle that could hardly be more opposed to the aims of Beccaria and other Enlightenment reformers. In his *Instruction to Judges and Lawyers*, Fox contended that contemporary judges should be "restored by the power of the Lord." Judges should return to the law that "came by Moses, given forth by God."[20] By returning to this biblical law, the death penalty would be confined to those for whom God had intended it.

Much in the writings of Fox and Bellers foreshadowed later reform efforts. In particular, Bellers presented an argument for the reformation of the jails. He attacked the jail keepers' practice of selling liquor to the inmates, which, he contended, distracted the prisoners from concentrating on repentance. The liquor "keeps the Prisoners' Blood always boiling, and their Brains hot, and without Sense of their Unhappiness in this World, they live so voluptuous, and without sense of the other World, because they are so strongly diverted from thinking of it." Bellers believed that "few of [the prisoners] are so incorrigible" they cannot be reformed. The goal of prison should be to "alter their evil habits" through a strict regimen designed for that purpose.[21] Such arguments were at the heart of the penitentiary movement during the founding era.

Some early American religious writers—in favor of the New Testament approach to punishment—made a much clearer attack on the Old Testament. Quakers making these arguments were inspired by earlier writers such as Roger Williams, whose "The Bloody Tenent Yet More Bloody," published in 1652, made an argument similar to one some Pennsylvanians would later employ against the use of the Mosaic law as a guide for penal statutes. Williams was fighting the strict application of the Mosaic law that was common in early America. John Cotton from Boston's Church of Christ argued, for instance, that the Mosaic law was intended to serve as a universal code, just as valid under the new covenant as it had been under the old. If not, Cotton argued, why had the Israelites continued to obey the law of Moses long after Moses himself was dead? Christ had come, Cotton contended, not to invalidate the old laws but to confirm and strengthen them.[22]

Williams responded that the Mosaic law cannot be a guide for contemporary penal statutes because the law was intended by God only for a specific people during a specific time period. Williams "cannot allow of Moses his Judicialls to binde all Nations of the World," because the "people of Israel (to which those Judiciall Lawes and punishments wer prescribed) was . . . a miraculous people or Nation." He argued that ancient Israel was a particularly holy land, and therefore the crimes committed there were considered particularly heinous and offensive to God. "The rigour of Lawes . . . cannot be justly executed, without the moderate and equall consideration of persons and other circumstances!"[23] Crimes committed in the holy land of Israel, among God's chosen people whom He had delivered out of slavery, were understandably deserving of more punishment than crimes committed elsewhere. This was, in Williams's view, a consequence of the special relationship between Israel and God.

Williams believed that the New Testament and the coming of Christ changed much of the lesson from the Old Testament. The coming of Christ changed the penalties by which ancient Israel had been governed. "The Lord Jesus tells us of a more tollerable Sentence," he says, "upon such Adulterers, Thieves, as profess to be teachers unto others, etc. of the contrary Graces and Vertues." Williams focused on adultery as an example. Contrary to Cotton, he did not believe that judges are bound by conscience to the Old Testament law of putting adulterers to death. Judges, he contended, must recognize two important points. First, when the question was put directly to Christ Himself, He neither confirmed the old punishment nor repudiated it. Christ "leaves the severall nations of the World, to their owne severall Lawes and Agreements (as is most probable) according to their severall natures, Dispositions and Constitutions, and their common peace and wellfare."[24] Second, Christ lets the different nations of the world determine their own forms of government and laws. Williams cited the first book of Peter, which reads: "Be subject to every human institution for the Lord's sake, whether it be to the king as supreme or to governors as sent by him for the punishment of evildoers and the approval of those who do good."[25]

In crafting penal statutes, legislators are not bound by the lex talionis of the Old Testament. This is an important argument from an American writing so early in colonial history, because the lex talionis of the Old Testament was almost universally cited as the basis of America's severe criminal penalties—up until and even through the Revolution. But, Williams said, there are "severall sorts of Governments in the Nations of the World, which are not framed after Israels Patterne"; those who

> literally stick to the punishment of Adultery, Witchcraft, etc. by Death, must either deny the severall Governments of the World to be lawfull (according to that of Peter) . . . or els they must see cause to moderate this their Tenent, which else proves as bloudie a Tenent in civill affaires, as peersecution in affaires religious.[26]

The rejection of severe penal laws on the basis of religious belief is a significant factor in the early American politics of punishment—particularly in Pennsylvania, where Penn and the Quakers were largely responsible for penal reform. Even Philadelphia's prison society, a leader in the American penal reform movement, was clearly motivated by Quaker religious tenets.[27] Even Barnes, who attributes much of Pennsylvania's reform to the influence of Beccaria and the Enlightenment, must admit that the prison society was heavily influenced by Quaker religious beliefs. "The ideas and theories of the reformers were wholly in harmony with Quaker precedents, even if they were to some slight degree affected by the contemporary reform currents of Europe."[28]

Degrees of Punishment

In addition to the religious influences in Pennsylvania, other aspects of the development of Pennsylvania's criminal code are worthy of note. With respect to the uniformly severe colonial code of 1718, there is a general consensus that it was not strictly enforced. The manner in which it was enforced is instructive. Lawrence Gipson argues that the inconsistent enforcement came not from the courts, which were fairly uniform, but from the executive council exercising its pardon power. He contends that the council issued pardons frequently and arbitrarily.[29] Fitzroy agrees, observing that of 141 recorded capital convictions before the Revolution, 41 were pardoned and 26 were reprieved.[30] The archives from this period certainly indicate that there were frequent pardons,[31] but the claim that they were issued arbitrarily needs scrutiny. The executive council also considered many cases for which it decided not to recommend pardon.[32]

In making the distinction between those cases that were recommended for pardon and those that were not, the council engaged in an examination of the merits of each case and made a determination as to whether the convict in question actually deserved the punishment. In fact, during one council meeting in 1759, the council granted a pardon for Catharine Kirchin, who had been sentenced to death for concealing the death of a bastard child, yet declined pardons for James Jones and Joseph Powell. In distinguishing between the cases, the council reported that, for Jones and Powell, "neither from their Characters, nor the Circumstances of their respective Trials, did there appear any thing that could induce them to consider them as *fit objects of Mercy*."[33] The pardon power was employed by the colony to make crimes and punishments more proportionate by circumventing the often inequitable penalties of the 1718 code. In fact, those recommending pardon were often the trial judges themselves, who were obligated to sentence in accord with the 1718 statute. They frequently turned to the council to bring the penalties more into line with the merits of the crime.

Even the 1794 criminal statute, often heralded as the clearest evidence of the influence of Enlightenment political thought, reflects the desire for criminal punishment to be founded upon the seriousness of the offense. The 1794 Pennsylvania statute was the first in America to establish degrees of murder and corresponding degrees of punishment for murder. The statute itself reads: "whereas the several offenses which are included under the general denomination of murder, differ so greatly from each other in the degree of their atrociousness, that it is unjust to involve them in the same punishment."[34] Such a statement hardly supports an argument for rejecting consideration of the moral seriousness of the crimes when formulating corresponding punishments.

VIRGINIA REVISITED

Many argue that Pennsylvania was the model for other states seeking to reform their criminal codes. In particular, the post-Revolutionary changes in Virginia's criminal code are seen as an attempt to follow Pennsylvania down the road to reform. Virginia's statutory revisions were based upon the recommendations of Thomas Jefferson and the Committee of Revisors. Jefferson's proposed revisions to the penal code represented a significant departure from past law, but Virginia's colonial code was one of the most severe and sanguinary in America. How much did Virginia's revisions reflect an acceptance of Beccarian penal reform philosophy, and how much did they reflect the principles of just deserts and proportionality? Although the revisions certainly effected a moderation in Virginia's criminal punishment, it is unclear to what extent the moderation was undertaken for the utilitarian purposes of deterrence and to what extent the reforms were undertaken in order to proportion crimes and punishments more equitably on the basis of just deserts.

In his proposed criminal code—undertaken as a member of the Committee of Revisors—Jefferson's concerns were for just deserts and proportionality. He wrote that the goal of the Revisors' plan was to effect a more accurate proportion between crimes and punishments.[35] In the preamble to his draft of the "Bill for proportioning Crimes and Punishments, in cases heretofore Capital," Jefferson indicated elements of both just deserts and reform philosophy. He gave a social contract description of the foundations of society and the corresponding duties of government and wrote that the principle of proportionality was of primary importance. The criminal must be made to suffer "a punishment in proportion to his offense." There is "a duty in the legislature to arrange, in a proper scale, the crimes which it may be necessary for them to repress, and to adjust thereto a corresponding gradation of punishments." He favored repealing the death penalty for many crimes, because those offenders do not *deserve* the disproportionate punishment of death. The preamble stated that the purpose of the proposed changes was "rendering crimes and punishments, therefore, more proportionate to each other."[36]

The Revisors' proposal, though less severe than colonial law, maintained severe penalties. The legislation did, however, attempt to order such penalties in a manner that more closely reflected the varying degrees of seriousness in different crimes. Treason, which required either the offender's confession or the testimony of at least two witnesses for a conviction, was to be punished by hanging and forfeiture of property to the state. Jefferson noted that accomplices were to be treated the same as the principal offenders. The proposal expanded the traditional definition of petty treason. In addition to the murder of a master by a servant or of a husband by his wife, the definition was broadened to include the murder of a wife by her husband, the murder of a child by a parent, or the murder of a parent by a child. The punishment for petty treason was death by hanging, dissection of the body, and forfeiture of half of the offender's property to the victim's next of kin. Jefferson noted that the old practice of including the death of a bastard child under the murder statute was eliminated. Murder by poison was to be punished with death by poison and half forfeiture. Murder by duel was to be punished by hanging. In addition, if the offender was the challenger in the duel, his body was to be gibbeted and there was to be half forfeiture to the victim's next of kin; if the offender was the challenged party, there was to be half forfeiture to the state. For any other murder, Jefferson called for death by hanging and half forfeiture to the victim's next of kin.[37] Jefferson later reaffirmed his support for the death penalty for treason and murder by including it in his draft constitution for the state of Virginia.[38]

Jefferson proposed that those convicted of manslaughter be put to public hard labor for seven years and forfeit half their property to the victim's kin on the first offense, while second offense manslaughter was to be punished as if it were murder. Jefferson stipulated that there must be intent—a key factor for just deserts advocates because it implies moral culpability—in order for a crime to qualify as murder or manslaughter. "No such case shall hereafter be deemed manslaughter, unless manslaughter was intended, nor murder, unless murder was intended." Jefferson noted that, under previous law, suicide was punished by forfeiture of the deceased's property. He argued that the state is far less injured by this crime than the offender's family, and to deprive them of their property would be an injustice.[39]

For the crimes of rape, polygamy, and sodomy, males were to be punished by castration and females by "cutting through the cartilage of [their] nose a hole of one half inch in diameter at the least." Reflecting even further the lex talionis, Jefferson proposed, as punishment for malicious maiming or disfigurement, similar dismemberment or disfigurement. "If that cannot be," he wrote, "for want of the same part, then as nearly as may be, in some other part of at least equal value and estimation." In addition, the offender was to forfeit half his property to the victim. For most other serious crimes Jefferson employed various degrees of imprisonment and forfeiture: six years in prison and full forfeiture for counterfeiting; five years and triple damages for arson and for theft of or on sea vessels; four years and double damages for robbery and burglary; four years plus damages for housebreaking (burglary committed during daylight); three years plus damages for horse stealing; two years, damages, and one-half hour on the pillory for grand larceny; one year, damages, and one-quarter hour on the pillory for petty larceny; and ducking and up to fifteen stripes for pretensions to witchcraft.[40]

This proposed code makes it difficult to categorize Jefferson as having adhered to any single one of the more polarized approaches to punishment in modern political thought. Instead, he had a more comprehensive view, which incorporates elements of utility and reformation with the fundamental principle of just deserts. In fact, the principle of proportionality between crimes and punishments—the core tenet of the just deserts position—occupied the central role in Jefferson's criminal code.[41]

CHAPTER EIGHT

Punishment and the Founders

THE FIRST CONGRESS

WHEN THE FIRST CONGRESS CONVENED in 1789, it had to address the issue of punishment for those crimes under federal jurisdiction.[1] Congress eventually addressed the issue by enacting the 1790 Crimes Act, which was the first criminal statute of the federal government.[2] The act provided that the following crimes, when committed in areas of federal jurisdiction, were to be punished by death: treason, murder, piracy, accessory before the fact to piracy, forgery of federal notes, and helping in the escape of a condemned federal prisoner. Condemned prisoners were to be executed by hanging, and the bodies of those executed for murder were to be subject to dissection at the discretion of the court. The Crimes Act also provided a punishment of up to seven years in prison and a $1,000 fine for misprision of treason; twelve months and $100 for attempting to prevent the dissection of an executed offender; three years and $1,000 for failing to report a felony; three years and $500 for accessory after the fact to piracy; three years and $1,000 for confederating to become pirates; seven years and $1,000 for malicious maiming; seven years and $5,000 for stealing or falsifying federal records; and three years and $1,000 for manslaughter. The law required up to one year in prison and a $500 fine for helping in the escape of a federal prisoner; twelve months and $300 for obstruction of justice; and three years and $800 for perjury. Those convicted of larceny were required to pay up to four times the value of the stolen articles (receiving stolen goods was punished similarly). The Crimes Act also added corporal punishments for some crimes: whippings of up to thirty-nine stripes for stealing or falsifying federal records, for larceny, and for receiving stolen goods, and an hour in the pillory for perjury. Congress prohibited corruption of blood, forfeiture, and benefit of clergy.[3]

In its original form as reported out of a Senate committee, the crimes bill made mandatory the dissection of an executed murderer. When the full Senate took up the bill for debate, this provision was changed to allow dissection at the discretion of the court.[4] In the House of Representatives, a motion was made to delete the dissection clause altogether, and there is an instructive record of some debate over this motion. Dissection was called by its opponents "a barbarous revenge" and a "savageness." They argued, for example, that it made "punishment wear the appearance of cruelty, which had a tendency to harden the public mind." No less a figure than James Madison rose in defense of dissection. Much of the debate focused on whether dissection would or would not help to deter murder, but Madison thought it most important to make the punishment proportionate to the "degree of offense." He reasoned that if it was just to inflict death for ordinary murders, then it must also be just to inflict the additional penalty of dissection for particularly heinous murders.[5] The motion to delete the dissection clause was defeated.

The House also voted down a motion that sought to eliminate the death penalty for counterfeiting and to replace it with some form of imprisonment. In addition to the argument that juries would hesitate to convict if the penalty were so severe, the debate focused on whether death was a proportionate reflection of the gravity of the crime. An opponent of the death penalty for counterfeiting reasoned that "there were degrees of guilt, and the punishment ought to be proportioned." Based on the similar reasoning that "the degrees of punishment ought to be proportioned to the malignity of the offense," a supporter of the death penalty concluded that counterfeiting was indeed serious enough to warrant such a punishment.[6] While defeating the motion to moderate the penalty for counterfeiting, the House did amend the bill by adding on to the penalty for perjury. In addition to giving courts discretion to impose imprisonment and a fine, the new language required that those convicted of perjury submit to the pillory for one hour.[7] This amendment was accepted by the Senate and enacted as part of the law.[8]

STATE CONSTITUTIONS AND
THE COMPREHENSIVE APPROACH TO THE LAW

A central premise of Beccarian penal reform is the rejection of the notion that the laws are based on anything other than aggregate self-interest. Deterrence is the proper justification for punishment, because deterrence best secures the collective interest of individuals. Beccaria and other Enlightenment thinkers write extensively against the idea that criminal punishment is based upon a higher moral law. They reject the idea that crimes reflect a breach of the moral law. America's founding statesmen and lawmakers were certainly of the view that the laws must be based upon higher principles of justice.

Most state constitutions reveal an understanding of the law that rejected Beccaria's narrow utilitarianism. For example, the 1776 Maryland constitution, even as it laid out strong precepts of religious freedom, also declared that the state has a duty to enforce principles of morality and justice through legislation. The constitution stipulated that the law may not molest any person, unless he "shall infringe the laws of morality, or injure others in their natural, civil, or religious rights."[9] The Massachusetts constitution of 1780 indicated that the very basis of the state's laws and institutions is a moral order, which seeks to promote the happiness of citizens in accord with the virtues. The constitution stated that "the happiness of a people and the good order and preservation of civil government essentially depend upon piety, religion, and morality." Happiness was not understood from the narrow perspective of interest but was instead a consequence of the harmony of the people with moral principles:

> A frequent recurrence to the fundamental principles of the constitution, and a constant adherence to those of piety, justice, moderation, temperance, industry, and frugality, are absolutely necessary to preserve the advantages of liberty and to maintain a free government. The people ought, consequently, to have a particular attention to all those principles, in the choice of their officers and representatives; and they have a right to require of their lawgivers and magistrates an exact and constant observance of them, in the formation and execution of the laws necessary for the good administration of the commonwealth.[10]

Contrary to Beccaria's insistence upon a separation between conventional laws and moral or religious principles, the Massachusetts constitution said that the legislature could direct the towns to support "public Protestant teachers of piety, religion, and morality in all cases where such provision shall not be made voluntarily."[11]

The New Hampshire constitution of 1784 also recognized that the conventional laws must reflect principles of justice. It stated that "morality and piety, rightly grounded on evangelical principles, will give the best and greatest security to government, and will lay in the hearts of men the strongest obligations to due subjection." Accordingly, the constitution granted the legislature the power to force localities to support churches and other forms of worship.[12]

This approach expresses an important difference from Beccarian principles. The constitution asserted that one obeys the law precisely because it represents and encourages "morality and piety," but not only out of fear and self-interest. Even in Virginia, one of the states often cited as a success by penal reformers, the 1776 bill of rights pointed to the basis of the laws in the principles of justice: "no free government, or the blessings of liberty, can be preserved to any people, but by a firm adherence to justice, moderation, temperance, frugality, and virtue, and by frequent recurrence to fundamental principles."[13] The mention of a frequent recurrence to "fundamental principles" is important in our understanding of the difference between the Virginia bill of rights and Beccarian penal reform. It points to the necessary close connection between the laws and higher principles of "justice" and "virtue."

The greatest indication that the founders took a more comprehensive approach than was advocated by Beccaria is, of course, the Declaration of Independence. The Declaration placed the foundation of all law firmly upon natural principles of justice. Abraham Lincoln recognized the importance of recurrence to the Declaration's fundamental principles, precisely because he realized the danger in legislating on the basis of interest alone. He blamed the growing acceptance of slavery, specifically, on the failure of the people to cherish the fundamental principles of the Declaration and to see to it that the laws reflected such principles.[14] The Declaration states that the very reason for our separation from England is that British law had failed to reflect the fundamental principles of the higher moral law.

JEFFERSON AND FRANKLIN: AMERICAN REFORMERS?

Thomas Jefferson

Most of those Americans closely identified with the Beccarian penal reform movement during the founding period were not among those normally considered "founders." Benjamin Rush, although a signer of the Declaration of Independence, was considered somewhat of a gadfly even by his own admission. Among those statesmen closely associated with the founding, Thomas Jefferson and Benjamin Franklin are most frequently mentioned as penal reformers. How much did their statesmanship reflect a commitment to Beccarian principles?

It is best to begin with Jefferson, as he certainly believed that utility and reformation are important aims of the criminal law. Marcello Maestro's assertion of a connection between Beccaria and the American founders hinges on the role of Jefferson. Maestro points both to Jefferson's proposed revision of Virginia's criminal code and to the frequent references to Beccaria and Montesquieu in many of his writings.[15]

In his "Answers to Questions Propounded by M. de Meusnier," Jefferson denounced the benefit of clergy on Beccarian grounds. Whereas benefit of clergy combines severe punishment with frequent pardon, Jefferson advocated (in accord with Beccaria) relatively mild punishment with consistent enforcement and execution. The goal of deterrence would best be served by mild punishments, uniformly applied. Writing of pardons and benefit of clergy, Jefferson argued that, "when the laws are made as mild as they should be, both those pardons are absurd. The principle of Beccaria is sound. Let the legislators be merciful, but the executors of the law inexorable."[16]

While Jefferson was in Paris in 1786, the state of Virginia asked him to propose a plan for a prison in Richmond. Although he had earlier proposed public hard labor for prisoners, Jefferson wrote that by 1786 the Pennsylvania experience with the wheelbarrow laws had changed his mind. In his autobiography, Jefferson noted that the ideas in his prison plan were drawn from the proposals of the various prison societies that had sprung up in America—especially in Pennsylvania. He believed that a prison devoted to hard labor and solitary confinement would best serve the ends of deterrence and reform.[17] He also indicated a hope that Virginia would substitute his new solitary confinement plan for the Revisors' proposal of public hard labor. With regard to his proposed revision of the Virginia criminal code, there is evidence to suggest that Jefferson later developed reservations about some of the proposal's more severe elements. In a letter to fellow Revisor George Wythe, which accompanied Jefferson's draft of the new criminal code, Jefferson remarked on the lex talionis provisions:

> I have strictly observed the scale of punishments settled by the Committee, without being entirely satisfied with it. The *Lex Talionis* . . . will be revolting to the humanized feelings of modern times. An eye for an eye, and a hand for a hand, will exhibit spectacles in execution whose moral effect would be questionable. . . . This needs reconsideration.[18]

Apparently the lex talionis was important enough to other Revisors or to the state legislature, or both, that Jefferson's reservations were insufficient to effect a removal of the provisions.

Some also point to Jefferson's *Commonplace Book* for its many references to Beccaria and Montesquieu, although the significance of these passages is far from clear. Written in Jefferson's own handwriting, the book contains long citations from Beccaria in the original Italian. The citations are taken from no fewer than twenty-five different chapters of *On Crimes and Punishments*.[19] The *Commonplace Book* is essentially a collection of Jefferson's handwritten notebooks, most of which were written before he entered politics in 1776.[20] Gilbert Chinard, editor of one edition of the *Commonplace Book*, believes that at least the first 879 entries—where all of the references to Beccaria are found—were written before 1776.[21]

There is much evidence to suggest, however, that Jefferson was as concerned with the just deserts aspects of punishment and the law as he was with deterrence and reform (see chapter 7). This becomes more evident in his understanding of the appropriate foundation for the positive law. Whereas Beccaria's penology explicitly rejects the role of moral law in guiding conventional legislation, Jefferson's did not. In addition to in his authorship of the Declaration of Independence, Jefferson indicated in other places the importance of properly grounding conventional law upon moral principles. In the *Notes on the State of Virginia*, he expressed his reservations about the actions of the state legislature: "Laws, to be just, must give a reciprocation of right: that, without this, they are mere arbitrary rules of conduct, *founded in force, and not in conscience.*" The very basis of Beccarian penal laws is force. One does not obey because of one's conscience but because one fears the consequences of disobedience. Jefferson later wrote of the foundation of liberties and duties, arguing that citizens must recognize their "firm basis" in the higher law of God.[22]

We must also consider the basic premise of Jefferson's proposed criminal code—proportionality. The "Bill for proportioning Crimes and Punishments" was based upon Jefferson's belief that punishment is justified by the crime and should reflect the severity of the crime. He believed that death is a disproportionate, or undeserved, penalty for crimes such as burglary and robbery. In his commentary on the bill, Jefferson wrote that his goal was to make punishment less cruel, which would happen "if the punishment were only proportioned to the injury."[23] He believed that principles of just deserts and utility must both play a role in criminal punishment. In his answers to Meusnier, he wrote:

> In forming a scale of crimes and punishments, two considerations have principal weight. 1. The atrocity of the crime. 2. The peculiar circumstances of a country, which furnish greater temptations to commit it, or greater facilities for escaping detection. The punishment must be heavier to counterbalance this.[24]

Jefferson made clear that the first principle—the atrocity of the crime—must be the general or defining consideration in determining punishment.

The principle of just deserts must form the general foundation of any nation's criminal law. If this principle were "the only consideration, all nations would form the same scale" of punishments, but since "the circumstances of a country have influence on the punishment," the prudential application of the fundamental just deserts principle must take into account the unique situation of each nation.[25] Jefferson used the example of horse stealing. Although it was universally wrong, and punished, Americans punished this crime more severely than Europeans because Americans had normally let their horses roam free.

Jefferson emphasized his belief in proportionality in a 1776 letter to Edmund Pendleton, in which he responded to those claiming he favored drastically reducing criminal penalties. He contended, "it is only the sanguinary hue of our penal laws which I meant to object to." Punishments, he said, ought to be "strict and inflexible, but proportioned to the crime." Providing examples of punishments that were "proportioned" to the crimes, he said "death might be inflicted for murder and perhaps for treason. . . . Rape, buggery &c. punish by castration. All other crimes by working on high roads, rivers, gallies &c. a certain time proportioned to the offence."[26] In a 1780 letter to James Callaway, he wrote that his view of capital punishment was based upon the moral culpability of the offender. He favored the death penalty but believed there are varying degrees of blame to which varying degrees of punishment should correspond. Referring to the capture of individuals accused of treason, Jefferson suggested that the main conspirators deserve death, whereas others with less involvement deserve leniency.[27] Like many just deserts advocates, Jefferson focused on the intent of the offender, in order to determine the degree of moral culpability upon which punishment must be based. "It is the intention alone," he wrote in a 1783 letter to Philip Turpin, "which constitutes the criminality of any act."[28]

So the evidence suggests that Jefferson, the most reform-minded of the founders, in addition to recognizing utility and reformation understood the centrality of just deserts within a comprehensive approach to punishment. Like many statesmen of the time, he was certainly influenced in some way by Beccaria. Even Jefferson, however, did not embrace a central Beccarian tenet—the rejection of the role of moral law in justifying and measuring criminal punishment.

Benjamin Franklin

The evidence that Franklin abandoned the just deserts approach for a Beccarian view of punishment is less formidable than the evidence regarding Jefferson. Maestro points to Franklin's correspondence with European writers about penal reform as evidence of his reform beliefs. Franklin, like William Blackstone, denounced the practice of criminal punishment at the time, but he did so on the basis of just deserts. Like most of his contemporaries, Franklin turned away from Beccaria's rejection of the higher law understanding of criminal legislation. In 1785 Franklin argued that the punishments for theft were unjust because they reflected the mere conventional protections enacted by a wealthy society. The punishments were not in accord with the law of justice, he contended, but were based upon man's conventional desire to protect his wealth. The severe laws against theft were designed only for purposes of deterrence; they were not based upon an equitable relationship between crime and punishment. "When, by virtue of the first Laws, Part of the Society accumulated Wealth and grew powerful, they enacted others more severe, and would protect their Property at the Expence of Humanity. This was abusing their Power, and commencing a Tyranny." Franklin attacked the narrow utilitarian considerations that form the basis of legislation for Beccaria. Franklin also emphasized the importance of just deserts not only in domestic law but in international law. He contended that all law must be based upon higher principles of justice, including the law that governs relations between nations.[29]

Many point to Franklin's 1783 letter to Gaetano Filangieri for its support of reduced criminal penalties; but the letter itself reveals a just deserts approach to criminal punishment. In the letter, Franklin responded to the first two volumes of Filangieri's *Scienza della legislazione*, expressing approval that the next volume of the work would address the criminal laws. "None have more need of reformation," he wrote. "They are everywhere in so great disorder, and so much injustice is committed in the execution of them." Franklin was most concerned with the lack of proportion between crimes and punishments. He even asserted that punishments would be more just if left to private retaliation: "So much injustice is committed in the execution of [the criminal laws], that I have been sometimes inclined to imagine less would exist in the world if there were no such laws, and the punishment of injuries were left to private resentment."[30]

In a well-known letter to Benjamin Vaughan, later published by the English law reformer Samuel Romilly,[31] Franklin expressed dismay that punishments were no longer proportionate to crimes. Romilly's *Observations on the Criminal Law of England* is an argument against Martin Madan's *Thoughts on Executive Justice*,[32] where Madan advocated a continuation of sanguinary punishment. Franklin, also attacking Madan, asserted that the laws must reflect what offenders truly deserve. Madan contended that innocence is protected so long as the laws are strictly followed; Franklin responded that it is possible for the laws themselves to be unjust if they do not reflect the proper relationship between crime and punishment. "Is it then impossible to make an unjust Law?" Franklin asked, "and if the Law itself be unjust, may it not be the very 'Instrument' which ought to 'raise the Author's and everybody's highest Indignation'?" He pointed to a newspaper account from London of a woman sentenced to death for shoplifting an item worth fourteen shillings. The key for Franklin was proportionality: "Is there any Proportion between the Injury done by a Theft, value 14/3, and the Punishment of a human Creature, by Death, on a Gibbet? . . . Is not all Punishment inflicted beyond the Merit of the offence, so much Punishment of Innocence?" Franklin reasoned that there is a "difference in Value between Property and Life."[33]

On the basis of proportionality, Franklin advocated the death penalty for murder, but he opposed it for lesser crimes. "If I think it right, that the Crime of Murder should be punished with Death, . . . does it follow that I must approve of the inflicting of the same Punishment for a little Invasion on my *property* by Theft?" Franklin said he supported the death penalty for murder because it is "an equal Punishment of the Crime." Franklin emphasized in the letter that his reason for advocating reduced criminal punishment is that penalties ought to reflect crimes. He specifically attacked the idea of putting petty criminals to death, not as a violation of deterrence but as a violation of the moral law that must inform the criminal law:

> If we really believe, as we profess to believe, that the Law of Moses was the Law of God, the Dictate of divine Wisdom, infinitely superior to human; on what Principles do we ordain Death as the Punishment of an Offence, which, according to that Law, was only to be punish'd by a Restitution of Fourfold? To put a man to Death for an Offence which does not deserve Death, is it not Murder?[34]

Killing an offender who does not, by the principles of justice, deserve death is a "crime against nature."

Franklin also questioned the narrowly utilitarian principles upon which Beccaria and Bentham grounded their deterrence theory. In fact, Franklin believed that a misguided belief in deterrence leads to unjust punishments. "It seems to have been thought," he wrote, that "Innocence may be punished by way of *Preventing* crimes." He argued that it would be unjust to punish primarily for the sake of deterrence, and he related the following example:

> [There was] the Reply of Judge Burnet to the convict Horse-stealer, who, being ask'd what he had to say why Judgment of Death should not pass

against him, and answering, that it was hard to hang a man for *only* stealing a Horse, was told by the judge, "Man, thou art not to be hang'd *only* for stealing, but that Horses may not be stolen."[35]

Franklin contended that it is unjust to treat humans as means to an end. He also rejected the judge's position on the basis of the proportionality that is required by the moral law. "The man's Answer, if candidly examined, will I imagine appear reasonable, as founded on the Eternal Principle of Justice and Equity, that Punishments should be proportioned to Offences."[36]

JAMES WILSON AND THE TRADITIONAL UNDERSTANDING OF THE LAW

James Wilson was a member of the Pennsylvania delegation to the federal convention of 1787 and is considered by many to be the father of the American executive. He was also an associate justice of the U.S. Supreme Court and later a professor of law at the College of Philadelphia, where he delivered his *Lectures on Law*. Wilson's *Lectures* address both civil and criminal law. Edwin R. Keedy and others—emphasizing the *Lectures*—cite Wilson as one of the primary penal reformers of the founding period. Wilson's occasional references to Montesquieu and Beccaria draw the attention of penal reform scholars.[37] But Wilson's thought was certainly not confined to the Enlightenment thinkers. He demonstrated a broad understanding of the entire political tradition. The evidence indicates that his thought on the law and criminal punishment reflects in several important ways the comprehensive view of the older tradition.

Wilson's understanding of the foundation of human law was apparently in tension with Beccaria's. Whereas Beccaria rejects the moral law basis of human legislation, Wilson spoke of the necessarily close relationship between the law of nature and the human law. The law of nature is "that law, which God has made for man in his present state; that law, which is communicated to us by reason and conscience." On the connection of the moral order to human law, Wilson said that "what we do, indeed, must be founded upon what [God] has done. . . . Human law must rest its authority, ultimately, upon the authority of that law, which is divine." One of the maxims of the moral law, upon which human law must rest, is "that no injury should be done."[38]

The moral law must guide the legislator in the construction of human laws. Wilson believed we know the basic goals, or ends, that we have a duty to pursue. We know these ends through our moral sense, which is the ultimate guide to legislation. But how do we translate our moral sense into specific legislative provisions, into what Wilson calls municipal law? Reason helps translate the principles of the moral sense into particular parts of a society's municipal law. "The design of municipal law is to fix all the questions which regard justice. . . . Reason serves to illustrate, to prove, to extend, to apply what our moral sense has already suggested to us, concerning just and unjust, proper and improper, right and wrong." Wilson addressed specifically those thinkers who, like Beccaria, contest the role of the moral sense in the formation of the positive law:

> The existence of the moral sense has been denied by some philosophers of high fame: its authority has been attacked by others: the certainty and uniformity of its decision have been arraigned by a third class. . . . In support of these observations, it is farther said, that moral sentiment is different in different countries, in different ages, and under different forms of government and religion; in a word, that it is as much the effect of custom, fashion, and artifice, as our taste in dress, furniture, and the modes of conversation.[39]

Wilson rejected this utilitarian position. He cited Aristotle in response, arguing that "to ascertain moral principles, we appeal not to the common sense of savages, but of men in their most perfect state." In a further criticism of the modern rejection of the law's higher purpose, he said:

> I could never read some modish modern authors, without being, for some time, out of humour with myself, and at every thing about me. Their business is to depreciate human nature, and consider it under its worst appearances. They give mean interpretation and base motives to the worthiest actions—in short, they endeavor to make no distinction between man and man, or between the species of men and that of brutes.[40]

According to Wilson, individuals are aided in their quest for the good life not only by reason but by divine revelation. In fact, reason itself is insufficient. Humans must draw not only on reason but also on divine revelation in the construction of their institutions and laws. The moral sense, directed by principles of justice, is an essential part of any properly ordered society. "It is necessary that reason should be fortified by the moral sense: without the moral sense, a man may be prudent, but he cannot be virtuous." Prudence itself cannot suffice, because it is devoid of the moral sense and cannot lead individuals to virtue. Contrast this to Beccaria and Bentham, for whom legislators must use their cleverness in order to effect the aggregate self-interest of society, without reference to higher notions of the good. Citing Cicero (*De Re Publica* I.3), Wilson argues that the narrow interest of society cannot replace its obligation to the moral law. This law is "a true law, conformable to nature, diffused among all men, unchangeable, eternal. By its commands, it calls men to their duty: by its prohibitions, it deters them from vice."[41]

Wilson also emphasized consent. Man obeys the law because of its just foundation, not only because he fears the consequences of disobedience. Consent, informed by reason, gives legitimacy to human law. "The obligation of human law arises from consent."[42] This gave Wilson cause to question the utilitarian formulas of Beccaria and others, which he found insufficient. In their sort of utilitarianism, he said, "actions . . . are to be estimated by their tendency to promote happiness. Whatever is expedient, is right. It is the utility, alone, of any moral rule, which constitutes its obligation." But Wilson contended that this cannot be the source of one's duty. When legislators frame the laws, they must look beyond narrow utility as a guide. "What is the efficient cause of moral obligation?—I give it this answer—the will of God. This is the supreme law. His just and full right of imposing laws, and our duty in obeying them, are the sources of our moral obligations." How are legislators to know what to do in a particular circumstance? Again Wilson answered with the moral law. We are guided "by our conscience, by our reason, and by the Holy Scriptures. The law of nature and the law of revelation are both divine: they flow, though in different channels, from the same adorable source."[43]

Wilson's understanding of the law's foundation translates into a just deserts understanding of criminal punishment. Society's right to punish is dependent not primarily upon the consequences of the punishment, Wilson contended, but upon the commission of a crime by a morally autonomous individual. In discussing the power of juries, he asserted that they are properly empowered because society has a legitimate right to punish crimes. For Wilson, the justification for punishment exists even before civil society is formed, where "the right of punishment . . . belonged to him who had suffered the injury, arising from the crime which was committed." Once society is formed, "the right of him who has suffered the injury is transferred to the community." Contrary to Locke, who also discusses the origin of the right to punish in the prepolitical state of nature, Wilson's punishment right is not grounded primarily upon self-interest. The right is instead based upon the notion of equitable retaliation. The prepolitical individual only has a right to punish if someone injures him—the right "arising from the crime which was committed."[44]

Wilson contended that only those things that are actually unjust are properly called crimes. A law that punishes for something that is not unjust is a bad law. "Every crime includes an injury: every offence is also a private wrong: it affects the publick, but it affects the individual likewise." For Wilson, punishment involves two important elements. First, there must be a punishment inflicted that reflects the severity of the crime. Second, there must be a reparation demanded that compensates the victim for the injury. Wilson defined punishment as "the infliction of that evil, superadded to the reparation, which the crime, superadded to the injury, renders necessary, for the purposes of a wise and good administration of government." In some ways, Wilson said, the ancient practice of punishment was superior. This is because ancient systems regularly included reparation as part of punishment. He mentioned specifically the Anglo-Saxon system, inherited from the Germans.[45]

Wilson's *Lectures* treated different crimes in a chapter-by-chapter breakdown. In this way, he categorized crimes by the manner in which they violate the principles of justice. Wilson also distinguished between those acts that are criminal because they violate the principles of justice and those that are criminal because they violate the rights of citizens under civil government. All the serious crimes were put into the former category: murder, robbery, and so on. Crimes falling into the latter category might include bribery or neglect of public office.[46]

The principle of proportionality, whereby the degree of punishment reflects directly the degree of the crime, must underlie the establishment of criminal penalties. Wilson called for greater precision in the balancing of crimes and punishments. He complained that in England most serious crimes were defined simply by the word *felony* and were punished uniformly. This violates the precision required by proportionality: "As the punishment ought to be confined to the criminal; so it ought to bear a proportion, it ought, if possible, to bear even an analogy, to the crime."[47]

Like most founding statesmen, and in accord with the comprehensive view of the ancient and medieval traditions, Wilson understood that deterrence and other factors must be taken into consideration. He argued that society had too often failed to connect clearly the crime and the punishment, but it had also failed to take deterrence into consideration. The need for punishment arises out of injustice, but deterrence ought to be weighed when determining the specific penalty. Considering "the prevention of crimes" helps the legislator once the parameters have been determined by just deserts and proportionality. It is in his discussion of how to precisely measure punishment that Wilson mentioned Beccaria (as well as Blackstone and others); but although Wilson praised Beccaria for doing much in the study of criminal law, he did not accept Beccaria's formula. In discussing the various positions in the punishment debate, Wilson was not willing to accept the purely retributive approach or the Beccarian approach. Punishment must be based upon a broader understanding of justice and must have as its end the happiness of the people.[48]

Wilson believed that punishments ought to be milder, but for purposes of proportionality at least as much as utility. Severe punishments, he said, are "inconsistent with the principles of our nature." The moral sense of the public inspires an understanding of proportionality. The public is repulsed by unduly harsh punishments, which lessen the public's respect for the laws, because the people properly consider them inconsistent with the principles of just deserts. "Can laws," Wilson asked, "which are a natural and a just object of aversion, receive a cheerful obedience, or secure a regular and uniform execution?" Wilson was also a strong supporter of the death penalty for reasons of just deserts and proportionality. Certain crimes—he specifically mentioned arson, rape, and murder—are so serious by their nature that they *deserve* the harsh punishment of death. Wilson approved of the Saxon code that punished arson and rape with death.[49]

JUSTICE, PUNISHMENT, AND THE FOUNDERS

George Washington

For founding leaders such as George Washington, James Madison, and Alexander Hamilton, criminal punishment was an important part of a comprehensive understanding of political justice. Although none of them believed the criminal law should have exclusively retributive aims, there was a firm recognition that the purpose of the laws and institutions reaches beyond the narrow aims of Beccaria's utilitarianism. Instead, the understanding of political justice—of which criminal punishment was a significant part—incorporated for the founders the aims of punishing those who deserve it, providing security for the citizens and providing opportunities for reformation where possible. As with that taken by Jefferson, Franklin, and Wilson, the approach to the criminal law taken by Washington, Madison, and Hamilton was more comprehensive than Beccaria's reform view. Although none of these statesmen wrote directly or at any great length about criminal punishment per se, their approach to the criminal law is evident in their notion that the positive law must reflect a higher moral order. For Beccaria, deterrence is the only legitimate aim of punishment because the criminal law must seek only to provide security. Thus Beccaria attacks the idea that punishments should reflect the moral transgressions inherent in crimes. The view of the founders goes beyond deterrence to a system of laws that seeks to embody the fundamental principles of political justice.

Like Wilson, Washington asserted that citizens' happiness is the proper end of the laws and institutions. The goal of happiness requires that the laws be grounded in a higher moral order. Washington's first inaugural address is perhaps the clearest expression of this view, wherein he proclaimed: "the propitious smiles of Heaven can never be expected on a nation that disregards the external rules of order and right, which Heaven itself has ordained." In its response to his inaugural address, the U.S. Senate confirmed Washington's understanding of the law. The senators responded: "it is . . . the duty of legislators to enforce, both by precept and example, the utility, as well as the necessity, of a strict adherence to the rules of distributive justice." The Senate pledged its cooperation on all measures that "may strengthen the Union, conduce to the happiness, or secure and perpetuate the liberties of this great confederated republic."[50]

Whereas Beccaria believed that laws based upon enlightened self-interest were the key to an orderly and successful society, Washington had a broader approach. He wrote that "religion and Morality are the essential pillars of Civil society." He praised the cooperation between different religions, contending that morality is "the surest basis of universal Harmony."[51] In his farewell address, Washington emphasized the importance of religion and morality to public life. Whereas Beccaria believed citizens behave themselves because they recognize it is in their best interest to do so, Washington believed citizens ought also to obey the law because they believe it is *moral* to do so. Citizens follow the law precisely because it is grounded in the principles of justice—a foundation for the law that Beccaria rejects. Washington wrote that "virtue or morality is a necessary spring of popular government."[52]

During his military career, Washington often expressed such a view about the primacy of moral principles. In one of his many military orders urging his officers to enforce moral behavior, Washington explained: "Purity of Morals [is] the only sure foundation of publick happiness in any Country."[53] Washington consistently applied his broad understanding of the law to his troops, as seen in his many expressions of concern that the troops be held to strict moral standards.[54] This concern was surely aimed not only at the maintenance of morality but also at the more utilitarian goal of inculcating obedience and good morale within the army. In general, however, Washington's military and political life reflects a belief that crime, or wrongdoing, is grounded in a breach of moral principle. In contrast to Beccaria's assertion that moral crimes should not be illegal, Washington's military papers contain many examples of his approving punishments for "moral crimes."[55]

Washington believed also in the principle of proportionality between crimes and punishments. In 1776 he rejected the punishment of a soldier by a court martial on the grounds that it was not sufficiently severe. The order stated that "the General is not a little surprised at the Sentence of the Court, on the prisoner Joseph Lent, and thinks the punishment so inadequate to the crime, that he disapproves of the sentence."[56] Washington was also quite firm on the punishment he believed was due Benedict Arnold. He issued instructions to General Lafayette in the event that Lafayette should capture Arnold: "You are to do no act whatever with Arnold that directly or by implication may skreen him from the punishment due to his treason and desertion, which if he should fall into your hands, you will execute in the most summary way."[57]

Even though we can hardly doubt that Washington recognized the usefulness of making examples of Arnold and other criminals, he did express skepticism of the effectiveness of deterrence. Washington wrote that he was not sure how useful deterrence was in the armed forces, saying that "I find examples of so little weight."[58] Washington did not hesitate to use his pardon power, perhaps another indication of his skepticism of deterrence. In an order pardoning a soldier from a death sentence, he wrote that the justification for punishment rests in the principle of just deserts. "I wish you to caution him against like conduct in the future, and to assure him, the rules of War and the principles of Justice would have justified his execution."[59]

James Madison

The writings of James Madison indicate his belief that the criminal law is based upon the principles of justice. Unlike Jefferson, Madison expressed doubts over proposals to limit the death penalty. He said that "it is at least questionable whether death ought to be confined to Treason and murder."[60] He supported the death penalty in general because he believed that it was in accord with the principles of justice. In response to G. F. H. Crockett, who had proposed the abolition of capital punishment, Madison responded: "I do not see the injustice of such punishments."[61] With regard to the crime of treason, Madison indicated that punishment must be determined by the degree of moral culpability. This is why only those who are the leaders of the conspiracy must be executed. Otherwise, he argued, "what name would be given to a severity which made no distinction between the legal and the moral offence, between the deluded multitude, and their wicked leaders?"[62]

Madison was involved in attempting to secure passage of Jefferson's penal code by the Virginia legislature. His correspondence on the topic indicates his skepticism of reform ideas. In praising Jefferson's work on the revised code, Madison also questioned the soundness of Beccaria's theories. He believed Jefferson's legislation worthy of praise, "in spite of its Beccarian illusions."[63] In another letter, he discussed the Committee of Revisors and made an apparent reference to Beccaria: "In the changes made in the penal law," he said, "the Revisors were unfortunately *misled* into some of the *specious errors* of [Beccaria], then in the zenith of his fame as a philosophical legislator."[64]

Alexander Hamilton

In addition to Washington and Madison, Alexander Hamilton expressed anti-Beccarian principles with regard to the foundation of law, perhaps most plainly in his essay "The Farmer Refuted," written in 1775 in response to the argument of the Tory Samuel Seabury. Hamilton rejected the claim that the British Parliament had the right to tax the colonies. In general, Hamilton denounced the philosophy of Hobbes, which is the basis for much of Beccaria's thought on criminal punishment. Hobbes, as well as Beccaria, claims that the sole purpose of the law is to secure citizens' self-interest, whereas Hamilton contended that such an approach ignores the foundation of human law in the higher principles of morality and justice.

Hamilton attacked the farmer as a disciple of Hobbes, contending that "there is so strong a similitude between your political principles and those maintained by Mr. Hobbs, that, in judging from them a person might very easily *mistake* you for a disciple of his." Hamilton argued that Hobbesianism (which provides much of the foundation for Beccarianism) is flawed because it rejects the idea that laws and government are subject to the universal laws of morality:

> Moral obligation, according to [Hobbes], is derived from the introduction of civil society, and there is no virtue, but what is purely artificial, the mere contrivance of politicians, for the maintenance of social intercourse. But the reason he runs into this absurd and impious doctrine, was, that he disbelieved the existence of an intelligent superintending principle, who is the governor, and will be the final judge of the universe.[65]

Beccaria advocates laws that are "the contrivance of politicians" interested in securing the narrow interest of the greatest number, but Hamilton rejects this doctrine for its ignorance of the higher purposes of the law. Hamilton did not argue that citizens' adherence to the moral law must be restricted to the private sphere, but he applied the moral argument to the spheres of law and government. To do precisely what Beccaria proposes—to separate human law and moral principles—would make human law "null and void" in Hamilton's view.[66]

Hamilton argued that the basis of government and human happiness is not simply mutual security. He cited Blackstone in arguing that human

laws must reflect the natural law. He said that the law of nature "is bind-
ing all over the globe, in all countries, and at all times. No human laws
are of any validity, if contrary to this; and such of them as are valid, derive
all their authority, mediately, or immediately, from this original." The security, or happiness, that political society must seek is not simply self-
preservation. Rather, security is part of what Hamilton called our "moral
security." The very basis of this moral security, which is the goal of all law,
is justice. Security and liberty have a moral foundation, because "natural
liberty is a gift of the beneficent Creator to the whole human race."[67]
Hamilton emphasized the role of "sanctions" in achieving and securing
the principles of justice.

THE FEDERALIST'S TREATMENT OF PUNISHMENT

There is more to learn about Hamilton's approach to punishment (as
well as Madison's) in his writings as Publius in The Federalist. Although
the only crime that Publius addressed directly and at any length was treason, The Federalist did provide some important insight on punishment.
Publius noted that treason is specifically defined in the Constitution so
that Congress cannot use "artificial treasons" as a tool of persecution.[68]
In general, Publius made it clear that the laws must be based upon
principles of morality. The laws must be directed to the security of the
people—and to their happiness, broadly understood. Publius's understanding of happiness, reflecting principles of justice, came from the Declaration of Independence. The Federalist presumed an understanding of
the laws' object that is prior to the Constitution, and that object is the
higher law doctrine of the Declaration. In Federalist 40, Publius responded to the charge that the convention of 1787 exceeded its authority. Just measures, he argued, are those that seek the safety and happiness
of the people; he cited the Declaration as his authority.[69] In Federalist 43,
Publius confirmed that the goal of laws and institutions is to reflect
higher law principles. This is why the defects of the Articles of Confederation had to be repaired. The idea was to make the union "more perfect,"
or make it reflect more closely the natural law principles of the Declaration. The repeal of the Articles was justified by "the transcendent law of
nature and of nature's God, which declares that the safety and happiness
of society are the objects at which all political institutions aim and to
which all such institutions must be sacrificed."[70] Happiness is connected
to the principles of justice, and Publius contended that this "transcendent" justice must be the goal of the law. Laws are to reflect not merely
the narrow utility of conventional society, as Beccaria and Bentham con-

tend, but a happiness that is in accord with "transcendent" principles.

Publius did address the principle of just retaliation. When he warned that a loose confederation of states would lead to violent domestic contests, he noted that the wars between Britain and Spain were particularly unjust. There was no proportional principle of retaliation, Publius explained, and retaliation was often taken without regard to guilt or innocence. The Spaniards often took measures that "exceeded the bounds of just retaliation." The retaliations were unjust, because "the innocent were . . . confounded with the guilty in indiscriminate punishment."[71]

Punishment is based upon morality, in Publius's view, because human beings are subject to the laws of justice. Even the hypothetical southerner in *Federalist* 54 admitted that the slaves must be considered as moral beings precisely because, in part, they are subject to the laws of punishment:

> In being protected . . . in his life and in his limbs, against the violence of all others, even the master of his labor and his liberty; and in being punishable himself for all violence committed against others—the slave is no less evidently regarded by the law as a member of the society, not as part of the irrational creation; as a moral person, not as a mere article of property.[72]

An important principle of the just deserts approach to punishment is that individuals are autonomous moral beings and that punishments are based upon holding them accountable for immoral behavior. For Publius, punishment meant that crimes are moral violations, and humans are held morally accountable for criminal behavior. That someone is subject to punishment is itself an indication of his humanity.

Publius also defended the pardon power, and his defense is important for its anti-Beccarianism. Whereas Beccaria contended that mild penalties must be imposed without the possibility of pardon, Publius advocated a real pardon power with strong penalties. Publius did not protest the severity of the criminal law. Instead, he claimed that this severity justifies the pardon power for cases of "unfortunate guilt":

> Humanity and good policy conspire to dictate that the benign prerogative of pardoning should be as little as possible fettered or embarrassed. The criminal code of every country partakes so much of necessary severity that without an easy access to exceptions in favor of unfortunate guilt, justice would wear a countenance too sanguinary and cruel.[73]

Publius equated "criminal codes" and "justice." Because the pardon power would rest in a single set of hands, the president would be well able to sort out the motives behind requests for pardon. Publius argued that a pardon is not appropriate when the law is properly seeking vengeance. In such cases, the president would be "least apt to yield to considerations which were calculated to shelter a fit object of [the law's] vengeance."[74] Severe punishments are ordinarily deserved; they are deserved when someone is a "fit object" of the law's "vengeance." This broader understanding of positive law must inform any attempt to understand the early American politics of punishment.

Conclusion

The Founders and the Contemporary Debate

A REFORM IN CRIMINAL PUNISHMENT certainly took place during the founding era, but we ought to be careful about placing too much emphasis on any one of the philosophical approaches to punishment. The Enlightenment reform approach, for example, calls for milder punishment. Some American states did, in fact, moderate their criminal penalties, and most of the prominent writers and statesmen of the time advocated milder criminal penalties of some kind. The colonial criminal codes were so harsh, however, that the founding-era moderation of criminal penalties must be examined with great care. Although it is possible that punishments were made less severe partly as a consequence of Beccaria's influence, there is also much evidence to suggest that punishments were seen simply as exceeding what criminals truly deserved. In many instances where punishments were moderated, those responsible argued that the changes were needed in order to make punishments more commensurate with crimes. Even Thomas Eddy, a leading figure in the American reform movement, decried the lack of moral proportionality in uniformly severe criminal codes, in addition to their lack of utility. This is not to say that Beccaria was unimportant in the founding debate, nor does it mean he did not have ardent followers in the United States. The analysis does suggest, however, that the early American politics of punishment must be understood from a perspective considerably broader than that of Beccaria's narrow utilitarianism alone.

The modern political tradition presents us with polarized approaches to punishment. In the moral idealism that is at the

root of the retributive approach, there is a rejection of utilitarian considerations. Punishments are justified only to the extent that they respond to
the moral transgressions inherent in crimes. On another extreme, Hobbes
and Beccaria contend that there ought to be no criminal laws grounded in
any sort of moral foundation. Only societal self-interest, narrowly understood, can provide the basis for a system of punishments. In addition to
these two arguments, the root social causes approach to rehabilitation
teaches that neither retribution nor utility can justify punishment, since
offenders are not responsible for their crimes.

The early American politics of punishment, however, does not confine
itself to any one narrow extreme. During the founding period, several important political principles combined to form a basis for the implementation of new criminal codes. First, the idea of strict and severe retribution
remained prominent in many parts of the nation. In several cases, the severe colonial codes based on the British common law were simply retained until well into the nineteenth century. Some states even continued
the severity of the kind seen in the Hempstead laws. Second, the principle of reformation was also significant. The earliest manifestation of this
principle was William Penn's criminal code based upon the idea of reformation in the Quaker religion. The aim of inner conversion of offenders'
characters became manifest most prominently in the writings of Benjamin
Rush and in the activities of the penitentiary movement and various
prison societies—most notably Philadelphia's.

Third, utilitarian principles had an important role. The necessity of
crafting punishments more precisely attuned to deterring future crime became increasingly recognized during the founding. William Bradford, although an admirer of Rush, is an example of someone whose penal philosophy was centered more closely around the idea of deterrence. Deterrence
became an important part of most approaches, with Virginia resisting a
moderation of its punishments for some time, at least partly because of the
belief that strict punishments were required to deter crimes such as horse
stealing. In a clear effort to deter, New York currency read throughout the
entire founding period: "'tis death to counterfeit."

Finally, the principle of just deserts and proportionality between crimes
and punishments was fundamental to the early American politics of punishment. Despite the influence of Beccaria and other Enlightenment thinkers,
most leaders during the founding era held to the belief that the positive law
must be designed to reflect and embody the principles of the higher moral
law. The Declaration of Independence, the state constitutions, and the relevant writings of the most prominent American thinkers unmistakably embrace the connection between the positive law and the moral law—a connection that much of Beccaria's work is devoted to attacking.

Given that several principles were at work, is there any coherence in
the early American politics of punishment? There were certainly those in
the debate who adhered strictly to the more narrow approaches to punishment. But the presence of several approaches to punishment during the
founding does not necessarily imply a lack of coherence. In the ancient
and medieval traditions, there was also a variety of punishment principles.
This is particularly true of Platonic political thought, where the emphasis
on just deserts and expiation in the *Gorgias* was in tension with the more
utilitarian view of the *Laws*. The many principles at work in the older traditions show there is a more comprehensive understanding of political justice. In these traditions, political justice incorporates punishing those who
deserve to be punished, protecting citizens from harm, and reforming
souls. This comprehensive approach to punishment thus proceeds from
the fundamental perspective of a moral order that underlies society's laws
and institutions and, appropriately, is concerned with utility and reformation as important parts of a just political order.

The politics of punishment during the American founding reflects this
broad approach, to a certain extent. In the state constitutions, for example, the principles laid out for the formulation of the laws generally required that statutes be directed toward both good morals and comfortable
self-preservation, or toward the "safety" and the "happiness" of the people.
On the basis of these principles, just punishments must reflect the moral
transgressions inherent in crimes, as well as protect the citizens from violations of their persons and property.

Thomas Jefferson's writings on punishment brought out this synthesis
of approaches. The principle of just deserts and proportionality is clear in
his proposed criminal code for Virginia. He supported the continuation of
the death penalty for murder and treason because he saw it as the deserved punishment for those particular crimes. He argued that lesser
crimes should be punished with lesser penalties. Along with this proportionality between crimes and punishments, he believed that the laws
could aim at the reform of most offenders, and he argued that reforming
offenders would serve the utilitarian end of helping to prevent future
crimes. Within his comprehensive view of punishment, deterrence had an
important role. Under the influence of Beccaria, Jefferson opposed pardons and the benefit of clergy because they undermine the certainty that
is required for effective deterrence. Also, under the influence of Philadelphia's reformers, Jefferson became an advocate of the penitentiary movement, which looked to reform offenders and to prevent future crimes
through a rehabilitative incarceration. The principles of deterrence and
reformation form a part of Jefferson's overall approach to punishment,
which was founded upon the idea of just deserts and proportionality.

The synthesis of approaches is perhaps most evident in the writings of James Wilson. Wilson, like his contemporaries, assumed that human laws must be designed to reflect and embody the principles of the moral law. Accordingly, punishments must seek to redress the moral transgressions inherent in crimes. Within this broad understanding of the law, Wilson incorporated several utilitarian goals. He made reparation a prominent feature of his punishment philosophy. His definition of punishment included two parts: just deserts for the crime and reparation for the injury caused by the crime. Wilson also argued that we must not ignore the goal of prevention. While the justification for punishment comes from the principle of just deserts, he contended, deterrence must be taken into consideration when determining the specific penalty. He complained that past punishment practices had focused too narrowly on retaliation and had not given deterrence its due weight.

The founders maintained the belief that the positive law must reflect and embody the higher moral law, but they also added something to the older view. For them, liberty was an essential part of the higher law. Hamilton said: "natural liberty is a gift of the beneficent Creator to the whole human race."[1] This is why, within the comprehensive approach of the founding, there was an emphasis on the principle of consent. In his writings on the criminal law Wilson paid particular attention to consent. The understanding of consent in the American founding serves as a contrast to Beccaria. For Beccaria, consent is based upon fear and self-interest. Individuals consent to the order of civil society because they recognize it is in their interest to avoid the consequences of disobedience. In the founding tradition, on the other hand, the consent of the people comes at least partly from their understanding that the laws are properly grounded in the principles of justice. Washington said that citizens obey the law because they believe it moral to do so. Along with the aims of utility and reformation, this belief that criminal laws and punishments reflect a moral order defines the comprehensive approach of the early American politics of punishment. It is by going beyond the narrow approaches to punishment, and reviving a more comprehensive view of criminal justice, that the politics of punishment during the founding can make a contribution to the contemporary punishment debate.

POLARIZED APPROACHES OF THE CONTEMPORARY DEBATE

Many of the positions taken in today's debate about crime and punishment—both in scholarly circles and in political circles—reflect the more narrow approaches to punishment found in modern political thought.

Utilitarian, retributive, and rehabilitative ideas are pushed to their respective extremes in modern political thought. This entails a departure from the more comprehensive notion of criminal justice that had been a part of the ancient and medieval traditions.

In the area of retribution, recall that Kant in particular rejects taking any utilitarian aims into account when formulating punishment policy. In contemporary scholarly writings, it is difficult to find anyone who takes the purely Kantian position on punishment, but the literature does contain a clear neo-Kantian argument. The most famous advocates of this argument are perhaps H. L. A. Hart and, later, John Rawls.[2] Although it falls short of Kant's view, the neo-Kantian argument reflects—in certain respects a modification of the Kantian balancing principle—that is, it is founded on the notion that all in society must have equal liberties and that criminal behavior upsets such a balance. Crime hinders the freedom necessary for Kant's concept of the Good Will.

For Hart, equal liberty and fairness make the criminal particularly liable to punishment, but punishment for Hart (unlike for Kant) is not inherently a good thing. Instead, it is justified only insofar as it restores the balance that has been upset by the crime in question.[3] For Rawls, as Stanley C. Brubaker notes, "punishment is understood as an extension of liberty."[4] According to Rawls, penal sanctions must give "the appropriate weight to liberty"; such sanctions are a "stabilizing device." In other words, punishment exists to redress the imbalance of liberties caused by criminal behavior. In much the same way that Kant has difficulty accounting for the deviance of criminal behavior in his theory of moral idealism, so too does Rawls have to admit that, under the "normal conditions of human life," punishment will be required "even for ideal theory."[5]

Some contemporary retributive writings do, like their antecedents in the modern political tradition, reject any serious role for utilitarian considerations in the formulation of criminal penalties. Michael Davis, for example, argues that it is impossible to set a utilitarian scale of punishments in a just society.[6] Alan Wertheimer points out that "to punish as severely as utility demands may entail punishments significantly less than or greater than those punishments which are commensurate with the crime."[7] Anthony Ellis, in a review of recent work on punishment, contends that "the most notable development of the past twenty years or so has been the resurgence of a more full-bodied retributivism."[8] There are even some in the contemporary debate who have gone back to the historical tradition whereby the government would act as a substitute for the injured party in seeking retribution for the crime. Lisa H. Perkins contends that the justification for state punishment is retribution, because state retribution takes the place of private retribution. When the state seeks retribution, she argues, it serves to mitigate and control excessive punishments that would otherwise be sought by private parties.[9]

Within the contemporary utilitarian position, there are many writers who, like Beccaria, advocate excluding any moral- or desert-based considerations from punishment. Such writers often make the argument that, since modern liberal society does not allow for government action on the basis of morality or some notion of the common good, retributive theories of punishment have no place in the current situation. Jeffrie G. Murphy makes such an argument. Although a supporter of retribution in theory, Murphy asserts that it is not a "legitimate state goal." In particular, he is unsure as to what extent just deserts—precisely because it is based upon the moral law—is compatible with the modern liberal state. Such a state, in Murphy's estimation, presumably leaves matters of virtue and moral inculcation in the private realm.[10] Russ Shafer-Landau, in a recent attack on retributivism, asserts that "retributivism's insistence on the correction of 'cosmic justice,' even if the suffering of the guilty promotes no one's interests, entails an allegiance to illiberal political theories that has yet to receive any adequate defense."[11]

Perhaps the clearest example of the narrow utilitarian perspective in the contemporary literature is the classic statement of the economic approach to punishment put forward by Gary Becker. Becker understands crime as a "negative externality." In order to deter crime, he contends, society must impose internally on the particular offender the cost of the externality. In other words, society must make the offender pay for the marginal cost of crime.[12]

One of the more recent and interesting critiques of retribution theory comes from the collaboration of two well-known criminologists, Norval Morris and Michael Tonry. In *Between Prison and Probation*, the two suggest a policy that aims to reduce the crime rate. They argue that retributive concepts obstruct the implementation of a policy that might actually be effective at reducing crime. Their proposal depends specifically on the idea of "interchangeability," the notion that offenders guilty of the same crime may be given different sentences based on the circumstances and the likelihood of their posing a danger to the community. Morris and Tonry defend this violation of retributivism's central premise (that because punishment is primarily justified by the criminal act, criminals who commit the same crimes must be treated similarly) on utilitarian grounds. They suggest that judges should have available a range of possible sentences—incarceration, straight probation, or something in the middle—and should focus on the group of punishments in the middle. The middle ground between prison and probation should be expanded so as to reflect the different circumstances of various offenders. They believe that judges should have the flexibility of sentencing one robber, for example, to prison, while sentencing another to community service. The utilitarian approach to punishment is superior, they contend, because retribution must take a backseat to the goal of prevention.

Morris and Tonry set forth several reasons as to why the concept of interchangeability should be accepted. First, they believe that reasonable people can disagree about determining the "just" punishment for a particular crime. Second, since reasonable people can disagree, there should be a relatively broad range established, and the idea of interchangeability should be implemented. Third, every offender is different. To take into account only one or two factors, they argue, is "too crude to be morally compelling." Finally, they believe that, although retribution may have a role to play in setting the minimum and maximum of possible punishments for a particular crime, utilitarian objectives should be primary in setting the specific sentence.[13] As a matter of policy, they believe that criminal punishment in the United States is too severe. A uniform application of just deserts, they believe, would inflict terrible suffering.[14]

Tonry argues in a more recent essay that "strong proportionality constraints" interfere with an effective criminal justice system. These constraints do not allow the flexibility to interchange different punishments for similarly situated offenders. Tonry contends that strong proportionality (tailoring punishment to fit the crime as precisely as possible) is, in practice, "unrealizable" and should not be allowed to interfere with the salutary implementation of interchangeable sentences. In particular, he attacks the notion that "like-situated offenders" ought to be punished similarly. He asserts that there really are no "like-situated" offenders; each case is different and ought to be treated as such. In Tonry's view, just deserts assumes that criminals "can conveniently and justly be placed into a manageable number of more-or-less desert categories," but in truth, "neither side of the desert-punishment equation lends itself to standardization."[15]

One must be careful, however, not to place Tonry squarely in the utilitarian camp, because some of his arguments belong more properly to the rehabilitation school. Whereas most utilitarians call for uniform punishments in order to create a consistent deterrent effect, Tonry argues that the particular circumstances of each offender should be considered and the punishment adjusted accordingly. He even suggests that the different social and material conditions in which offenders are situated should be an important factor in determining criminal penalties. Strong proportionality schemes "necessarily ignore the differing material conditions of life, including poverty, social disadvantage, and bias."[16]

No discussion of the contemporary arguments about punishment would be complete without addressing James Q. Wilson's considerable contributions to the field. Wilson is a difficult case, because his approach to punishment evolved since the publication of his landmark *Thinking about Crime* in the 1970s, in which he takes a strong utilitarian line. In fact, one might say that this work is one of the most important and interesting from the political science discipline, precisely because it asserts that we ought to "think" about crime and punishment in utilitarian terms.

Wilson's book is not so much an argument about the sorts of policies we ought to pursue (though it certainly does make such an argument) as it is a contention that we should approach the formulation of punishment policy in a particular way. Put simply, Wilson contends that we must formulate our public policy on the basis of what works. His central question is, What is the most effective public policy to solve the problem of crime? Wilson calls his approach "policy analysis" (presumably as opposed to moralistic or idealistic approaches). Following his utilitarian policy analysis model, Wilson expresses some degree of frustration with the retribution approach and, more vehemently, the rehabilitation approach, because neither approach, in his view, seeks to find the most *effective* punishment.[17]

Wilson makes it clear that he is not satisfied with the narrowly utilitarian philosophy of Beccaria and Bentham, which underlies most of his suggestions in *Thinking about Crime*, but that we must play the hand we have been dealt, as it were. Wilson believes the policies recommended by Beccarianism to be the most prudent course to follow under modern circumstances. He is explicit about his distaste for the dependence upon narrow self-interest found at the heart of Enlightenment penal reform philosophy. Yet he appears resigned to the fact that American society responds best to policies aimed at such thinking. He argues that "the only instruments society has by which to alter behavior in the short run require it to assume that people act in response to the costs and benefits of alternative courses of action." He goes on to say, "we have made our society and we must live with it. If the philosophy of Hobbes and Bentham governs our explanations of history and our definitions of policy, so be it."[18]

While the more comprehensive approach to punishment suggests that utilitarian and retributive arguments can coexist, many in the contemporary literature reject such a possibility. The "insurmountable problem," Wertheimer asserts, is that the retributive understanding "pegs the severity of punishment to the gravity of the crime," whereas "economical" deterrence "pegs the severity of punishment to the benefit to the criminal from the crime."[19] As a practical matter, Wertheimer also argues that just deserts and utility will lead to different scales of punishments, precisely because their premises are different. Some morally serious crimes may not require as strong a deterrent effect, for instance, as other crimes less serious.[20]

Mark Tunick also believes that the utilitarian and retributive approaches are incompatible. Punishment, he argues, is not a combination of principles but is instead a "single practice that has conflicting principles." Although personally a retributivist, Tunick contends that all our competing approaches to punishment "lack absolute grounds." In other words, his retributive view is merely a value judgment. He says that the conflicting purposes of our punishment policies "can be established only by interpretation, about which we may disagree."[21] Michael Clark agrees with Wertheimer that there is perhaps an irresolvable inconsistency between the two approaches as regards establishing a scale of punishments. He is more willing to see this tension as existing in principle, however, but not in practice, where he believes that something compatible to both strategies may be worked out.[22]

The compatibility between the moral deserts, utilitarian, and rehabilitative approaches has also become more difficult under contemporary arguments than it was in the comprehensive approach that, I argue, characterized the founding era. Indeed, even—and especially—in Philadelphia, where there was the strongest founding-era sympathy for the idea of focusing punishment on the rehabilitation of offenders, utility and the moral law were seen as a critical part of the rehabilitation effort. Such is infrequently the case with the strain of rehabilitationism that has come to dominate the contemporary debate. Why is this so? Why is it that most contemporary rehabilitation arguments, in contrast to the founding position, leave little if any room for a synthesis with other approaches to criminal justice?

Most important, contemporary rehabilitation arguments reject a premise that is central to the founding-era rehabilitation approach: that criminal behavior represents a breach of the moral law and that offenders are morally responsible for their behavior. Based upon such a premise, even some of the most aggressive reformers in founding-era Philadelphia, such as Benjamin Rush, understood that the key to rehabilitation was a moral reform of offenders' characters. The practical recommendations at the heart of the penitentiary movement—solitary confinement, meditation, prayer, religious services—are evidence of this understanding. Also, such moral reform would clearly help to satisfy the aims of utilitarianism since reformed offenders would be less likely to recidivate. Even those elements of early American penal reform that were clearly influenced by the Enlightenment were just as clearly influenced by moral and religious considerations. Michael Meranze's book on reform in Philadelphia—while pointing out the important role of Enlightenment political thought—rightly acknowledges the significance of moral reform in the individual character as part of Philadelphia's reform movement.

The contemporary rehabilitation approach, by contrast, rejects the premise that criminal justice has any sort of moral foundation and, therefore, that criminals are morally accountable for their behavior. Instead, the more narrow understanding of rehabilitation from modern political thought (such as Rousseau and Godwin) was the primary influence on the contemporary rehabilitation position. For former attorney general Ramsey Clark, a leading advocate of rehabilitation in the 1960s and 1970s, crime is not necessarily a matter of free choice. According to Clark, as with Rousseau, modern society has created conditions whereby the individual freedom at the heart of both the moral deserts and the utilitarian approaches does not exist. For Clark, crime is largely the product of a variety of social factors that lead individuals to commit offenses.[23]

If individuals cannot avoid acting criminally, whom are we to hold responsible? In another classic work of rehabilitation theory, Karl Menninger provides a clear answer: society. It is the fault of society for forcing individuals to commit crimes, and it is society that must be held accountable—not the offenders. In *The Crime of Punishment*, Menninger argues that we must understand "our part" in crime:

> By our part, I mean the encouragement we give to criminal acts and criminal careers, including Oswald's, our neglect of preventive steps, . . . and our quickly subsiding hysterical reactions to sensational cases. I mean our love of vindictive "justice," our generally smug detachment, and our prevailing public apathy.[24]

Clark concurs. He argues that crime is a reflection of society as a whole; it "reflects the character of a people."[25] External factors within society—heredity, environment, social class—are the "elemental origins of crime." Clark says that what offenders "are and what they experienced came largely from society—from its influence on them and on their forbears. If we are to deal meaningfully with crime," Clark reasons,

> what must be seen is the dehumanizing effect on the individual of slums, racism, ignorance and violence, of corruption and impotence to fulfill rights, of poverty and unemployment and idleness, of generations of malnutrition, of congenital brain damage and prenatal neglect, of sickness and disease, of pollution, of decrepit, dirty, ugly, unsafe, overcrowded housing, of alcoholism and narcotics addiction, of avarice, anxiety, fear, hatred, hopelessness and injustice. These are the fountainheads of crime.[26]

Change within society is particularly dangerous. The changes of the twentieth century were rapid, and Clark believes the unequal distribution of wealth is an indication of how poorly society has dealt with this change.[27] Instead of increasing the punitiveness of the system, society should focus on expanding government efforts to improve economic conditions. This view is shared more recently by Barbara A. Hudson, who contends that penal policy can have little impact on crime "without broader policies to reduce inequalities and social divisions, and to increase social provision."[28]

Given the different premise that underlies the contemporary rehabilitation argument, the policies it recommends differ in an important way from the founding idea of reform. For most founding-era reformers, since the problem was understood to lie in individual character, the practical recommendation was a penitentiary. In other words, the founding-era reformers understood that reform required *penitence* and that the criminal law should be designed to encourage this sort of moral and religious reform. The contemporary rehabilitationists' understanding of the causes of crime leads necessarily to a different conclusion.

The system, according to the rehabilitation argument, should focus not on punishment but correction. Clark believes the system has failed because it has not rehabilitated those offenders who entered it. Clark relies upon the claims of those in the psychiatric profession—such as Menninger and H. J. Eysenck—for his confidence that the system can actually turn criminals around. Menninger claims that psychiatry has developed to a point where it can treat criminal behavior because it can treat all human behavior:

> There is today an utterly new psychiatry, a new understanding of abnormal and normal behavior. . . . For the first time in history we have a logical and systematic theory of personality, an explanation of what human nature is and how behavior is determined and modified. This enables psychiatry to graduate from a science dealing with the recognition and handling of crazy people to a science of understanding the behavior of *all* people.[29]

Menninger's faith in medicine is in direct contrast to the reliance of the just deserts position upon morality. For Menninger, law cannot be based on any objective view of justice but, rather, on an objective analysis of the human personality. Science replaces morality as the objective source for "justice." Morality is simply an arbitrary preference, and we cannot base any penal policy upon it; science, on the other hand, is objective and should guide our response to crime. There comes to be a very close connection between punishment and medicine. When asking how much medicine to prescribe for a patient, one does not ask what is right according to "justice." The same is true for human behavior; it must be treated scientifically.

In terms of its impact on the policy arena, the rise of indeterminate sentencing in the 1960s and 1970s (which many states and the federal government have more recently eliminated) is perhaps the clearest example of the contemporary rehabilitation approach. Instead of incarcerating offenders for fixed terms, indeterminate sentencing allows a judge to sentence an offender to a wide range of time in prison—from ten years to life, for example. The purpose of such a system is to permit corrections officials to monitor the progress of offenders and to determine when a particular offender has made enough progress to merit return to the community.

The narrowly utilitarian approach has also had an impact on the policy arena. In recent years this approach has enjoyed the most political success. Largely convinced that rehabilitation does not work, both public and politicians now believe the only successful punishment policy is to incarcerate criminals so as to incapacitate them. In other words, rehabilitation may not work, and deterrence may not work, but if criminals are behind bars, then they cannot be out on the streets victimizing the public.

Perhaps the clearest indication of how divorced the contemporary utilitarian approach has become from the moral deserts approach can be found in the attempts by various states to tailor prison sentences precisely to the cost of prison construction and maintenance. Illinois and North Carolina serve as good examples. During the 1980s, the state of Illinois undertook a review of its criminal sentencing procedures. The recommendation of the state's Task Force on Prison Crowding was to use available prison space as a limitation on sentences. In other words, in determining what an appropriate penalty might be for a particular crime, the state would not so much consider what the crime merited in terms of its gravity but would instead fix the sentence on the basis of how much existing prison space was available. As a result, of course, the more offenders caught and successfully prosecuted for crimes, the less time each offender would serve. Joseph M. Bessette contends that the Illinois task force recommendations essentially excluded the idea of moral desert from the formation of punishment policy. He also presents evidence demonstrating that the task force recommendations mirrored trends in other states.[30]

In a case that drew national attention in 1994, North Carolina also tailored its sentences to the cost of prison space. What made the North Carolina case so extraordinary, and so reflective of the narrow utilitarian position, was that it enlisted the aid of a computer in determining the length of prison sentences. In legislative debate over the length of criminal sentences, a computer was employed to tell lawmakers exactly how much extra prison space would be needed in order to accommodate proposed sentences. The computer also laid out for legislators the adjustments that would have to be made in the severity of their criminal penalties in order keep corrections costs at a predetermined level.[31]

THE RELEVANCE OF THE FOUNDING APPROACH

What relevance does the founding approach have to the contemporary debate about criminal punishment? Much of the contemporary debate suffers from the same sort of narrowness that characterized the Enlightenment and post-Enlightenment era of political thought. Perhaps we can learn how a more comprehensive notion of criminal justice—one based on the idea of moral desert and incorporating both utilitarian and reformative ends—might have something to contribute to the contemporary situation.

In contemporary politics, the greatest obstacle to a broader approach to punishment is the inability of liberal society to see itself as based on the idea of a moral good. Instead of the founding-era understanding of utility and reform, grounded in the principles of moral desert and moral accountability, much of the contemporary utilitarian and reform arguments rejects the suggestion that punishment must somehow be connected to the moral seriousness of crimes. This is a point made nicely by Brubaker when he contends that "liberalism is a doubting philosophy of politics."[32] Instead of recognizing a human good at the heart of politics, from which utilitarian or reformative policies could then proceed, contemporary society substitutes utilitarianism, rehabilitationism, or neo-Kantianism. The result is a more narrow conception of both political and criminal justice, with approaches to punishment that mutually exclude each other.

This contrast between the polarized contemporary approach and the more comprehensive founding-era approach makes even more sense if we reflect upon the origins of the penitentiary in founding-era Philadelphia. The penitentiary movement is often cited as evidence that Philadelphia's reformers subscribed wholeheartedly to Enlightenment penal reform philosophy (articulated most fully by Beccaria), which argues for a severing of the criminal law from any moral foundation (a point about which Beccaria is explicit). Yet the very notion of a penitentiary implies both moral and religious amendment of offenders. Such a policy was attractive to utilitarians because they believed it presented a real likelihood that crime would be reduced as offenders reformed their characters. In this way, within founding-era reform, utility and rehabilitation united and were made coherent by a common moral foundation. Under the polarized approach that characterizes much of the contemporary debate, however, the idea of a morally grounded criminal law has been dropped, and the utilitarian and rehabilitative approaches have fragmented. During the founding, the moral foundation of the criminal law served as the glue that held the various approaches together under a broader notion of political and criminal justice. That there was significant penal reform during the founding is clear, but the founding-era idea of reform and the varied contemporary approaches to it are fundamentally different.

The founding approach offers contemporary society a potential ground for coming together under a broader understanding of criminal justice. We ought to consider the proposition—well understood even by many of the most aggressive founding-era penal reformers—that a criminal law based upon moral desert is essential for the maintenance of a free society. Such a proposition can serve as the anchor for pursuing both utilitarian and rehabilitative punishment policies. Walter Berns has argued that, in the twentieth century, liberal democracy has shown itself lacking in the necessary moral strength to defend itself against crime. He contends that this is a "strength that derives from the conviction that one's cause is just."[33]

Today's public often reacts with anger to the crime problem. Yet this anger can be a good thing, Walter Moberly has explained, so long as it is distinguished both from vengeance and from hatred. Drawing on the argument of St. Thomas Aquinas, Moberly contends that public anger indicates a public understanding that crime and punishment are fundamentally moral issues. We can only punish or be angry with those with whom we have relations of justice, and so anger (properly understood) is directed at a member of one's own class for acting contrary to the idea of the good to which that class is dedicated.[34] This recognition of the moral violation represented in criminal behavior is the natural threshold across which we must travel in order to formulate more specific punishments on the basis of utility and reform.

Without such a basis in moral desert, the more narrow utilitarian and rehabilitative approaches become problematic. With respect to utilitarianism, it is difficult to see how one could ensure reasonable or equitable punishments under a utilitarian system. We can think of many punishments that would be very likely to reduce future crime, but this justification would not be sufficient to warrant the implementation of such punishments. Severe penalties for minor infractions (the death penalty for jaywalking, for example) might deter, but no just society would utilize such penalties. Why not? Because there would be no connection between the punishment and what an offender actually deserved, based on the crime he might have committed. In the contemporary literature, both Davis and Wertheimer have written about this problem.[35] Narrow utilitarianism was, of course, also a concern during the founding. Benjamin Franklin in particular warned of the dangers from a utilitarianism that was not grounded in the principle of moral desert.

With respect to the excesses of a rehabilitative approach to criminal justice divorced from the idea of moral desert, C. S. Lewis's critique is still difficult to overcome. Lewis wonders how the parameters of rehabilitative therapy will be set without an underlying principle of moral desert. Once society ceases to consider what the offender deserves, Lewis asserts, "we have tacitly removed [the offender] from the sphere of justice altogether; instead of a person, a subject of rights, we now have a mere object, a patient, a 'case'."[36] Accordingly, the indeterminate sentencing that is central to the contemporary rehabilitation argument presents a problem. Once society removes the notion of what the offender deserves, how do we determine the length and form of rehabilitation? Under indeterminate sentencing, medical science and psychology take the place of desert, posing the danger of a threat to rights and other abuses. The length and form of punishment would be limited only by a psychiatrist's opinion (or that of some other corrections official) of when an offender is "cured," not by what an offender might have deserved for his crime.

Some have rightly pointed out how hard it is to adhere to a more comprehensive notion of criminal justice in a contemporary political society that questions the role of a moral good in politics. Nevertheless, the principle of moral desert also lends support to one of contemporary society's fundamental tenets: democracy. Lewis makes this point, arguing that just deserts is the only approach to punishment that is consistent with the democratic principles of modern society.[37] If we consider only the narrow utilitarian approach (deterrence or incapacitation), where the punishment must be measured by the extent to which it will prevent future crime or affect the cost of a corrections budget, then only social scientists (or, in the North Carolina case, computers) are really qualified to formulate punishment policy. Average citizens are not capable of using the sophisticated mathematical models required to tell us how much punishment is necessary to prevent crime, so average citizens under the narrow utilitarian approach really have no role in determining criminal justice policy. Similarly, if we rely exclusively on rehabilitation, where only those who have the requisite medical or psychological training can determine when an offender's treatment has been successful, there is also no role for democratic opinion to influence public policy.

My argument is not that utility and rehabilitation have no legitimate place. Indeed, such a view would be just as narrow and just as problematic as the other extreme approaches to punishment. Instead, drawing on the founding-era approach, the key to a broader understanding of criminal justice is a restoration of desert. In this way, the reasoned public opinion that necessarily guides democratic government can help determine what levels of punishment ought to be. Reasoned public opinion (not fleeting public passion) can set the general parameters of punishment policy, leaving plenty of room for the legitimate principles of utility and rehabilitation to aid in our approach to criminal justice. Bessette has addressed the question of how reasoned public opinion might have a significant role to play in the formulation of punishment policy. Arguing that recent and current levels of punishment in the United States are far below what the considered sense of the community believes is warranted, Bessette contends that "what a murderer, rapist, or assaulter deserves by way of punishment is a moral issue on which men, by virtue of their rational and moral character, have an opinion. . . . Thus we can talk about 'the moral sense of the community,' or 'the conscience of the society'."[38] The irony is that moral desert is excluded from political justice, as contemporary society understands itself, yet moral desert is the only principle that is compatible with the democratic theory supposedly informing contemporary political institutions.

The founding debate holds considerable significance for the contemporary debate in its understanding that the various approaches to punishment do not have to be mutually exclusive. There are some in the contemporary scholarly literature who argue for a synthesis of approaches. Rehabilitationists Barbara Hudson and Edgardo Rotman, for instance, also employ utilitarian arguments. Hudson contends that "rehabilitation is clearly motivated by the aim of preventing future crime." Rehabilitation offers the "best chance of reducing reoffending."[39] Rotman reasons that under the rehabilitative approach, "the law threatens citizens with imprisonment," and it "expects the citizen to foresee the loss of liberty prescribed by statute."[40] In other words, citizens ought to be deterred by the possibility of incarceration; if this deterrent is not sufficient to prevent them from offending, then rehabilitation is employed while they are imprisoned. Both Hudson and Rotman are part of a new school of rehabilitationism, which expresses an increased sensitivity to the prevailing political concern with curtailing crime. Ultimately, though, it is not really possible to connect even the new rehabilitationism with the founding approach, since it lacks the principle of morally deserved punishment that is central to the founding.

Perhaps most interesting is the more recent writing of James Q. Wilson. Wilson espoused a clearly utilitarian position in *Thinking about Crime*, but now he takes a more comprehensive position in *Crime and Human Nature*, written with Richard Herrnstein. In his earlier book, Wilson appeared resigned to what he characterized as the Hobbesian or utilitarian nature of our contemporary political society. This resignation was at the heart of his urging us to "think" about crime in utilitarian terms. In *Crime and Human Nature*, while certainly not rejecting the merits of the utilitarian approach, Wilson and Herrnstein contend that the central element guiding any punishment policy must be moral desert. Whereas Wilson's earlier work was also critical of rehabilitation, its criticism was based squarely on the argument that rehabilitation did not work and, therefore, failed the test of utility. In the later book, Wilson and Herrnstein take on Menninger's argument that offenders are not responsible for their acts and that punishment is not deserved. Their response to Menninger is that desert must be the primary consideration.[41] Although they remain cautious about how far just deserts can be applied in public policy,[42] there is more optimism for the place of just deserts in contemporary society than there was in the 1970s.

In addition to the scholarly debate, the ordinary administration of criminal justice today can profit from lessons from the founding. The controversy surrounding the California three-strikes law that introduced this book illustrates the relevance of the founding-era punishment debate. From the more comprehensive understanding of criminal justice, there are several sound criticisms that can be made of the three-strikes law. It is gimmicky and simplistic. It groups a variety of crimes under a single sweeping punishment and leaves open the possibility that relatively minor offenses can be punished with long terms of incarceration. From the founding perspective, one might say that it pursues incapacitation to such an extreme as to exclude a meaningful role for moral desert. Many of the founding-era statesmen who sought to reduce criminal penalties at the time cited this very same line of reasoning. The colonial criminal codes were so uniformly harsh that justice required a more proportionate relationship between crimes and punishments.

Yet we can also see, at least in some of the motivations animating the three-strikes movement, that the idea of making penalties commensurate with crimes was a key factor. If nothing else, the three-strikes debate shows how shockingly short was the average time served for the most violent crimes in the state of California. According to 1993 data from the California Department of Corrections, the median time served by those offenders released in 1992 after being convicted of a homicide was three years and four months. It was three years and one month for rape and other sex offenses, one year and eleven months for robbery, one year and ten months for felonious assault, and four years and one month for kidnapping.[43] These revelations drew near universal condemnation of California's criminal justice system. One might say that three-strikes, notwithstanding its obvious flaws, was motivated by the principles of utility and moral desert.

Contemporary political debates over punishment policy, as in the case of three-strikes or with a variety of other issues, show that there is a desire in the political arena to achieve several goals with the criminal justice system. The founding-era debate is important in this regard. It provides us with an example from our own tradition of a broad notion of political justice that encompasses all of the important aims of criminal punishment. The lesson from the founding is that society can punish on the basis of moral desert and that such a grounding can be the threshold for policies that seek to achieve utilitarian and reformative aims, insofar as we understand such aims to be a part of a more comprehensive approach to criminal justice.

INTRODUCTION

1. Under the law, an offender convicted of a felony who has one previous serious or violent felony conviction must be sentenced to twice the normal term. An offender convicted of a felony who has two previous serious or violent felony convictions must be sentenced to either three times the normal term or twenty-five years, whichever is greater. The law carries its own truth-in-sentencing provision, whereby offenders convicted under the measure must serve a minimum of 80 percent of their sentence, regardless of "good-time" credits for good behavior.

2. Peter W. Greenwood et al., *Three Strikes and You're Out: Estimated Benefits and Costs of California's New Mandatory-Sentencing Law* (Santa Monica: Rand, 1994).

3. Martin Diamond, "Ethics and Politics: The American Way," in *The Moral Foundations of the American Republic*, 3d ed., ed. Robert H. Horwitz (Charlottesville: University Press of Virginia, 1986), 75–108. The influence of Hobbes is a central issue both for early American political thought in general and for criminal punishment in particular. Beccaria's approach to punishment rests partly on the Hobbesian belief that society ought to deter deviance by appealing to self-interest, that is, our self-interest in avoiding state coercion in the form of punishment.

4. See, for example, Charles R. Kesler, "*Federalist* 10 and American Republicanism," in *Saving the Revolution*, ed. Charles R. Kesler (New York: Free Press, 1987), 13–39; Charles R. Kesler, "The Founders and the Classics," in *The American Founding*, ed. J. Jackson Barlow et al. (New York: Greenwood Press, 1988), 57–90; Thomas G. West, "The Classical Spirit of the Founding," in Barlow et al., *The American Founding*, 1–56.

5. See Willmoore Kendall and George W. Carey, *Basic Symbols of the American Political Tradition* (Baton Rouge: Louisiana State University Press, 1970); Forrest McDonald, *Novus Ordo Seclorum: The Intellectual Origins of the Constitution* (Lawrence: University Press of Kansas, 1985); Gordon S. Wood, *The Creation of the American Republic, 1776–1787* (New York: W. W. Norton, 1972).

6. Harry Elmer Barnes, *The Evolution of Penology in Pennsylvania* (Indianapolis: Bobbs-Merrill, 1927); David J. Rothman, *The Discovery of the Asylum: Social Order and Disorder in the New Republic* (Boston: Little, Brown, 1971); Marcello T. Maestro, *Cesare Beccaria and the Origins of Penal Reform* (Philadelphia: Temple University Press, 1973).

7. Thomas L. Dumm, *Democracy and Punishment: Disciplinary Origins of the*

United States (Madison: University of Wisconsin Press, 1987); Louis P. Masur, *Rites of Execution: Capital Punishment and the Transformation of American Culture, 1776–1865* (New York: Oxford University Press, 1989); Adam J. Hirsch, *The Rise of the Penitentiary: Prisons and Punishment in Early America* (New Haven: Yale University Press, 1992); Michael Meranze, *Laboratories of Virtue: Punishment, Revolution, and Authority in Philadelphia, 1760–1835* (Chapel Hill: University of North Carolina Press, 1996). The argument of these works, some of which acknowledge the importance of the Enlightenment, will be discussed more fully below.

1: THE PENNSYLVANIA EXPERIENCE

1. Benjamin Rush, "To Mrs. Rush, August 22, 1787," *Letters of Benjamin Rush*, ed. L. H. Butterfield (Princeton: Princeton University Press, 1951), 437.

2. Benjamin Rush, *The Autobiography of Benjamin Rush*, ed. George W. Corner (Princeton: Princeton University Press, 1948), 238.

3. Ibid., 253, 256.

4. For the prison society's account of the 1786 law and the problems associated with it, see "Brief History of the Penal Legislation of Pennsylvania," *Journal of Prison Discipline and Philanthropy* 1 (January 1845): 3. See also La Rochefoucauld-Liancourt, *On the Prisons of Philadelphia* (Philadelphia: Moreau de Saint Mery, 1796), 6.

5. Barnes, *Evolution of Penology*, 1.

6. "Brief History of the Penal Legislation of Pennsylvania," 1.

7. Meranze, *Laboratories of Virtue*, 4.

8. Roberts Vaux, *Notices of the Original, and Successive Efforts, to Improve the Discipline of the Prison at Philadelphia, and to Reform the Criminal Code of Pennsylvania* (Philadelphia: Kimber and Sharpless, 1826), 6.

9. Staughton George, Benjamin N. Nead, and Thomas McCamant, eds., *Charter to William Penn and Laws of the Province of Pennsylvania, 1682–1700* (Harrisburg, Pa.: Lane S. Hart, State Printer, 1879), 3–77.

10. Ibid., 14–15.

11. Ibid., 24, 27.

12. Ibid., 10, 27, 59.

13. Ibid., 84.

14. Ibid., 85.

15. Vaux, *Notices*, 5.

16. George, Nead, and McCamant, *Charter to William Penn and Laws*, 100.

17. Ibid., 101, 103, 116.

18. Ibid., 107–13.

19. Ibid., 144.

20. Vaux, *Notices*, 6. See also La Rochefoucauld-Liancourt, *On the Prisons of Philadelphia*, 4.

21. George, Nead, and McCamant, *Charter to William Penn and Laws*, 192–220.

22. Herbert William Keith Fitzroy, "The Punishment of Crime in Provincial

Pennsylvania," *Pennsylvania Magazine of History and Biography* 60 (1936): 249.

23. See, for example, the following sequence in *Calendar of State Papers, Colonial Series, America and West Indies*, 40 vols. (Great Britain: Public Records Office, 1964): in 19.332–33, 474–77 (letters from William Penn to the Council of Trade and Plantations, July 2, August 26, 1701), Penn submits colonial laws to Britain for approval; in 22:276–81 ("Attorney General to the Council of Trade and Plantations," October 13, 1704), there is a long report by the attorney general recommending repeal of many Pennsylvania laws; in 22:597–98 ("W. Popple, jr., to Mr. Penn," July 26, 1705), the Council of Trade communicates its objections to the colonial laws; in 23:18 ("Council of Trade and Plantations to the Queen," January 17, 1706), the council recommends to the queen that she repeal several of the acts submitted by Penn; in 23:47 ("Order of the Queen in Council," February 7, 1706), the queen orders the repeal of several Pennsylvania laws. See also 19:161–62, 24:487, and 24:459–61. For an illustration of the confusion in Pennsylvania's colonial government that was created by the various repeals, see *Minutes of the Provincial Council of Pennsylvania, from the Organization to the Termination of the Proprietary Government* (Philadelphia: Jo. Severns, 1852), 2:611–13 (meetings on May 4, June 6, and June 12, 1716).

24. An example can be found in *Calendar of State Papers*, 19:57–58 ("Vestrymen of Christchurch in Philadelphia to the Council of Trade and Plantations," January 28, 1701), where the vestrymen complain about Penn's failure to establish provisions for the military and to provide protection from pirates and Native Americans. The effect of such complaints is evident even in papers from the House of Lords; see, for example, *The Manuscripts of the House of Lords* 5, new series, 1702–1704 (London: Her Majesty's Stationary Office, 1965), 82, where the following is recorded about Pennsylvania: "Information has been given of three particular cases, very heinous, viz: a man committed for bestiality with a mare, for want of a legal method, got off. A woman committed for murdering her bastard child and confessing the fact, was either acquitted or pardoned. The son of an eminent Quaker committed for a rape, by several shuffling and irregular practices, got off without trial."

25. *Statutes at Large of Pennsylvania from 1682 to 1801* (Harrisburg, Pa.: Clarence M. Busch, 1896), 2:525, 543. *Calendar of State Papers*, 27:268, 270 ("Mr. Solicitor General to the Council of Trade and Plantations," December 22, 1713) and 27:299 ("Order of Queen in Council," February 20, 1714). For evidence of the crisis created by the revocation of affirmation, see *Minutes of the Provincial Council of Pennsylvania*, 2:614–29, 3:33–36 (meetings on October 18, November 4, 1716, and February 14, 1717). See also *Pennsylvania Archives, Eighth Series*, 2:1167, 1170–71, 1177, 1178, 1186–1205, 1257, 1260–62.

26. William Bradford, *An Enquiry how far the Punishment of Death is Necessary in Pennsylvania* (Philadelphia: Dobson, 1793), 18, 19.

27. For Vaux's commentary on the new laws, see Vaux, *Notices*, 7.

28. Barnes, *Evolution of Penology*, 38.

29. The "benefit of clergy" was a legal device originally intended to prevent the civil prosecution of priests. Priests would have to read a "neck verse" from the Bible as proof of their ecclesiastical office. By the American colonial

period, however, most everyone was entitled to benefit of clergy. The Bible was always opened to the same verse, so even the illiterate could avail themselves of the device. Those pleading benefit of clergy were burned on the hand, so they could not so plead on a second offense. Essentially, the benefit of clergy was a pardon for first offenders. By the Revolutionary period, most criminal codes had abolished this plea.

30. Fitzroy, "Punishment of Crime," 252.

31. *Statutes at Large of Pennsylvania*, 3:199–204.

32. Ibid., 3:331.

33. Lawrence H. Gipson, "The Criminal Codes of Pennsylvania," *Journal of Criminal Law* 6 (1915): 331.

34. Benjamin Rush, *Essays Literary, Moral and Philosophical*, ed. Michael Meranze (Schenectady: Union College Press, 1988), iii. In fact, he was an opponent of Pennsylvania's democratic constitution; see "Observations on the Government of Pennsylvania," in Benjamin Rush, *The Selected Writings of Benjamin Rush*, ed. Dagobert D. Runes (New York: Philosophical Library, 1947).

35. Donald J. D'Elia, *Benjamin Rush: Philosopher of the American Revolution*, in *Transactions of the American Philosophical Society* 64 (1974): 8. D'Elia explains that, for Rush, the Enlightenment reflected a new and fuller understanding of Christ's gospel, and that the new value placed on human life in the American Christian republic must be reflected in the abolition of capital punishment. See D'Elia, *Benjamin Rush*, 65–66, 96–97. For a good overview of the scholarship on Rush in the first half of the twentieth century, see D'Elia's introduction, esp. 6–7. Other scholars, including David Freeman Hawke, focus less on Rush's Christianity and emphasize instead the influence of English reformer John Howard. See Hawke, *Benjamin Rush: Revolutionary Gadfly* (Indianapolis: Bobbs-Merrill, 1971), 363–66.

36. Meranze, *Laboratories of Virtue*, 4.

37. Rush, "To Thomas Eddy, October 19, 1803," *Letters*, 875.

38. Rush, "To Jeremy Belknap, October 7, 1788," *Letters*, 490.

39. Rush, "An Enquiry into the Effects of Public Punishments upon Criminals, and upon Society," *Essays*, 79.

40. Ibid., 94. Rush also accepts Beccaria's premise on the pardon power: for reasons of deterrence, the pardon power should be strictly limited. However, as a prudential matter, Rush sees no choice during his time other than a frequent use of the pardon power, because the punishments were so severe. "Where punishments are excessive in degree, or infamous from being public, a pardoning power is absolutely necessary" (91).

41. Ibid., 89.

42. Ibid., 92.

43. Rush, "To Jeremy Belknap, October 13, 1989," *Letters*, 526.

44. Rush, "Effects of Public Punishments," *Essays*, 92.

45. Rush, "An Enquiry into the consistency of the punishment of Murder by Death, with Reason and Revelation," *Essays*, 95.

46. Rush, "The Influence of Physical Causes Upon the Moral Faculty," *Selected Writings*, 192–98.

47. Ibid., 192.

48. Ibid., 195.

49. Rush, "Punishment of Murder by Death," *Essays*, 98.

50. Genesis 9:5–6.

51. Rush, "Effects of Public Punishments," *Essays*, 92.

52. Exodus 21:12–15.

53. Rush, "Punishment of Murder by Death," *Essays*, 96, 97.

54. Ibid., 98.

55. Ibid., 96.

56. Rush, "To Elizabeth Graeme Ferguson, January 18, 1793," *Letters*, 628.

57. Rush, "Punishment of Murder by Death," *Essays*, 99.

58. Ibid., 103.

59. Rush, "Effects of Public Punishments," *Essays*, 93.

60. Rush, *Autobiography*, 29.

61. Rush, "To Enos Hitchcock, April 24, 1789," *Letters*, 511.

62. Rush, "Effects of Public Punishments," *Essays*, 88. This directly contradicts a central Beccarian principle—certainty and uniformity in punishment.

63. Rush, "To Thomas Eddy, October 19, 1803," *Letters*, 875.

64. Rush, *Autobiography*, 230.

65. Rush, "To John Coakley Lettsom, September 28, 1787," *Letters*, 443.

66. Rush, "Effects of Public Punishments," *Essays*, 80.

67. Ibid., 80–85.

68. Rush, "To John Adams, July 11, 1806," *Letters*, 922. He is referring to Bradford's *An Enquiry how far the Punishment of Death is Necessary in Pennsylvania*.

69. Rush, "To John Adams, July 11, 1806," *Letters*, 1114.

2: The Success of Pennsylvania's Reformers

1. Vaux, *Notices*, 33.

2. Bradford, *An Enquiry*, 3.

3. Ibid., 4. Emphasis is original in all citations from Bradford, unless otherwise noted.

4. Ibid., 6.

5. Ibid., 29, 31.

6. Ibid., 3, 43, 44.

7. Ibid., 45.

8. Ibid.

9. Ibid., 52.

10. Ibid., 21.

11. Ibid., 22–24, 26–28.

12. Ibid., 5.

13. Ibid., 44–45.

14. Ibid., 45.

15. Ibid., 46.

16. Ibid., 5, 7.

17. Ibid., 8, 9. Bradford also quotes Montesquieu (*Spirit of the Laws* 6:12): "The force of all human corruption lies in the impunity of the criminal act not in the moderation of punishment."

18. Ibid., 9–11.

19. Ibid., 12, 33.

20. Ibid., 36.

21. Ibid., 7.

22. Bradford refers to the reforms of the 1780s, which will be discussed in the following section of this chapter.

23. Bradford, *An Enquiry*, 13.

24. Ibid., 14, 15.

25. Ibid., 16. The actual records from this period are lost.

26. Ibid., 20.

27. Ibid., 42.

28. Ibid., 36.

29. In its journal, the prison society praises Bradford for his influence: "Few men have been as closely connected, as was William Bradford, with the penal reform in Pennsylvania. . . . He shared in the designs of the Philadelphia Prison Society: and he was noticed as a warm friend of their plans, while older public men were holding back from the proposed reforms." "William Bradford," *Journal of Prison Discipline and Philanthropy* 2 (July 1846): 205, 208–9.

30. Vaux, *Notices*, 3 (emphasis original).

31. Ibid., 5.

32. Edwin R. Keedy, "History of the Pennsylvania Statute Creating Degrees of Murder," *University of Pennsylvania Law Review* 97 (May 1949): 764. See also J. Thomas Scharf and Thompson Westcott, *History of Philadelphia, 1609–1884* (Philadelphia: L. H. Everts, 1884), 1:337–38.

33. "Constitution of Pennsylvania, 1776," *The Federal and State Constitutions, Colonial Charters, and other Organic Laws of the United States*, ed. Ben. Perley Poore (Washington, D.C.: Government Printing Office, 1878), 1547.

34. *Statutes at Large of Pennsylvania*, 12:280.

35. Ibid.

36. Ibid., 12:280–84.

37. Ibid., 12:284.

38. Caleb Lownes, *An Account of the Alteration and Present State of the Penal Laws of Pennsylvania, containing also an Account of the Gaol and Penitentiary House of Philadelphia and the Interior Management Thereof* (Lexington, Ky.: J. Bradford, 1794), 4. See also La Rochefoucauld-Liancourt, *On the Prisons of Philadelphia*, 6.

39. *Statutes at Large of Pennsylvania*, 12:511, 519, 523.

40. Ibid., 14:132–34.

41. Vaux, *Notices*, 33.

42. *Journal of the Senate of the Commonwealth of Pennsylvania* (Philadelphia, 1793), 3:14.

43. *Statutes at Large of Pennsylvania*, 15:174. Meranze notes a trend in the actual number of executions carried out in Pennsylvania, which corresponds roughly to the changes in the penal code. As a consequence of the severe 1718

statutes, executions continued steadily in the eighteenth century until the Revolutionary period, when they increased. Thereafter, executions declined as a consequence of the successive changes in the state's criminal law. Meranze, *Laboratories of Virtue*, 21–23.

44. *Statutes at Large of Pennsylvania*, 15:174–77, 180.

45. Ibid., 15:175.

46. For an argument about how the courts actually interpreted this new statute, see Keedy, "Pennsylvania Statute Creating Degrees of Murder," 773–77. Keedy argues that the Pennsylvania courts had difficulty interpreting the distinction between first- and second-degree murder. He cites several cases where this difficulty became manifest.

47. John F. Watson, *Annals of Philadelphia and Pennsylvania, in the Olden Time; being a collection of Memoirs, Anecdotes, and Incidents of the City and Its Inhabitants, and of the Earliest Settlements of the Inland Part of Pennsylvania*, ed. Willis P. Hazard (Philadelphia: Edwin S. Stuart, 1905), 1:356, 59, 361.

48. See the description of White in the official journal of the prison society: "Notice of Right Reverend William White, D.D., one of the Founders of the Society for Alleviating the Miseries of Public Prisons," *Journal of Prison Discipline and Philanthropy* 2 (January 1846): 2–3.

49. Vaux, *Notices*, 10.

50. "Brief History of the Penal Legislation of Pennsylvania," 2.

51. Constitution of Philadelphia's prison society, found on the inside front cover of each edition of the *Journal of Prison Discipline and Philanthropy*.

52. Vaux, *Notices*, 18.

53. Ibid., 25.

54. Ibid., 22.

55. Bradley Chapin, "Felony Law Reform in the Early Republic," *Pennsylvania Magazine of History and Biography* 113 (April 1989): 178.

56. Barnes, *Evolution of Penology*, 85. Vaux offers a description of this event, noting that most prisoners gave the preacher their good attention and respect: "All behaved with much greater decency than he expected" (*Notices*, 16). The prison society's article on Bishop White has another description of this religious service, "in which [White] officiated at great personal risk." See "Notice of the Right Reverand William White," 3. See also La Rochefoucauld-Liancourt, *On the Prisons of Philadelphia*, 21.

57. Lownes, *Penal Laws of Pennsylvania*, 6.

58. Ibid., 5.

59. Ibid., 6, 9–10.

60. Ibid., 11–13. For a detailed physical description of the prison, see ibid., 7.

61. Ibid., 3.

62. Ibid., 10. See also p. 15.

63. Ibid., 10.

64. La Rochefoucauld-Liancourt, *On the Prisons of Philadelphia*, 32. La Rochefoucauld-Liancourt himself would go further than the Pennsylvania reforms by advocating the elimination of the death penalty (35).

65. Ibid., 33–34.

66. Ibid., 3.

67. Ibid., 14–15.

68. Ibid., 22.

69. Vaux, *Notices*, 13. See also "Brief History of the Penal Legislation of Pennsylvania," 5–6. The prison society's journal comments that the mixing of the various classes of prisoners "was constant and corrupting to the highest degree."

70. *Statutes at Large of Pennsylvania*, 12:286–87.

71. Ibid., 13:243.

72. Vaux, *Notices*, 15.

3: THE SPREAD OF REFORM?

1. Thomas Jefferson, "A Bill for proportioning Crimes and Punishments, in cases heretofore Capital," in *The Writings of Thomas Jefferson*, vol. 1, ed. Andrew A. Lipscomb (Washington, D.C.: Thomas Jefferson Memorial Association, 1904), 219. Jefferson attached this bill to his autobiography as an appendix.

2. David H. Flaherty, ed., and William Strachey, comp., *For the Colony in Virginia Britannia, Lawes Divine, Morall and Martiall, etc.* (Charlottesville: University Press of Virginia, 1969), ix.

3. John D. Cushing, ed., *Colony Laws of Virginia, 1619–1660* (Wilmington, Del.: Michale Glazier, 1978), 1:96.

4. Flaherty, *Lawes Divine, Morall and Martiall*, xi, xv.

5. Cushing, *Colony Laws of Virginia*, 1:69.

6. Flaherty, *Lawes Divine, Morall and Martiall*, 10–11.

7. Ibid., 12–18, 21–23.

8. Ibid., 11–12.

9. Ibid., 14.

10. Ibid., 18–19.

11. Ibid., 19–20, 23–24.

12. Thomas Jefferson, *Notes on the State of Virginia*, ed. William Peden (Chapel Hill: University of North Carolina Press, 1955), 113.

13. Arthur P. Scott, *Criminal Law in Colonial Virginia* (Chicago: University of Chicago Press, 1930), 152.

14. Jefferson, *Notes on the State of Virginia*, 114.

15. Cushing, *Colony Laws of Virginia*, 1:123.

16. Ibid., 1:127.

17. For an account of the common law penalties, see William Blackstone, *Commentaries on the Laws of England* (Philadelphia: J. B. Lippincott, 1893). Volume and page number citations refer to Blackstone's original division and pagination. For high treason, see 4:91–92; petty treason, 4:203–4; murder, 4:194; manslaughter, 4:191; other crimes against persons, 4:205–19; crimes against habitations (burglary, arson, and so on), 4:220–23; crimes against property, 4:229–47.

18. See William Walter Hening, ed., *The Statutes at Large; being a Collection of all the Laws of Virginia, from the First Session of the Legislature, in the year 1619* (Richmond: J. and G. Cochran, 1809), 1:119, for an account of the first assembly

in Virginia under Governor Yeardley. Many of the records from this assembly have been lost, but the punishments enacted by it are confirmed in 1623; see 1:121. See also 1:69, where the "Articles, Instructions and Orders" from James I (November 20, 1606) essentially spell out several of the crimes and punishments upon which colonial codes were later founded.

19. Blackstone, *Commentaries*, 4:91–92. Blackstone notes that, in the case of nobles, "the king may, and often does, discharge all the punishment, except beheading."

20. Ibid., 4:203–4.

21. Severe punishments for crimes associated with tobacco can be found throughout the colonial statutes. See, for example, Hening, *Statutes at Large*, 9:516. Even before the colonial legislature enacted its code, tobacco-related crimes were on the books; see 1:64, 96.

22. Thomas Jefferson, *Autobiography*, *Writings of Thomas Jefferson* (Lipscomb), 1:62.

23. Hening, *Statutes at Large*, 9:176.

24. Jefferson, *Autobiography*, *Writings* (Lipscomb), 1:63–64.

25. Ibid., 1:65, 67–68.

26. Ibid., 1:65.

27. Jefferson, "A Bill for proportioning Crimes and Punishments," *Writings* (Lipscomb), 1:237.

28. Jefferson's notes refer to an older Italian edition of Beccaria, where the chapter numbering is slightly different than in the Cambridge English translation. One can trace the edition used by Jefferson because of the Italian citations from Beccaria in *The Commonplace Book*.

29. Jefferson, "A Bill for proportioning Crimes and Punishments," *Writings* (Lipscomb), 1:222–27.

30. Jefferson, *Autobiography*, *Writings* (Lipscomb), 1:66.

31. James Madison, "To Thomas Jefferson, February 15, 1787," in *Letters and Other Writings of James Madison* (New York: R. Worthington, 1884), 1:272.

32. Hening, *Statutes at Large*, 6:363, 9:457, 12:531. Samuel Shepherd, ed., *The Statutes at Large of Virginia, from October session 1792, to December session 1806, inclusive, in Three Volumes, Being a Continuation of Hening* (New York: AMS Press, 1835), 1:111–12.

33. Jefferson, *Autobiography*, *Writings* (Lipscomb), 1:70.

34. Shepherd, *Statutes at Large*, 2:5–6.

35. Ibid., 2:6–8.

36. Ibid., 2:8–12.

37. Adelaide Meador Hunter, *Punishment of Crimes in Virginia, 1775–1820* (Master's thesis, Duke University, 1947), 75.

38. Some of the first regulations for New Netherlands from the Amsterdam Chamber of the West India Company can be found in "Provisional Regulations for the Colonists Adopted by the Assembly of the Nineteen of the West India Company, March 28, 1624," in *Documents Relating to New Netherland, 1624–1626, in the Henry E. Huntington Library*, ed. and trans. A. J. F. van Laer (San Marino: Henry E. Huntington Library and Art Gallery, 1924), 2–5, and "Further Instruc-

tions for Willem Verhulst and the Council of New Netherland," in ibid., 82–114. For secondary source accounts of the early laws of New Netherlands, see Philip English Mackey, *Hanging in the Balance: The Anti-Capital Punishment Movement in New York State, 1776–1861* (New York: Garland Publishing, 1982), 2. See also Thorsten Sellin, *Pioneering in Penology: The Amsterdam Houses of Correction in the Sixteenth and Seventeenth Centuries* (Philadelphia: University of Pennsylvania Press, 1944), 1–8; Paul Zumthor, *Daily Life in Rembrandt's Holland*, trans. Simon Watson Taylor (London: Weidenfeld and Nicolson, 1962), 252–55.

39. Thomas Eddy, *An Account of the State Prison or Penitentiary House, in the City of New-York* (New York: Isaac Colins and Son, 1801), 10–11.

40. Michael Kraus, *The Atlantic Civilization: Eighteenth Century Origins* (Ithaca: Cornell University Press, 1949), 132.

41. Ibid., 133. Chapin, "Felony Law Reform," 181.

42. Eddy, *Account of the State Prison*, 50.

43. Ibid., 5, 6.

44. Eddy, *Account of the State Prison*, title page. See Cesare Beccaria, *On Crimes and Punishments and Other Writings*, ed. Richard Bellamy, trans. Richard Davies (Cambridge, England: Cambridge University Press, 1995), 68.

45. Eddy, *Account of the State Prison*, 4. See Montesquieu, *The Spirit of the Laws*, trans. Anne M. Cohler, Basia Carolyn Miller, Harold Samuel Stone (New York: Cambridge University Press), bk. 6, ch. 12, pp. 84–86.

46. Eddy, *Account of the State Prison*, 5 (emphasis original).

47. Ibid., 50–52.

48. Ibid., 65, 66–67.

49. Ibid., 50.

50. Ibid.

51. Ibid., 51.

52. Ibid., 53–54.

53. Ibid., 7, 8–9, 11–12.

54. Ibid., 7.

55. Ibid. 9, 12.

56. Ibid., 13–14.

57. Mackey, *Hanging in the Balance*, 67.

58. Eddy, *Account of the State Prison*, 15, 16 (emphasis original).

59. Ibid., 16

4: THE ENLIGHTENMENT

1. Lawrence Friedman, *Crime and Punishment in American History* (New York: Basic Books, 1993), 63.

2. Morton J. Horwitz, *The Transformation of American Law, 1780–1860* (Cambridge: Harvard University Press, 1977). William E. Nelson, *Americanization of the Common Law* (Cambridge: Harvard University Press, 1975).

3. Barnes, *The Evolution of Penology*, 6, 80, 105. Barnes also recognizes that there was a feeling, especially among eastern Pennsylvania Quakers, that the se-

vere colonial code was the product of foreign coercion. This point is echoed by Michael Kraus, who contends that penal reform grew out of Beccaria's writings but was also popular in America because it was anti-British (the colonists did not like that the laws were not their own). Kraus, *The Atlantic Civilization*, 127, 129.

4. Barnes, *Evolution of Penology*, 6.

5. Ibid., 80.

6. Maestro, *Cesare Beccaria*, 126.

7. Blackstone, *Commentaries*, vol. 4, ch. 1, sect. 3, pp. 11–14. Citations refer to Blackstone's original division and pagination.

8. See Jeremy Bentham, *A Commentary on the Commentaries: A Criticism of William Blackstone's Commentaries on the Laws of England*, ed. Charles Warren Everett (Oxford: Clarendon Press, 1928).

9. "Declaration of the Rights of Man and Citizen," in *The Constitutions and other Select Documents illustrative of the History of France, 1789–1907*, ed. Frank Maloy Anderson (New York: Russell and Russell, 1908), 59–60.

10. Maestro, *Cesare Beccaria*, 138.

11. Rothman, *The Discovery of the Asylum*, 59, 60. Rothman also grounds founding-era penal reform in Beccaria and the Enlightenment in a more recent essay. See "Perfecting the Prison: United States, 1789–1865," in *The Oxford History of the Prison*, ed. Norval Morris and David J. Rothman (New York: Oxford University Press, 1995), 111–29.

12. Hirsch, *Rise of the Penitentiary*, 113.

13. Masur, *Rites of Execution*, 51, 54.

14. Dumm, *Democracy and Punishment*, 88, 141.

15. Meranze, *Laboratories of Virtue*, 66.

16. Beccaria, *On Crimes and Punishments*, 4–5.

17. Ibid., 5.

18. Ibid., 39, 41.

19. Jeremy Bentham, *The Theory of Legislation*, ed. C. K. Ogden (London: Rougledge & Kegan Paul Ltd, 1931), 60.

20. Jeremy Bentham, *An Introduction to the Principles of Morals and Legislation* (Oxford: Clarendon Press, 1879), 186. It is difficult to see how Bentham's own punishments will lead to specific levels of deterrence, although he is confident that such things can be accurately calculated.

21. Ibid., 18.

22. That Hobbes is the forerunner to Beccaria and Bentham is also an argument made by Mario A. Cattaneo, in "Hobbes's Theory of Punishment," in *Hobbes Studies*, ed. Keith C. Brown (Cambridge: Harvard University Press, 1965), 275–97. For a different view, see Alan Norrie, "Thomas Hobbes and the Philosophy of Punishment," *Law and Philosophy* 3 (1984): 299–320.

23. Thomas Hobbes, *Leviathan* (New York: Collier Books, 1962), 231.

24. Ibid., 230.

25. Beccaria, *On Crimes and Punishments*, 10.

26. Ibid.

27. Ibid., 39–40.

28. Ibid., 40, 54–55.

29. Hobbes, *Leviathan*, 231.

30. Beccaria, *On Crimes and Punishments*, 66.

31. Ibid., xxiv.

32. Ibid., xvii–xix.

33. Ibid., xxvi–xxvii.

34. This is Kant's primary objection to the utilitarian approach. It treats individuals as means to the end of utility, and not as ends in themselves.

35. Hobbes, *Leviathan*, 229.

36. Beccaria, *On Crimes and Punishments*, 7.

37. Cited in Maestro, *Cesare Beccaria*, 131.

38. Bentham, *Principles of Morals and Legislation*, 170, 71.

39. Bentham, *Theory of Legislation*, 60.

40. Beccaria, *On Crimes and Punishments*, 19. The question is, however, what if one could show that it took more severe penalties to deter robbery than murder? Would such a scheme be appropriate?

41. Ibid., 64.

42. Ibid., 76.

43. Ibid., 63.

44. Bentham, *Principles of Morals and Legislation*, 183.

45. Ibid., 1.

46. Ibid., 179, 181–82.

47. Bentham, *Theory of Legislation*, 339.

48. Beccaria, "To André Morellet," *On Crimes and Punishments*, 119, 121, 122.

49. Ibid., 121, 123.

50. Beccaria, *On Crimes and Punishments*, 3–4.

51. Ibid., 113.

52. Ibid., 105.

53. John Locke, *Second Treatise of Government*, ed. Peter Laslett (Cambridge, England: Cambridge University Press, 1988), para. 7. All citations of Locke refer to paragraph numbers.

54. Ibid., 8, 11.

55. One might argue that the second formulation represents "specific deterrence," where one deters the particular offender in question from future crime by punishing him for his present offense. The offender will want to avoid such punishment in the future. Since Locke's formulation comes in the context of one's right to *kill* a murderer, however, it seems more appropriately considered incapacitation.

56. Locke, *Second Treatise of Government*, 8, 10.

57. In a section of his book on Locke's theory of rights, A. John Simmons deals nicely with the origin of the right to punish. Although Simmons understands the right to punish as deriving from the right to preservation, he also argues that there is an element of retribution involved. I am not so sure this is justified by the text. If one were to witness a brutal murder, Simmons suggests, one would "feel justified in seeing to it that the murderer suffered for his crime." He imputes this retributive notion to Locke's natural punishment right. See Simmons, *The*

Lockean Theory of Rights (Princeton: Princeton University Press, 1992), 125–26. Although Locke does occasionally make reference to criminal desert, it always appears to be incidental to utilitarian concerns. The essential point remains that man's interest in his own preservation is both necessary and sufficient to constitute for Locke a natural right to punish. Daniel M. Farrell defends this utilitarian interpretation in his essay "Punishment without the State," *Nous* 22 (1988): 437–53. He argues that deterrence is the essential justification for punishment in Lockean political philosophy.

58. Locke, *Second Treatise of Government*, 8, 12.

59. Ibid., 17, 19.

60. Thomas Hurka has a slightly different view. He suggests that the right to punish in Locke derives from a more fundamental natural right "to threaten others with certain harms if they succeed in violating . . . rights." Hurka calls the right to threaten harm an "enforcement-right" that justifies our actually making good on the threat through punishment. See Hurka, "Rights and Capital Punishment," *Dialogue* 21 (1982): 649.

61. Locke, *Second Treatise of Government*, 17, 18.

62. Montesquieu, *Spirit of the Laws*, 1.6.2, 3.

63. Ibid., 1.6.9, 12.

64. Ramsey Clark, *Crime in America* (New York: Simon and Schuster, 1970). Karl Menninger, *The Crime of Punishment* (New York: Viking Press, 1966).

65. There is, in fact, an entire school of Marxist criminology in the contemporary politics of punishment. For an excellent representation of this school, see David F. Greenberg, ed., *Crime and Capitalism: Readings in Marxist Criminology* (Philadelphia: Temple University Press, 1993). In his introduction to this collection, Greenberg defines Marxist criminology by examining Marx's point of departure from Hegel. Hegel's mistake, according to Greenberg, was to assume that men's consciousness determines their existence, instead of recognizing that conditions of social existence determine human consciousness. Jeffrie G. Murphy also argues along these lines in the above-cited collection. While he admits the moral appropriateness of retribution theory, Murphy points to Marx's argument that the social conditions of modern society do not permit sufficient moral autonomy to justify retribution. See Murphy's "Marxism and Retribution," in *Punishment: A Philosophy and Public Affairs Reader*, ed. A. John Simmons et al. (Princeton: Princeton University Press, 1990), 8. For another overview of this school, see Jeffrey Reiman, *The Rich Get Richer and the Poor Get Prison: Ideology, Class, and Criminal Justice*, 3d ed. (New York: Macmillan, 1990), 157–78.

66. William Godwin, *An Enquiry Concerning Political Justice and Its Influence on General Virtue and Happiness*, 2 vols., ed. Raymond A. Preston (New York: Alfred A. Knopf, 1926), 1:9. Citations refer to volume number followed by page number.

67. The social contract is not the only means that Rousseau suggests to improve the human condition. Another way is a certain kind of private or domestic education that Rousseau explains in *Emile*.

68. Jean-Jacques Rousseau, *Discourse on the Origin and Foundations of Inequality among Men*, trans. Roger D. Masters and Judith R. Masters, in *The First and Second Discourses*, ed. Roger D. Masters (New York: St. Martin's Press, 1964), 101, 105.

69. Ibid., 141–42.

70. Ibid., 160.

71. Godwin, *Enquiry Concerning Political Justice*, 2:154.

72. Ibid., 1:84.

73. Ibid., 1:81, 83.

74. Ibid., 1:82, 2:60–61, 168.

75. Rousseau, *Discourse on the Origin and Foundations of Inequality*, 102.

76. Jean-Jacques Rousseau, *On the Social Contract*, trans. Judith R. Masters, ed. Roger D. Masters (New York: St. Martin's Press, 1978), 66.

77. Ibid., 46.

78. Ibid., 53.

79. Ibid., 55.

80. Ibid., 64.

5: ANSWERING THE ENLIGHTENMENT

1. Egon Bittner and Anthony Platt, "The Right of the State to Punish," in *Contemporary Punishment*, ed. Rudolph J. Gerber and Patrick D. McAnany (Notre Dame: University of Notre Dame Press, 1972), 24–26, 29.

2. Immanuel Kant, *Groundwork of the Metaphysic of Morals*, trans. H. J. Paton (New York: Harper and Row, 1956), 57. Mark Tunick questions the extent to which Kant ought to be identified as a retributivist in "Is Kant a Retributivist?" *History of Political Thought* 17 (spring 1996): 60–78.

3. Kant, *Groundwork of the Metaphysic of Morals*, 62.

4. Jeffrie G. Murphy argues that the essential distinction between Kantian and utilitarian morality is the primacy of *rights* for Kant. Justifying state action on the grounds of utility would ignore the critical question for a Kantian: what gives the state the *right* to act? See Murphy, "Marxism and Retribution," 3–29.

5. Kant, *Groundwork of the Metaphysic of Morals*, 65, 70–71.

6. Immanuel Kant, *The Metaphysical Elements of Justice: Part I of The Metaphysics of Morals*, trans. John Ladd (Indianapolis: Bobbs-Merrill, 1965), 100.

7. Kant, *Groundwork of the Metaphysic of Morals*, 69–70.

8. Ibid., 69.

9. Immanuel Kant, *Critique of Practical Reason*, trans. Lewis White Beck (New York: MacMillan, 1985), 62, 63.

10. Ibid., 97.

11. Kant, *Metaphysical Elements of Justice*, 100.

12. Kant, *Critique of Practical Reason*, 63.

13. Kant, *Metaphysical Elements of Justice*, 99.

14. Ibid., 101.

15. Ibid., 102.

16. Ibid., 104–5.

17. Georg Wilhelm Friedrich Hegel, *The Philosophy of History*, trans. J. Sibree (New York: Dover Publications, 1956), 38.

18. Georg Wilhelm Friedrich Hegel, *The Philosophy of Right*, trans. T. M.

Knox (London: Oxford University Press, 1967), 70.

19. Ibid.

20. Ibid., 71, 72.

21. Mark Tunick identifies Hegel's approach to punishment with what he calls the "split will." One part of the split will is represented by crime, which comes from the criminal's "particular will." The other part of the split will is represented by punishment, which is part of the "universal" or "implicit" will that the law be obeyed. "In committing the crime, the criminal acts against his own implicit will, and punishment respects his rationality by universalizing the part of his split will that went against his implicit will." For a comprehensive treatment of Hegel on the question of punishment, see Mark Tunick, *Hegel's Political Philosophy: Interpreting the Practice of Legal Punishment* (Princeton: Princeton University Press, 1992). Tunick also argues that the criminal is actually "made free" by punishment, in that punishment releases him from the slavery of his particular will and leaves him free to will the universal. For the discussion of these points, see pages 35–36.

22. Hegel, *Philosophy of Right*, 67.

23. Ibid., 70–71.

24. Hegel, *Philosophy of History*, 28–29.

25. Michel Foucault, *Discipline and Punish*, trans. Alan Sheridan (New York: Vintage Books, 1979), 3–8.

26. Ibid., 9–10.

27. Ibid., 11, 13.

28. Although toward a different end, C. S. Lewis makes much the same criticism of the psychiatric rehabilitation argument. Both Lewis and Foucault consider psychiatric attempts at rehabilitation as degrading to the human soul and perhaps the most inhumane of the various approaches to punishment. See the discussion of Lewis in the conclusion.

29. Foucault, *Discipline and Punish*, 18–19.

30. Ibid., 30.

31. Ibid., 80, 90.

32. Plato, *Republic*, trans. Allan Bloom (Basic Books, 1968), l. 338c.

33. Ibid., 338e.

6: A More Comprehensive Approach

1. St. Thomas Aquinas, *Summa Theologiae*, 5 vols., trans. Fathers of the English Dominican Province (Westminster, Md.: Christian Classics, 1981), I-II, Q.87, a.1.

2. Ibid., a.4.

3. Ibid., II-II, Q.60, a.1.

4. Ibid., Q.62, a.2.

5. Pope Pius XII, "Crime and Punishment," in Gerber and McAnany, *Contemporary Punishment*, 60–61, 65.

6. Ibid., 62.

7. Whether the society discussed by Socrates in the *Gorgias* is merely an

ideal or represents Plato's practical penology is an important subject of Mary Margaret Mackenzie's thorough treatment of Plato's punishment philosophy. See *Plato on Punishment* (Berkeley and Los Angeles: University of California Press, 1981), esp. 179–206. For a more recent comprehensive account of Plato and punishment, see Trevor J. Saunders, *Plato's Penal Code* (Oxford: Clarendon Press, 1991).

8. Note how this is precisely the opposite of Foucault (as well as Thrasymachus and Polus), who asserts that punishment is an expression of power not in accord with higher principles of justice but designed instead to achieve the arbitrary ends of those in authority.

9. Plato, *Gorgias,* trans. James H. Nichols Jr. (Ithaca: Cornell University Press, 1998), ll. 468d–e, 480b–c.

10. Aquinas, *Summa Theologiae,* II-II, Q.108, a.1.

11. Plato, *Gorgias,* 504d.

12. Most of my discussion of the ancients and punishment will concentrate on Plato. This is not because Aristotle is less important but simply because Plato's argument best lends itself to drawing a connection between ancient and contemporary approaches to punishment. Also, much of Aristotle's argument is found in Thomistic thought.

13. Aristotle, *Nicomachean Ethics,* trans. Terence Irwin (Indianapolis: Hackett Publishing, 1985), 1132a20.

14. Ibid., 1129b20.

15. Aquinas, *Summa Theologiae,* I-II, Q.88, a.1.

16. Ibid., II-II, Q.108, a.2.

17. Ibid., App.I, Q.2, a.5.

18. Pius XII, "Crime and Punishment," 63.

19. Plato, *Republic,* 409a-d.

20. Plato, *Gorgias,* 465d.

21. Ibid., 472d–e.

22. Ibid., 473c–e.

23. Mackenzie makes clear in her argument that, in spite of its incorporation of utilitarian concerns, Plato's view of punishment remains "firmly rooted" in his ethics, which derives from the more "idealistic" accounts in the *Republic* and *Gorgias.* See Mackenzie, *Plato on Punishment,* 204–5.

24. Plato, *The Laws of Plato,* trans. Thomas L. Pangle (New York: Basic Books, 1980), l. 728d.

25. Aquinas, *Summa Theologiae,* I-II, Q.46, a.2.

26. Ibid., I-II, Q.46, a.6.

27. Ibid.

28. Ibid., a.4, 7 (emphasis added).

29. Plato, *Laws,* 728b–c.

30. Ibid., 731d.

31. Ibid., 735b–d, 862e, 867c–868a.

32. Ibid., 735d.

33. Ibid., 730b, 862d.

34. Aquinas, *Summa Theologiae,* I-II, Q.95, a.1.

35. Ibid., Q.108, a.3.

36. Ibid., Q.64, a.2.

7: REEVALUATING THE REFORM MOVEMENT

1. *Journals of the Continental Congress, 1774–1789* (Washington, D.C.: Government Printing Office, 1973), 1:69.

2. Hening, *Statutes at Large*, 9:127.

3. Horwitz, *Transformation of American Law*, 4. See also Elizabeth Gasper Brown, *British Statutes in American Law, 1776–1836* (Ann Arbor: University of Michigan Law School, 1964), 23–26. The two exceptions were Rhode Island and Connecticut. To many Americans, the common law was understood as an important part of their political tradition, because of its protection of liberty. For an account of the common law and the liberal tradition in America, see James R. Stoner Jr., *Common Law and Liberal Theory* (Lawrence: University Press of Kansas, 1992). Generally, the American reaction against the common law (to the extent that there was one) focused on its severe criminal penalties. This should be distinguished from the common law treatment of criminal procedure and its protection of individual rights.

4. *Laws of the State of New Jersey* (Trenton: Joseph Justice, 1821), 244–64 ("An Act for the Punishment of Crimes," March 18, 1796). Also passed on this date was "An Act Concerning Sheriffs," which adopted regulations for prison regimen similar to those suggested by Pennsylvania reformers (see 236–44).

5. Chapin, "Felony Law Reform," 180, 183.

6. "The Liberties of the Massachusetts Colony in New England, 1641," in Edwin Powers, *Crime and Punishment in Early Massachusetts, 1620–1692* (Boston: Beacon Press, 1966), 533–48.

7. David Flaherty, "Law and the Enforcement of Morals in Early America," in *American Law and the Constitutional Order: Historical Perspectives*, ed. Lawrence M. Friedman and Harry N. Scheiber (Cambridge: Harvard University Press, 1978), 54. See also William E. Nelson, "Emerging Notions of Modern Criminal Law in the Revolutionary Era: An Historical Perspective," where he observes that "crime was still looked upon as a sin, the criminal as sinner, and criminal law as the earthly arm of God" (in Friedman and Scheiber, *American Law and the Constitutional Order*, 165).

8. See "Appendix A" in Edgar J. McManus, *Law and Liberty in Early New England* (Amherst: University of Massachusetts Press, 1993). Edwin Powers explains that harsh punishment in the statute books did not always lead to harsh punishment in practice. In examining the disposition of particular cases in the Massachusetts Colony, for example, Powers finds that the usual punishment for adultery was a whipping and a fine, even though the prescribed punishment was death. See Powers, *Crime and Punishment in Early Massachusetts*, 510–32.

9. Bradley Chapin, *Criminal Justice in Colonial America, 1606–1660* (Athens: University of Georgia Press, 1983), 147.

10. Hirsch, *Rise of the Penitentiary*, 57–59. Richard Gaskins argues that the change in Connecticut's criminal punishments was equally gradual. See Gaskins,

"Changes in the Criminal Law in Eighteenth-Century Connecticut," in *Crime and Justice in American History*, vol. 1, *The Colonies and Early Republic*, ed. Eric H. Monkkonen (Westport, Conn.: Meckler, 1991), 197–230.

11. Barnes, *Evolution of Penology*, 6, 28.

12. Meranze, *Laboratories of Virtue*, 65.

13. In addition to the Quakers, other important figures in the reform movement were also influenced by religion. Rush biographer Donald J. D'Elia emphasizes the importance of Christianity in Rush's push for milder penalties. See D'Elia, *Benjamin Rush*, 8–9.

14. George, Nead, and McCamant, *Charter to William Penn and Laws*, 81, 465.

15. George Fox, *A Journal or Historical Account of the Life, Travels, Sufferings, Christian Experiences, and Labour of Love, in the Work of the Ministry, of that Ancient, Eminent, and Faithful Servant of Jesus Christ, George Fox* (Philadelphia: Joseph and William Kite, 1839), 1:71–72.

16. George Fox, *An Instruction to Judges and Lawyers* (London: Thomas Dimmons, 1660), 3.

17. John Bellers, *John Bellers, 1654–1725, Quaker, Economist and Social Reformer*, ed. A. Ruth Fry (London: Cassell, 1935), 76–77. See Genesis 9:5–6, and Exodus 21:12–27, 22:1–4. See also Fox, *Instruction to Judges and Lawyers*, 6, where Fox asks: "How can [the thief] restore four, or five, or seven fold, when ye hang him?"

18. Fitzroy, "Punishment of Crime," 245.

19. Bellers, *John Bellers*, 77.

20. Fox, *Instruction to Judges and Lawyers*, 1, 3.

21. Bellers, *John Bellers*, 77.

22. John Cotton, *The Bloody Tenent, Washed, and Made White in the Blood of the Lamb* (New York: Arno Press, 1972), 192–95.

23. Roger Williams, "The Bloody Tenent Yet More Bloody," in *The Complete Writings of Roger Williams*, vol. 4, ed. Samuel L. Caldwell (New York: Russell and Russell, 1963), 485, 486.

24. Ibid., 486, 487.

25. 1 Peter 2:13.

26. Williams, "The Bloody Tenent Yet More Bloody," 488.

27. For a general description of the Quaker influence in the Society, see "Roberts Vaux," *Journal of Prison Discipline and Philanthropy* 2 (April 1846): 109–22. See also La Rochefoucauld-Liancourt, *On the Prisons of Philadelphia*, 7.

28. Barnes, *Evolution of Penology*, 84.

29. Lawrence H. Gipson, "Crime and Its Punishment in Provincial Pennsylvania," *Pennsylvania History* 2 (1935): 15.

30. Fitzroy, *Punishment of Crime in Provincial Pennsylvania*, 255.

31. See, for example, *Minutes of the Provincial Council of Pennsylvania*, 3:45, 240, 370, 429–30, 591; 5:612; 8:336; 9:384; 10:94.

32. See, for example, ibid., 9:236, 402, 10:172.

33. Ibid., 8:336 (emphasis added).

34. *Statutes at Large of Pennsylvania*, 15:175.

35. Jefferson, *Notes on the State of Virginia*, 143.

36. Jefferson, Preamble to "A Bill for proportioning Crimes and Punishments," *Writings* (Lipscomb), 1:218, 19.

37. Ibid., 1:220–22.

38. See *Writings* (Lipscomb), 2:287.

39. Jefferson, "A Bill for proportioning Crimes and Punishments," *Writings* (Lipscomb), 1.223–24, 225–26 note.

40. Ibid., 1.226–36.

41. Kathryn Preyer also argues that proportionality was the main thrust behind Virginia's new criminal code. Commenting on Jefferson's proposal, she contends that it "took the principle of revenge seriously and provided that the state take this into account by making retribution the basis of punishment." She characterizes the general effort of Virginia to replace the colonial code as an effort "based on the doctrine of proportionality." Preyer, "Crime, the Criminal Law and Reform in Post-Revolutionary Virginia," *Law and History Review* 1 (1983): 53, 85. By contrast, Edward Dumbauld contends that Jefferson's proposed revisions were based primarily on Beccaria. His assertion relies almost entirely on the simplicity of Jefferson's code and on the long passages from Beccaria's works in Jefferson's *Commonplace Book*. That Jefferson's proposal draws heavily on the lex talionis (hardly compatible with Beccaria's philosophy) is ignored altogether. Dumbauld, *Thomas Jefferson and the Law* (Norman: University of Oklahoma Press, 1978), xii, 135–39.

8: Punishment and the Founders

1. There was some question as to whether the common law definition of crimes and punishments was applicable in federal jurisdiction after the Revolution. Congress failed to follow the lead of many states when it chose not to include as part of the Judiciary Act of 1789 a blanket adoption of the common law. Although many believed that one could be convicted of a crime under the common law, the U.S. Supreme Court eventually ruled that there could be no criminal conviction without a statute (*U.S. v. Hudson and Goodwin*, 7 Cranch 32, 1812).

2. The legislative history shows that the Senate debated and passed a crimes bill in 1789, but the bill was postponed by the House and was eventually superceded by the 1790 version. There is little difference between the 1789 bill and the bill enacted in 1790. Linda Grant De Pauw, ed., *Documentary History of the First Federal Congress of the United States of America* (Baltimore, Md.: Johns Hopkins University Press, 1972), 6:1719–52.

3. Ibid., 6:1733–41. See also *An Act for the Punishment of certain Crimes against the United States*, 1 Stat. 112–17.

4. De Pauw, *Documentary History of the First Federal Congress*, 1:229–30, 6:1744 n. 3.

5. Ibid., 13:968–70.

6. Ibid., 13:973–74. See also 6:1747 n. 13. The diary of Senator William

Maclay from Pennsylvania also contains some very brief mention of the crimes bill debates. See ibid., 9:135–36, 192. See also Joseph Gales Sr., ed., *The Debate and Proceedings in the Congress of the United States* (Washington, D.C.: Gales and Son, 1834), 2:1520–21.

7. De Pauw, *Documentary History of the First Federal Congress*, 13:973–74.

8. For a precise record of amendments considered when the Senate took up the House version, see ibid., 1:286–87 n. 42.

9. "Constitution of Maryland, 1776," in Poore, *The Federal and State Constitutions*, 819.

10. "Constitution of Massachusetts, 1780," in ibid., 957, 959.

11. Ibid., 957.

12. "Constitution of New Hampshire, 1784," in ibid., 1281.

13. "Virginia Bill of Rights, 1776," in ibid., 1909.

14. Abraham Lincoln, "The Dred Scott Decision, June 26, 1857," in *Life and Works of Abraham Lincoln*, ed. Marion Mills Miller (New York: Lincoln Centenary Association, 1907), 3:15–30.

15. Maestro, *Cesare Beccaria*, 141–42. Edward Dumbauld makes a similar argument in *Thomas Jefferson and the Law*, 135–39.

16. Thomas Jefferson, "Answers to Questions Propounded by M. de Meusnier, January 24, 1786," *Writings* (Lipscomb), 17:78.

17. Jefferson, *Autobiography*, *Writings* (Lipscomb), 1:69.

18. Jefferson "To George Wythe, November 1, 1778," *Writings* (Lipscomb), 1:217–18.

19. Thomas Jefferson, *The Commonplace Book of Thomas Jefferson*, ed. Gilbert Chinard (Baltimore: Johns Hopkins University Press, 1926), 211–98.

20. Thomas Jefferson, *Jefferson's Literary Commonplace Book*, ed. Douglas L. Wilson (Princeton: Princeton University Press, 1989), 5.

21. Jefferson, *The Commonplace Book of Thomas Jefferson*, 11.

22. Jefferson, *Notes on the State of Virginia*, 142, 163 (emphasis added).

23. Jefferson, "A Bill for proportioning Crimes and Punishments," *Writings* (Lipscomb), 1:219.

24. Jefferson, "Answers to Meusnier," *Writings* (Lipscomb), 17:79.

25. Ibid.

26. Thomas Jefferson, "To Edmund Pendleton, August 26, 1776," in *The Writings of Thomas Jefferson*, ed. Julian P. Boyd (Princeton: Princeton University Press, 1950), 1:505.

27. Jefferson, "To James Callaway, August 1, 1780," ibid., 3:519.

28. Jefferson, "To Philip Turpin, July 29, 1783," ibid., 6:326.

29. Benjamin Franklin, "To Benjamin Vaughan, March 14, 1785," in *The Writings of Benjamin Franklin*, ed. Albert Henry Smyth (New York: Macmillan, 1907), 9:293, 296.

30. Franklin, "To Gaetano Filangieri, January 11, 1783," ibid., 9:1–2.

31. Samuel Romilly, *Observations on the Criminal Law of England* (London: J. M'Creery, 1811).

32. Martin Madan, *Thoughts on Executive Justice* (London: J. Dodeley, 1785).

33. Franklin, "To Benjamin Vaughan," *Writings of Benjamin Franklin*, 9:293, 294.

34. Ibid., 9:292, 295 (emphasis original).

35. Ibid., 9:294.

36. Ibid., 9:294–95.

37. Keedy, "Pennsylvania Statute Creating Degrees of Murder," 768.

38. James Wilson, *Lectures on Law*, in *The Works of James Wilson*, ed. Robert Green McCloskey (Cambridge, Mass.: Belknap Press, 1967), 124.

39. Ibid., 138, 139.

40. Ibid., 139.

41. Ibid., 143, 145.

42. Ibid., 184. See also Publius, *The Federalist*, ed. Clinton Rossiter (New York: New American Library of World Literature, 1961), 22:152.

43. Wilson, *Lectures on Law*, 131, 132, 133.

44. Ibid., 507.

45. Ibid., 612, 626.

46. Ibid., 672.

47. Ibid., 618, 634.

48. Ibid., 616, 625.

49. Ibid., 627, 647–62.

50. George Washington, "The First Inaugural Speech, April 30, 1789," in *George Washington: A Collection*, ed. William B. Allen (Indianapolis: Liberty Classics, 1988), 462, 464–65.

51. George Washington, "To the Clergy of Different Denominations Residing in and near the City of Philadelphia, March 3, 1797," in *The Writings of George Washington*, ed. John C. Fitzpatrick (Washington, D.C: Government Printing Office, 1931–1944), 35:416.

52. Washington, "Farewell Address, September 19, 1796," ibid., 35:229.

53. Washington, "General Orders, October 21, 1778," ibid., 13:118.

54. See, for example, ibid., 8:129, 9:130, 10:242.

55. See, for example, "General Orders, March 14, 1778," ibid., 11:83.

56. Washington, "General Orders, May 29, 1776," ibid., 5:90. For a similar example, see 14:180.

57. Washington, "To Marquis De Lafayette," ibid., 21:255.

58. Washington, "To Robert Dinwiddle, August 27, 1757," ibid., 2:122.

59. Washington, "To Brigadier General David Wooster, April 12, 1777," ibid., 7:405.

60. James Madison, "Remarks on Mr. Jefferson's Draft of a Constitution for Virginia," in *Letters and Other Writings*, 1:189.

61. Madison, "To G. F. H. Crockett, November 6, 1823," ibid., 3:343.

62. Madison, "Remark's on Mr. Jefferson's Draft," ibid., 1:189.

63. Madison, "To Nicholas Biddle, May 17, 1827," ibid., 3:580.

64. Madison, "To Thomas S. Grimke, January 15, 1828," ibid., 3:612 (emphasis added). Beccaria's name is never directly mentioned in this quote, but the editor of Madison's work concludes that the reference is to Beccaria.

65. Alexander Hamilton, "The Farmer Refuted," in *The Papers of Alexander Hamilton* vol. 1, ed. Harold C. Syrett (New York: Columbia University Press, 1961), 86–87 (emphasis original).

66. Ibid., 1:136.

67. Ibid., 1:87, 88, 104.

68. Publius, *Federalist* 43:273. Publius also addresses the subject of piracy and felony on the high seas, noting that it needs to be addressed by the first Congress (which did address it in the 1790 Crimes Act). See 42:265–66.

69. Ibid., 40:253.

70. Ibid., 43:279.

71. Ibid., 6:58.

72. Ibid., 54:337.

73. Ibid., 74:447.

74. Ibid., 74:448.

CONCLUSION

1. Hamilton, "The Farmer Refuted," 104.

2. For my understanding of Hart's and Rawls's place in the punishment debate, I am indebted to Stanley C. Brubaker's article "Can Liberals Punish?" *American Political Science Review* 82 (September 1988): 821–36. My description here is intended to serve only as a brief summary; Brubaker's article provides a more able and detailed account of the neo-Kantian position within the punishment debate. For more of Brubaker's general argument on punishment issues, see "In Praise of Punishment," *Public Interest* 97 (fall 1989): 44–55.

3. See H. L. A. Hart, *Punishment and Responsibility* (Oxford: Oxford University Press, 1968).

4. Brubaker, "Can Liberals Punish?" 829.

5. John Rawls, *A Theory of Justice* (Cambridge, Mass.: Belknap Press, 1971), 241.

6. Michael Davis, "How to Make the Punishment Fit the Crime," *Ethics* 93 (1983): 727.

7. Alan Wertheimer, "Should the Punishment Fit the Crime?" *Social Theory and Practice* 3 (1975): 404.

8. Anthony Ellis, "Critical Study: Recent Work on Punishment," *Philosophical Quarterly* 45 (1995): 225.

9. Lisa H. Perkins, "Suggestions for a Justification of Punishment," *Ethics* 81 (1970): 55–61.

10. Jeffrie G. Murphy, *Retribution Reconsidered: More Essays in the Philosophy of Law* (Boston: Kluwer Academic Publishers, 1992), 17–18. Brubaker questions whether the liberal state is capable of punishment at all for this very same reason. Bradley C. S. Watson also raises these questions in a recent paper, "On Punishment and the Liberal State" (Washington, D.C.: American Political Science Association Annual Meeting, 1997).

11. Russ Shafer-Landau, "The Failure of Retributivism," *Philosophical Studies* 82 (1996): 311.

12. Gary Becker, "Crime and Punishment: An Economic Approach," *Journal of Political Economy* 76 (1968): 169. For another important deterrence argument, see Johannes Andeneas, *Punishment and Deterrence* (Ann Arbor: University of Michigan Press, 1974). Many sophisticated deterrence theories go well beyond a simple calculation of self-interest. Nigel Walker, for instance, argues that the public associates the "badness" of the crime with the severity of the punishment. Accordingly, making punishments appropriately severe for certain crimes educates the public that these acts are particularly evil. The motivation for law-abidingness, according to Walker, is a desire to avoid evil, which is more than merely maximizing one's individual utility. Walker's argument closely resembles that of Hyman Gross in *A Theory of Criminal Justice*. It also seems consistent with what Michael Lessnof believes are the two appropriate justifications or strategies for punishment. The first is the more narrow approach of deterrence based upon fear or self-interest. The second is the broader approach of "moral education." Lessnof contends that individuals "become disinclined, for reasons of moral principle, to perform acts of the kind punished." See Walker, *Why Punish?* (Oxford: Oxford University Press, 1991), esp. 21; Gross, *A Theory of Criminal Justice* (Oxford: Clarendon Press, 1979); Lessnof, "Two Justifications of Punishment," *Philosophical Quarterly* 21 (1971): esp. 141.

13. Norval Morris and Michael Tonry, *Between Prison and Probation* (New York: Oxford University Press, 1990), 86.

14. There are also just deserts advocates who argue for a system of non-incarcerative sentences. In opposition to Morris and Tonry's claim that just deserts interferes with establishing effective non-incarcerative penalties, Andrew von Hirsch, Martin Wasik, and Judith Greene contend that the various non-incarcerative punishments can be scaled to correspond with the seriousness of different crimes. In fact, they suggest that such a scaling may be easier to implement in the community than behind bars. See "Punishments in the Community and the Principles of Desert," *Rutgers Law Journal* 20 (1989): 695–718.

15. Michael Tonry, "Proportionality, Parsimony, and Interchangeability of Punishment," in *Penal Theory and Practice: Tradition and Innovation in Criminal Justice*, ed. Anthony Duff et al. (New York: Manchester University Press, 1994), 59, 64, 69.

16. Ibid., 75. Ian Brownlee takes issue with Tonry on this point. That different material and social conditions merit different punishments, Brownlee says, is "by no means clear." Questions such as the material and social inequities of different citizens are *political* and should not be settled by the judiciary. Although he does not dispute that inequities may exist, Brownlee argues that "it does not necessarily follow . . . that it is for judges in their sentencing function to redress, on a piecemeal basis, the social inequities of the capitalist order." See "Hanging Judges and Wayward Mechanics: Reply to Michael Tonry," in Duff et al., *Penal Theory and Practice*, 87, 89.

17. For another good illustration of the utilitarian argument against rehabilitation, see Robert Martinson, "What Works?—Questions and Answers about Prison Reform," *Public Interest* 35 (1974): 25.

18. James Q. Wilson, *Thinking about Crime* (New York: Vintage Books, 1983), 50–51, 249.

19. Wertheimer, "Should the Punishment Fit the Crime?" 416.

20. Ibid., 418. Von Hirsch addresses the question of how, exactly, we might determine a scale of punishments based upon just deserts. See *Censure and Sanctions* (Oxford: Clarendon Press, 1993), esp. 36–46.

21. Mark Tunick, *Punishment: Theory and Practice* (Berkeley and Los Angeles: University of California Press, 1992), 184, 186.

22. Michael Clark, "The Moral Gradation of Punishment," *Philosophical Quarterly* 21 (1971): 140.

23. See Clark, *Crime in America*, esp. 16.

24. Menninger, *Crime of Punishment*, 4.

25. Clark, *Crime in America*, 15.

26. Ibid., 17. See also Reiman, *The Rich Get Richer*, 50, 57–78, and John Rothchild, "Crime and Not Much Punishment," in *Crime and Punishment: Philosophical Explorations*, ed. Michael J. Gorr and Sterling Harwood (Boston: Jones and Bartlett, 1995), 118.

27. Clark, *Crime in America*, 30.

28. Barbara A. Hudson, *Penal Policy and Social Justice* (Toronto: University of Toronto Press, 1993), 179.

29. Menninger, *Crime of Punishment*, 118 (emphasis original). See also H.J. Eysenck, *Crime and Personality* (Boston: Houghton Mifflin, 1964).

30. Joseph M. Bessette, "Can Political Philosophy Help a Democracy Determine How and How Much to Punish?" (Washington, D.C.: American Political Science Association Annual Meeting, 1997), 1–2, 6–7.

31. Amanda Bennett, "State Tailors Sentences to Cost of Prison Space with Computer's Help," *Wall Street Journal*, August 5, 1994, A1.

32. Brubaker, "Can Liberals Punish?" 821.

33. Walter Berns, *For Capital Punishment* (New York: Basic Books, 1979), 6.

34. Walter Moberly, "Expiation," in Gerber and McAnany, *Contemporary Punishment*, 74. See also St. Thomas Aquinas's question on anger in the *Summa Theologiae* (I-II, Q.46). For an opposing view, see Anthony Platt's "Crime Rave," *Monthly Review* 47 (June 1995): 35–46. He argues that recent increases in punishment are the result of opportunistic politicians taking advantage of the public's thirst for retribution.

35. Davis, "How to Make the Punishment Fit the Crime," 727. Wertheimer, "Should the Punishment Fit the Crime?" 404. There is a false impression in the contemporary political debate that those who employ the just deserts or retribution approach necessarily advocate increased levels of criminal punishment. Many contend that criminals today do not receive the severe punishments merited by their offenses, but some also employ the just deserts argument in favor of leniency. Joshua Dressler, for example, asserts that the courts ought to use the principle of just deserts to strike down state laws that punish too severely. Citing the 1980 Supreme Court case of *Rummel v. Estelle* (445 U.S. 263), Dressler contends that the Court was wrong to uphold a Texas law imposing a life sentence for a minor theft (it was the offender's third conviction). Dressler argues that the law violated the principles of proportionality and just deserts. See Dressler, "Substantive Criminal Law through the Looking Glass of *Rummel v. Estelle*: Proportionality and Jus-

tice as Endangered Doctrines," *Southwestern Law Journal* 34 (1981): 1063–130. It is perhaps Andrew von Hirsch who has written most extensively in favor of more lenient punishments on the basis of just deserts. Von Hirsch rejects the deterrence argument, contending that punishments should "be distributed as a matter of fairness according to the degree of blameworthiness of convicted criminals' conduct." He believes that most offenders do not deserve imprisonment. Although he does believe that the severity of punishment must increase with the severity of the crime, he only places the most terrible crimes among the group that warrant incarceration. See von Hirsch, *Doing Justice* (Boston: Northeastern University Press, 1986), viii.

36. C. S. Lewis, "The Humanitarian Theory of Punishment," in *God in the Dock* (Grand Rapids: William B. Eerdmans, 1970), 288.

37. Ibid., 288–89.

38. Bessette, "Can Political Philosophy Help a Democracy?," 15–16.

39. Hudson, *Penal Policy and Social Justice*, 163.

40. Edgardo Rotman, *Beyond Punishment: A New View on the Rehabilitation of Criminal Offenders* (New York: Greenwood Press, 1990), 12. For additional information on the new rehabilitationism, see Ted Palmer. Palmer describes the resurgence of rehabilitation as a response to the "pessimism" that had dominated since roughly 1975, in writings such as Wilson's *Thinking about Crime*. He cites three tenets of the new rehabilitationists: (1) rehabilitation can effectively prevent recidivism; (2) concerns over the intrusiveness of rehabilitation have become "less onerous"; and (3) rehabilitation programs can be made "less risky to the public" if offenders are held accountable for violating the parameters of their treatment. Palmer admits that the renewed belief in rehabilitation is "far from universal," but there is clear evidence that rehabilitation is alive and well in the contemporary literature. See Palmer, "The Effectiveness of Intervention: Recent Trends and Current Issues," *Crime and Delinquency* 37 (1991): 332, 334. Paul Gendreau and Robert R. Ross, for example, attempt to show that rehabilitation can actually work. Remarking that "it seems only recently the cynics were in full flower," they point to new techniques such as "differential association" and "peer-group counseling" as improvements on older rehabilitative methods. Gendreau and Ross, "Revivification of Rehabilitation: Evidence from the 1980s," *Justice Quarterly* 4 (1987): 349.

41. James Q. Wilson and Richard Herrnstein, *Crime and Human Nature* (New York: Simon and Schuster, 1985), 489.

42. Wilson and Herrnstein do believe that desert has limitations in the public policy arena. They focus on the concept of mens rea—a central element of many retribution theories. Mens rea holds that the most important factor in justifying criminal punishment is that the individual has willingly committed a crime (not, in other words, because punishment would deter others). Wilson and Herrnstein warn that this might make the criminal justice system a hostage to developments in science and medicine. As scientific knowledge about the causes of human behavior progresses, they argue, the scope of the criminal law must shrink. Scientists will become better able to pinpoint factors that have "forced" individuals to behave criminally. If we rely on the doctrine of mens rea as a justification for

punishment, the level of punishment must decrease as criminals are increasingly held not to be responsible for their actions. Wilson and Herrnstein use the John Hinckley case as an illustration of their point. Once psychiatrists testified that Hinckley was not sane, the jury had no choice but to find him not guilty because he was not responsible for his actions. They believe that an effective punishing system must focus on the deterrent and incapacitative effects of the law, which can be substantially weakened by adhering to the doctrine of mens rea. Wilson and Herrnstein, *Crime and Human Nature*, 504.

43. California Department of Corrections, "Time Served on Prison Sentences: Felons First Released to Parole by Offense, Calendar Year 1992," July 1993.

Andeneas, Johannes. *Punishment and Deterrence*. Ann Arbor: University of Michigan Press, 1974.

Aquinas, St. Thomas. *Summa Theologiae*. 5 vols. Translated by Fathers of the English Dominican Province. Westminster, Md.: Christian Classics, 1981.

Aristotle. *Nicomachean Ethics*. Translated by Terence Irwin. Indianapolis: Hackett Publishing, 1985.

Barnes, Harry Elmer. *The Evolution of Penology in Pennsylvania*. Indianapolis: Bobbs-Merrill, 1927.

Beccaria, Cesare. *Dei delitti e delle pene*. Milano: Biblioteca Universale Rizzoli, 1981.

———. *On Crimes and Punishments*. Translated by Henry Paolucci. New York: Macmillan, 1963.

———. *On Crimes and Punishments and Other Writings*. Edited by Richard Bellamy, translated by Richard Davies. Cambridge, England: Cambridge University Press, 1995.

Becker, Gary. "Crime and Punishment: An Economic Approach." *Journal of Political Economy* 76 (1968): 169–217.

Bellers, John. *John Bellers, 1654–1725, Quaker, Economist and Social Reformer*. Edited by A. Ruth Fry. London: Cassell, 1935.

Bennett, Amanda. "State Tailors Sentences to Cost of Prison Space with Computer's Help." *Wall Street Journal*, August 5, 1994, A1.

Bentham, Jeremy. *A Commentary on the Commentaries: A Criticism of William Blackstone's Commentaries on the Laws of England*. Edited by Charles Warren Everett. Oxford: Clarendon Press, 1928.

———. *An Introduction to the Principles of Morals and Legislation*. Oxford: Clarendon Press, 1879.

———. *The Theory of Legislation*. Edited by C. K. Ogden. London: Routledge and Kegan Paul, 1931.

Berns, Walter. *For Capital Punishment*. New York: Basic Books, 1979.

Bessette, Joseph M. "Can Political Philosophy Help a Democracy Determine How and How Much to Punish?" Washington, D.C.: American Political Science Association Annual Meeting, 1997.

Blackstone, William. *Commentaries on the Laws of England*. Philadelphia: J. B. Lippincott, 1893.

Bradford, William. *An Enquiry how far the Punishment of Death is Necessary in Pennsylvania*. Philadelphia: Dobson, 1793.

"Brief History of the Penal Legislation of Pennsylvania." *Journal of Prison Discipline and Philanthropy* 1 (January 1845): 1–14.

Brown, Elizabeth Gasper. *British Statutes in American Law, 1776–1836*. Ann Arbor: University of Michigan Law School, 1964.

Brubaker, Stanley C. "Can Liberals Punish?" *American Political Science Review* 82 (September 1988): 821–36.

———. "In Praise of Punishment." *Public Interest* 97 (fall 1989): 44–55.

Calendar of State Papers, Colonial Series, America and West Indies. 40 vols. Great Britain: Public Records Office, 1964.

California Department of Corrections. "Time Served on Prison Sentences: Felons First Released to Parole by Offense, Calendar Year 1992." July 1993.

Cattaneo, Mario A. "Hobbes's Theory of Punishment." In *Hobbes Studies*, ed. Keith C. Brown, 275–97. Cambridge, Mass.: Harvard University Press, 1965.

Chapin, Bradley. *Criminal Justice in Colonial America, 1606–1660*. Athens: University of Georgia Press, 1983.

———. "Felony Law Reform in the Early Republic." *Pennsylvania Magazine of History and Biography* 113 (April 1989): 163–83.

Clark, Michael. "The Moral Gradation of Punishment." *Philosophical Quarterly* 21 (1971): 132–40.

Clark, Ramsey. *Crime in America*. New York: Simon and Schuster, 1970.

Cotton, John. *The Bloody Tenent, Washed, and Made White in the Blood of the Lamb*. New York: Arno Press, 1972.

"Crimes Act, April 6, 1790." In *The Debate and Proceedings in the Congress of the United States*, ed. Joseph Gales Sr. Vol. 2. Pp. 1520–21. Washington, D.C.: Gales and Son, 1834.

Cushing, John D., ed. *Colony Laws of Virginia, 1619–1660*. Vol. 1. Wilmington, Del.: Michale Glazier, 1978.

Davis, Michael. "How to Make the Punishment Fit the Crime." *Ethics* 93 (1983): 726–52.

"Declaration of the Rights of Man and Citizen." In *The Constitutions and other Select Documents illustrative of the History of France, 1789–1907*, ed. Frank Maloy Anderson. New York: Russell and Russell, 1908.

D'Elia, Donald J. *Benjamin Rush: Philosopher of the American Revolution*. In *Transactions of the American Philosophical Society* 64 (1974).

De Pauw, Linda Grant, ed. *Documentary History of the First Federal Congress of the United States of America*. 14 Vols. Baltimore: Johns Hopkins University Press, 1972.

Diamond, Martin. "Ethics and Politics: The American Way." In *The Moral Foundations of the American Republic*, ed. Robert H. Horwitz, 75–108. 3d ed. Charlottesville: University Press of Virginia, 1986.

Dressler, Joshua. "Substantive Criminal Law through the Looking Glass of *Rummel v. Estelle*: Proportionality and Justice as Endangered Doctrines." *Southwestern Law Journal* 34 (1981): 1063–130.

Duff, Anthony, et al., eds. *Penal Theory and Practice: Tradition and Innovation in Criminal Justice*. New York: Manchester University Press, 1994.

Dumbauld, Edward. *Thomas Jefferson and the Law*. Norman: University of Oklahoma Press, 1978.

Dumm, Thomas L. *Democracy and Punishment: Disciplinary Origins of the United*

States. Madison: University of Wisconsin Press, 1987.

Eddy, Thomas. *An Account of the State Prison or Penitentiary House, in the City of New-York*. New York: Isaac Colins and Son, 1801.

Ellis, Anthony. "Critical Study: Recent Work on Punishment." *Philosophical Quarterly* 45 (1995): 225–33.

Eysenck, H. J. *Crime and Personality*. Boston: Houghton Mifflin, 1964.

Farrell, Daniel M. "Punishment without the State." *Nous* 22 (1988): 437–53.

Fitzroy, Herbert William Keith. "The Punishment of Crime in Provincial Pennsylvania." *Pennsylvania Magazine of History and Biography* 60 (1936): 242–69.

Flaherty, David. "Law and the Enforcement of Morals in Early America." In *American Law and the Constitutional Order: Historical Perspectives,* ed. Lawrence M. Friedman and Harry N. Scheiber, 53–66. Cambridge, Mass.: Harvard University Press, 1978.

———, ed. *For the Colony in Virginia Britannia, Lawes Divine, Morall and Martiall, etc.* Compiled by William Strachey. Charlottesville: University Press of Virginia, 1969.

Foucault, Michel. *Discipline and Punish*. Translated by Alan Sheridan. New York: Vintage Books, 1979.

Fox, George. *An Instruction to Judges and Lawyers*. London: Thomas Dimmons, 1660.

———. *A Journal or Historical Account of the Life, Travels, Sufferings, Christian Experiences, and Labour of Love, in the Work of the Ministry, of that Ancient, Eminent, and Faithful Servant of Jesus Christ, George Fox*. Philadelphia: Joseph and William Kite, 1839.

Franklin, Benjamin. *The Writings of Benjamin Franklin*. Edited by Albert Henry Smyth. Vol. 9. New York: Macmillan, 1907.

Friedman, Lawrence M. *Crime and Punishment in American History*. New York: Basic Books, 1993.

Gales, Joseph Sr., ed. *The Debate and Proceedings in the Congress of the United States*. Vol. 2. Washington, D.C.: Gales and Son, 1834.

Gaskins, Richard. "Changes in the Criminal Law in Eighteenth-Century Connecticut." In *Crime and Justice in American History*, vol. 1, *The Colonies and Early Republic,* ed. Eric H. Monkkonen, 197–230. Westport, Conn.: Meckler, 1991.

Gendreau, Paul, and Robert R. Ross. "Revivification of Rehabilitation: Evidence from the 1980s." *Justice Quarterly* 4 (1987): 349–407.

George, Staughton, Benjamin N. Nead, and Thomas McCamant, eds. *Charter to William Penn and Laws of the Province of Pennsylvania, 1682–1700*. Harrisburg, Pa.: Lane S. Hart, State Printer, 1879.

Gerber, Rudolph J., and Patrick D. McAnany. *Contemporary Punishment*. Notre Dame: University of Notre Dame Press, 1972.

Gipson, Lawrence H. "Crime and Its Punishment in Provincial Pennsylvania." *Pennsylvania History* 2 (1935): 3–16.

———. "The Criminal Codes of Pennsylvania." *Journal of Criminal Law* 6 (1915): 323–44.

Godwin, William. *An Enquiry Concerning Political Justice and Its Influence on*

General Virtue and Happiness. Edited by Raymond A. Preston. 2 vols. New York: Alfred A. Knopf, 1926.

Gorr, Michael J., and Sterling Harwood, eds. *Crime and Punishment: Philosophical Explorations.* Boston: Jones and Bartlett, 1995.

Greenberg, David F., ed. *Crime and Capitalism: Readings in Marxist Criminology.* Philadelphia: Temple University Press, 1993.

Greenwood, Peter W., et al. *Three Strikes and You're Out: Estimated Benefits and Costs of California's New Mandatory-Sentencing Law.* Santa Monica: Rand, 1994.

Gross, Hyman. *A Theory of Criminal Justice.* Oxford: Clarendon Press, 1979.

Hamilton, Alexander. "The Farmer Refuted." In *The Papers of Alexander Hamilton,* ed. Harold C. Syrett, 1:81–165. New York: Columbia University Press, 1961.

Hart, H. L. A. *Punishment and Responsibility.* Oxford: Oxford University Press, 1968.

Hawke, David Freeman. *Benjamin Rush: Revolutionary Gadfly.* Indianapolis: Bobbs-Merrill, 1971.

Hegel, Georg Wilhelm Friedrich. *The Philosophy of History.* Translated by J. Sibree. New York: Dover Publications, 1956.

———. *The Philosophy of Right.* Translated by T. M. Knox. London: Oxford University Press, 1967.

Hening, William Walter, ed. *The Statutes at Large; being a Collection of all the Laws of Virginia, from the First Session of the Legislature, in the year 1619.* Richmond: J. and G. Cochran, 1809.

Hirsch, Adam J. *The Rise of the Penitentiary: Prisons and Punishment in Early America.* New Haven: Yale University Press, 1992.

Hobbes, Thomas. *Leviathan.* New York: Collier Books, 1962.

Horwitz, Morton J. *The Transformation of American Law, 1780–1860.* Cambridge, Mass.: Harvard University Press, 1977.

Hudson, Barbara A. *Penal Policy and Social Justice.* Toronto: University of Toronto Press, 1993.

Hunter, Adelaide Meador. *Punishment of Crimes in Virginia, 1775–1820.* Master's thesis. Duke University, 1947.

Hurka, Thomas. "Rights and Capital Punishment." *Dialogue* 21 (1982): 647–60.

Jefferson, Thomas. *The Commonplace Book of Thomas Jefferson.* Edited by Gilbert Chinard. Baltimore: Johns Hopkins University Press, 1926.

———. *Jefferson's Literary Commonplace Book.* Edited by Douglas L. Wilson. Princeton: Princeton University Press, 1989.

———. *Notes on the State of Virginia.* Edited by William Peden. Chapel Hill: University of North Carolina Press, 1955.

———. *The Writings of Thomas Jefferson.* Edited by Julian P. Boyd. Vol. 1. Princeton: Princeton University Press, 1950.

———. *The Writings of Thomas Jefferson.* Edited by Andrew A. Lipscomb. 20 vols. Washington, D.C.: Thomas Jefferson Memorial Association, 1904.

Journal of the Senate of the Commonwealth of Pennsylvania. Vol. 3. Philadelphia, 1793.

Journals of the Continental Congress, 1774–1789. 5 vols. Washington, D.C.: Government Printing Office, 1973.

Kant, Immanuel. *Critique of Practical Reason*. Translated by Lewis White Beck. New York: MacMillan, 1985.

———. *Groundwork of the Metaphysic of Morals*. Translated by H. J. Paton. New York: Harper and Row, 1956.

———. *The Metaphysical Elements of Justice*. Part 1 of *The Metaphysics of Morals*. Translated by John Ladd. Indianapolis: Bobbs-Merrill, 1965.

Keedy, Edwin R. "History of the Pennsylvania Statute Creating Degrees of Murder." *University of Pennsylvania Law Review* 97 (May 1949): 759–77.

Kendall, Willmoore, and George W. Carey. *Basic Symbols of the American Political Tradition*. Baton Rouge: Louisiana State University Press, 1970.

Kesler, Charles R. "*Federalist* 10 and American Republicanism." In *Saving the Revolution*, ed. Charles R. Kesler, 13–39. New York: Free Press, 1987.

———. "The Founders and the Classics." In *The American Founding*, ed. J. Jackson Barlow et al., 57–90. New York: Greenwood Press, 1988.

Kraus, Michael. *The Atlantic Civilization: Eighteenth Century Origins*. Ithaca: Cornell University Press, 1949.

La Rochefoucauld-Liancourt. *On the Prisons of Philadelphia*. Philadelphia: Moreau de Saint Mery, 1796.

Laws of the State of New Jersey. Trenton: Joseph Justice, 1821.

Lessnof, Michael. "Two Justifications of Punishment." *Philosophical Quarterly* 21 (1971): 141–48.

Lewis, C. S. "The Humanitarian Theory of Punishment." In *God in the Dock*, 287–300. Grand Rapids: William B. Eerdmans, 1970.

Lincoln, Abraham. "The Dred Scott Decision, June 26, 1857." In *Life and Works of Abraham Lincoln*, ed. Marion Mills Miller. Vol. 3. Pp. 15–30. New York: Lincoln Centenary Association, 1907.

Locke, John. *Second Treatise of Government*. Edited by Peter Laslett. Cambridge, England: Cambridge University Press, 1988.

Lownes, Caleb. *An Account of the Alteration and Present State of the Penal Laws of Pennsylvania, containing also an Account of the Gaol and Penitentiary House of Philadelphia and the Interior Management Thereof*. Lexington, Ky.: J. Bradford, 1794.

Mackenzie, Mary Margaret. *Plato on Punishment*. Berkeley and Los Angeles: University of California Press, 1981.

Mackey, Philip English. *Hanging in the Balance: The Anti-Capital Punishment Movement in New York State, 1776–1861*. New York: Garland Publishing, 1982.

Madan, Martin. *Thoughts on Executive Justice*. London: J. Dodeley, 1785.

Madison, James. *Letters and Other Writings of James Madison*. 4 vols. New York: R. Worthington, 1884.

Maestro, Marcello T. *Cesare Beccaria and the Origins of Penal Reform*. Philadelphia: Temple University Press, 1973.

The Manuscripts of the House of Lords. Vol. 5. London: Her Majesty's Stationary Office, 1965.

Martinson, Robert. "What Works? Questions and Answers about Prison Reform." *Public Interest* 35 (1974): 22–54.

Masur, Louis P. *Rites of Execution: Capital Punishment and the Transformation of*

American Culture, 1776–1865. New York: Oxford University Press, 1989.

McDonald, Forrest. *Novus Ordo Seclorum: The Intellectual Origins of the Constitution*. Lawrence: University Press of Kansas, 1985.

McManus, Edgar J. *Law and Liberty in Early New England*. Amherst: University of Massachusetts Press, 1993.

Menninger, Karl. *The Crime of Punishment*. New York: Viking Press, 1966.

Meranze, Michael. *Laboratories of Virtue: Punishment, Revolution, and Authority in Philadelphia, 1760–1835*. Chapel Hill: University of North Carolina Press, 1996.

Minutes of the Provincial Council of Pennsylvania, from the Organization to the Termination of the Proprietary Government. Philadelphia: Jo. Severns, 1852.

Montesquieu. *The Spirit of the Laws*. Translated by Anne M. Cohler, Basia Carolyn Miller, and Harold Samuel Stone. New York: Cambridge University Press, 1989.

Morris, Norval, and Michael Tonry. *Between Prison and Probation*. New York: Oxford University Press, 1990.

Murphy, Jeffrie G. "Marxism and Retribution." In *Punishment: A Philosophy and Public Affairs Reader*, ed. A. John Simmons et al., 3–29. Princeton: Princeton University Press, 1995.

———. *Retribution Reconsidered: More Essays in the Philosophy of Law*. Boston: Kluwer Academic Publishers, 1992.

Nelson, William E. *Americanization of the Common Law*. Cambridge, Mass.: Harvard University Press, 1975.

———. "Emerging Notions of Modern Criminal Law in the Revolutionary Era: An Historical Perspective." In *American Law and the Constitutional Order*, ed. Lawrence M. Friedman and Harry N. Scheiber, 165–72. Cambridge, Mass.: Harvard University Press, 1978.

Norrie, Alan. "Thomas Hobbes and the Philosophy of Punishment." *Law and Philosophy* 3 (1984): 299–320.

"Notice of the Right Reverend William White, D.D., one of the Founders of the Society for Alleviating the Miseries of Public Prisons." *Journal of Prison Discipline and Philanthropy* 2 (January 1846): 1–6.

Palmer, Ted. "The Effectiveness of Intervention: Recent Trends and Current Issues." *Crime and Delinquency* 37 (1991): 330–46.

Pennsylvania Archives, Eighth Series. Edited by Gertrude MacKinney. Vol. 2. Harrisburg, Pa.: Bureau of Publications, 1931.

Perkins, Lisa H. "Suggestions for a Justification of Punishment." *Ethics* 81 (1970): 55–61.

Plato. *Gorgias*. Translated by James H. Nichols Jr. Ithaca: Cornell University Press, 1998.

———. *The Laws of Plato*. Translated by Thomas L. Pangle. New York: Basic Books, 1980.

———. *Republic*. Translated by Allan Bloom. Basic Books, 1968.

Platt, Anthony. "Crime Rave." *Monthly Review* 47 (June 1995): 35–46.

Poore, Ben. Perley, ed. *The Federal and State Constitutions, Colonial Charters, and other Organic Laws of the United States*. Washington, D.C.: Government Printing Office, 1878.

Powers, Edwin. *Crime and Punishment in Early Massachusetts, 1620–1692.* Boston: Beacon Press, 1966.

Preyer, Kathryn. "Crime, the Criminal Law and Reform in Post-Revolutionary Virginia." *Law and History Review* 1 (1983): 53–85.

Publius. *The Federalist.* Edited by Clinton Rossiter. New York: New American Library of World Literature, 1961.

Rawls, John. *A Theory of Justice.* Cambridge, Mass.: Belknap Press, 1971.

Reiman, Jeffrey. *The Rich Get Richer and the Poor Get Prison: Ideology, Class, and Criminal Justice.* New York: Macmillan, 1990.

"Roberts Vaux." *Journal of Prison Discipline and Philanthropy* 2 (April 1846): 109–22.

Romilly, Samuel. *Observations on the Criminal Law of England.* London: J. M'Creery, 1811.

Rothman, David J. *The Discovery of the Asylum: Social Order and Disorder in the New Republic.* Boston: Little, Brown, 1971.

———. "Perfecting the Prison: United States, 1789–1865." In *The Oxford History of the Prison: The Practice of Punishment in Western Society,* ed. Norval Morris and David J. Rothman, 111–29. New York: Oxford University Press, 1995.

Rotman, Edgardo. *Beyond Punishment: A New View on the Rehabilitation of Criminal Offenders.* New York: Greenwood Press, 1990.

Rousseau, Jean-Jacques. *Discourse on the Origin and Foundations of Inequality among Men.* Translated by Roger D. Masters and Judith R. Masters. In *The First and Second Discourses,* ed. Roger D. Masters. New York: St. Martin's Press, 1964.

———. *On the Social Contract.* Translated by Judith R. Masters, edited by Roger D. Masters. New York: St. Martin's Press, 1978.

Rush, Benjamin. *The Autobiography of Benjamin Rush.* Edited by George W. Corner. Princeton: Princeton University Press, 1948.

———. *Essays Literary, Moral and Philosophical.* Edited by Michael Meranze. Schenectady: Union College Press, 1988.

———. *Letters of Benjamin Rush.* Edited by L. H. Butterfield. Princeton: Princeton University Press, 1951.

———. *The Selected Writings of Benjamin Rush.* Edited by Dagobert D. Runes. New York: Philosophical Library, 1947.

Saunders, Trevor J. *Plato's Penal Code.* Oxford: Clarendon Press, 1991.

Scharf, J. Thomas, and Thompson Westcott. *History of Philadelphia, 1609–1884.* 3 vols. Philadelphia: L. H. Everts, 1884.

Scott, Arthur P. *Criminal Law in Colonial Virginia.* Chicago: University of Chicago Press, 1930.

Sellin, Thorsten. *Pioneering in Penology: The Amsterdam Houses of Correction in the Sixteenth and Seventeenth Centuries.* Philadelphia: University of Pennsylvania Press, 1944.

Shafer-Landau, Russ. "The Failure of Retributivism." *Philosophical Studies* 82 (1996): 289–316.

Shepherd, Samuel, ed. *The Statutes at Large of Virginia, from October session 1792, to December session 1806, inclusive, in Three Volumes, Being a Continuation of Hening.* New York: AMS Press, 1835.

Simmons, A. John. *The Lockean Theory of Rights*. Princeton: Princeton University Press, 1992.

Statutes at Large of Pennsylvania from 1682 to 1801. 3 vols. Harrisburg, Pa.: Clarence M. Busch, 1896.

Stoner, James R., Jr. *Common Law and Liberal Theory*. Lawrence: University Press of Kansas, 1992.

Tunick, Mark. *Hegel's Political Philosophy: Interpreting the Practice of Legal Punishment*. Princeton: Princeton University Press, 1992.

———. "Is Kant a Retributivist?" *History of Political Thought* 17 (spring 1996): 60–78.

———. *Punishment: Theory and Practice*. Berkeley and Los Angeles: University of California Press, 1992.

van Laer, A. J. F., ed. and trans. *Documents Relating to New Netherland, 1624–1626, in the Henry E. Huntington Library*. San Marino: Henry E. Huntington Library and Art Gallery, 1924.

Vaux, Roberts. *Notices of the Original, and Successive Efforts, to Improve the Discipline of the Prison at Philadelphia, and to Reform the Criminal Code of Pennsylvania*. Philadelphia: Kimber and Sharpless, 1826.

von Hirsch, Andrew. *Censure and Sanctions*. Oxford: Clarendon Press, 1993.

———. *Doing Justice*. Boston: Northeastern University Press, 1986.

von Hirsch, Andrew, Martin Wasik, and Judith Greene. "Punishments in the Community and the Principles of Desert." *Rutgers Law Journal* 20 (1989): 695–718.

Walker, Nigel. *Why Punish?* Oxford: Oxford University Press, 1991.

Washington, George. *George Washington: A Collection*. Edited by William B. Allen. Indianapolis: Liberty Classics, 1988.

———. *The Writings of George Washington*. Edited by John C. Fitzpatrick. 39 vols. Washington, D.C.: Government Printing Office, 1931–1944.

Watson, Bradley C. S. "On Punishment and the Liberal State." Washington, D.C.: American Political Science Association Annual Meeting, 1997.

Watson, John F. *Annals of Philadelphia and Pennsylvania, in the Olden Time; being a collection of Memoirs, Anecdotes, and Incidents of the City and Its Inhabitants, and of the Earliest Settlements of the Inland Part of Pennsylvania*. Edited by Willis P. Hazard. 3 vols. Philadelphia: Edwin S. Stuart, 1905.

Wertheimer, Alan. "Should the Punishment Fit the Crime?" *Social Theory and Practice* 3 (1975): 403–23.

West, Thomas G. "The Classical Spirit of the Founding." In *The American Founding*, ed. J. Jackson Barlow et al., 1–56. New York: Greenwood Press, 1988.

"William Bradford." *Journal of Prison Discipline and Philanthropy* 2 (July 1846): 205–10.

Williams, Roger. "The Bloody Tenent Yet More Bloody." In *The Complete Writings of Roger Williams*, ed. Samuel L. Caldwell. Vol. 4. New York: Russell and Russell, 1963.

Wilson, James. *The Works of James Wilson*. Edited by Robert Green McCloskey. Cambridge, Mass.: Belknap Press, 1967.

Wilson, James Q. *Thinking about Crime*. New York: Vintage Books, 1983.

Wilson, James Q., and Richard Herrnstein. *Crime and Human Nature.* New York: Simon and Schuster, 1985.

Wood, Gordon S. *The Creation of the American Republic, 1776–1787.* New York: W. W. Norton, 1972.

Zumthor, Paul. *Daily Life in Rembrandt's Holland.* Translated by Simon Watson Taylor. London: Weidenfeld and Nicolson, 1962.

DATE DUE
